AN ASTROLOGICAL JOURNEY OF THE UNITED STATES

Introducing a New Birth Chart for the United States

by
Cornelia Hansen
with Karen E Steinberg

Copyright Cornelia Hansen, 2025
All Rights Reserved

Without limiting the rights reserved above under copyright, no part of this publication may be reproduced, stored in, or introduced into a retrieval system, or transmitted in any form or by any means (electronic, mechanical, photocopying, scanning, recording or otherwise), without written permission from both the author and the publisher, except in the case of brief quotations embodied in reviews and articles.

The scanning, uploading and distribution of this book via the Internet, or via any other means, without the written permission of the publisher is illegal and punishable by law. Please do not encourage electronic piracy of copyrighted materials.

ISBN: 978-0-86690-696-8
Cover art: Celeste Nash
Requests and inquires may be mailed to the publisher:
American Federation of Astrologers, Inc.
6553 S. Rural Road
Tempe, AZ 85283
www.astrologers.com

Dedication

To all my ancestors who were part of the fabric of this country from the very beginning. They contributed their beliefs and their hard work to produce a place in this world that prized freedom for the individual to create a better life. To our Founding Fathers who gave us our "Great Experiment" for us to continue as a self-governing people. We have gone through many changes since then, but the cycle of history eventually evolves upward. Despite the times we find ourselves in, our dedication to these ideals must encourage us to stay focused on realizing the dream of our country's motto:

FROM MANY, ONE.

ACKNOWLEDGEMENTS

I wish to thank my dear friend and fellow professional astrologer, Dominique Jaramillo, for reviewing all the charts used in the book and her dedication to my work. I also want to thank Jim Schultz and Spencer Grendahl, professional astrologers, for their continued support and encouragement through the years.

My family's loving support has been the fuel to keep me going: Karen, David, Alan, and my grandson, Samuel. I thank you all

Table of Contents

Prologue — i
Introduction — vii
    The Journey Begins
Chapter One — 1
    The Colonial Period
Chapter Two — 13
    From Rage to Revolt
Chapter Three — 23
    We the People of the United States
Chapter Four — 29
    The First Federal Congress Meets
Chapter Five — 37
    Westward Expansion
Chapter Six — 45
    The Jackson Era
Chapter Seven — 51
    The March of the Women
Chapter Eight — 59
    The Issue of Immigration
Chapter Nine — 65
    The Civil War
Chapter Ten — 75
    The American Labor Movement
Chapter Eleven — 87
    World War I
Chapter Twelve — 95
    Two Pandemics One Hundred Years Apart

Chapter Thirteen   101
    The Roaring Twenties

Chapter Fourteen   113
    The Great Depression of 1930

Chapter Fifteen   125
    World War II and its Aftermath

Chapter Sixteen   137
    The Fifties and the Cold War.

Chapter Seventeen   147
    The Tumultuous Sixties

Chapter Eighteen   159
    The Backlash 1970s

Chapter Nineteen   167
    The Avaricious Eighties

Chapter Twenty   179
    The Good Decade – The 1990s

Chapter Twenty-One   189
    The New Millenium

Chapter Twenty-Two   201
    The Turning Point Decade – The Obama Years

Chapter Twenty-Three   213
    The Turning Point Decade – The Trump Years

Chapter Twenty-Four   227
    America Divided - The Crisis Point

Epilogue   243

Appendix One   253
    Uranus Transits

Appendix Two   261
    Treaty of Paris Ratification

Appendix Three   273
    Pluto transits; Biwheel with Author's natal chart

Prologue

As Pluto once again passes through Capricorn into Aquarius, we stand at a pivotal point in American history: Do we confront those issues that interfere with the full realization of liberty, equality, democracy, justice, and the rule of law, the ideals laid out by our Founding Fathers during Pluto's last transit? Do we forge a stronger union, confident in its ability to achieve new heights?

Or do we ignore the conflicts and let that American Dream fade away as do other dreams with the sunrise? Do we give up freedom for tyranny, trade human rights for the security of state control, disregard the equality of all, and expand the gap between rich and poor?

I have always pursued what I deemed the ideals of our Founding Fathers, ideals internalized through my study and love of American history. I was raised in upstate New York, home to numerous villages, churches, battlefields, forts, and other historical sites. Exploring such places connected me with the country and excited my curiosity. As an adult, I traced my genealogy, discovering that my ancestors through my mother's line played a part in early American history, including the Revolution. I felt a deep sense of belonging and continuity with America and the pride that went with it.

That optimism slowly deteriorated over time as I watched conflicts arising continually that were never resolved. American ideals of democracy, equality, and the rule of law seemed in peril. People around me were also shaken by current events. Questions arose that I could not answer. Why is this happening? When and how did it begin? I had to find the answers.

I began my quest in 2021, while also experiencing a strong Pluto transit of my Saturn opposed to my Sun that transformed my life. As I reviewed astrological articles, I was puzzled by how positive they found the coming Pluto transit into Aquarius when the situation appeared so dire to me. I knew that Pluto transits create powerful transformations in the collective mind. The upheavals and paradigm shifts are often not obvious immediately as Pluto moves slowly, but soon are apparent as time advances.

A synchronous event alerted me to a new revelation. I discovered a book, *Zero Hour*, published by Harry Dent, a financial advisor, and his partner Andrew Pancoli, an expert on historical cycles, that posited a revolution could occur when three historical cycles converged.[1] The cycles included a 250-year Revolutionary Cycle, an 84-year Populist Movement Cycle, and a 28-year Financial Crisis Cycle. They reported the cycles had converged between 1765 and 1783, then predicted the transition point of the next convergence to be 2018 to 2023.

The connection between the cycles of Pluto, Uranus, and Saturn was immediately obvious to me. The cycles converge as Pluto moves through Capricorn into Aquarius. Was the convergence of these three great planets challenging America today?

Before exploring that possibility, I wanted to see if this configuration was associated with other transformative events in the past. I researched historical periods and found it applicable.

- 11th Century: The power of monarchies competed with the power of the Church. Each power had its period of domination until the Church and State united to initiate the Crusades and retake the land of Jesus from the Muslims. This had a devastating effect on the Byzantium Empire.
- 13th Century: The Treaty of Paris and 100 Years War were outstanding events, as the Crusades advanced and Marco Polo expanded trade to China. The economic center shifted from the Middle East to Europe.
- 1500s: Martin Luther rebelled against the Catholic Church. This huge transformation resulted in the rise of Protestantism and the establishment of the Church of England.
- 1700s: French and American revolutions.

My next step was to apply the cycles to the American chart. But which chart was the "correct" one? I reviewed the numerous charts listed in the Astro DataBank (www.astro.com/astro-databank/Main_Page) and read articles discussing rationales for the different rising signs chosen. Notably, several different versions existed, all using the Declaration of Independence as the United States birthdate. The chart with Gemini rising seemed most consistent with the United States.

As I reflected on the meaning of birthdates, I recalled that human births are made "official" by a form of written record. In the past, births were recorded in a family Bible or a church baptism form. Currently states issue a birth certificate that lists the date, time, and place of birth, as well as qualities that define the child such as name, gender, and parents' names. What kind of document existed that officially recognized the US as an existing entity, a nation with defined boundaries?

The Treaty of Paris of 1783, negotiated by our American emissaries, Benjamin Franklin, John Adams, and John Jay, with representatives of King George III, appeared to fulfill most criteria I had set for a birthdate. Ultimately, another synchronistic event led me to an internet article[2] which established for me the Treaty as the true American birthdate. I will talk about this in more depth as I present the new chart.

I use different charts throughout the book to analyze pertinent events in American history. All charts are based on Koch Houses. For many, I determined the exact time an event started. In others, I deduced a time based on factors affecting the event itself. For example, to create the first chart, I considered that although the Continental Congress convened at noon, they required time for counting a quorum and reviewing previous business before addressing the day's main business. In contrast, the chart for the atom bomb's release over Hiroshima has an exact time recorded in history. If I could not find a near-exact time, I used a noon chart.

The Introduction presents the new US birth chart with some interpretations. I will review some distinguishing patterns I have found, particularly the complicated Yod that is unique to this birth chart. The Yod has a significant impact on American development, and understanding it clarifies the issues that have long afflicted us. Before I delve into the historical framework, I want astrologers to have the opportunity to get their first impressions of the chart.

The main text first discusses the early colonies, beginning in the early 1600s and continuing to the Revolution. Who came here? Why did they come here? What beliefs from their past shaped them? What events affected the American character that led to the need for a revolution? Does it relate to what is happening today?

The next part will cover the 1700s and what developed into the fervor for independence. I will tie important events of this period to the new chart. What were the issues at play and why were so many ignored, only to appear again and again during our journey? Can the Yod help us uncover these buried conflicts and deal with them appropriately?

Later chapters will cover important events on our journey to the present and their ties to this new US chart. The whole context of the event and individuals connected to it will be explored. I tried to choose events that illustrated particularly strong impacts on the US and its people, such as the start or conclusion of an era.

The last event discussed, January 6, 2021, brings us to today where the issues pertaining to the Yod have surfaced once again. As Pluto travels into Aquarius, the Yod urges us to decide. Will we finally bring into reality the idealistic promises we made 250 years ago, that all people are created equal?

In the Epilogue, I will try to suggest a way to the future that may offer some hope to us all.

PROLOGUE NOTES

1. Dent, Harry S. Jr. & Pancholi, Andrew: *Zero Hour*, Portfolio/Penguin, New York, New York, 2017
2. https://calvetconnect.blog/2021/01/14/treatyofparis *Accessed 6/21/22*

Introduction
The Journey Begins

DRUMROLL, PLEASE!

Presenting a new birthdate for the United States of America! January 14, 1784 at 1:31 p.m. in Annapolis, Maryland.

BACKGROUND TIMELINE

- American Revolution ends after the Battle of Yorktown on October 19, 1781.[1]
- US representatives Benjamin Franklin, John Adams, and John Jay journey to Paris to meet with King George's emissaries to hammer out a treaty in the spring of 1782.[2]
- Congress approves and signs treaty on September 3, 1783. However, the treaty must be ratified by the states within 6 months, requiring a quorum of nine of the thirteen states to proceed.[3]
- Delegates convene in November 1783 at the Annapolis, Maryland Statehouse but a quorum is not achieved.[4]
- The needed delegate finally appears in January from South Carolina and the treaty is signed on January 14, 1784.[5]
- "Resolved, that the said ratification be transmitted with all possible despatch, under the care of a faithful person, to our ministers in France, who have negotiated the treaty, to be exchanged."[6]
- The entire treaty is published on January 22, 1784 in the Maryland Gazette to notify all Americans that they are now citizens of a sovereign nation.[7]
- The boundaries of the new nation are defined, extending from the north up to British Canada, to the south at Georgia, ending at Florida, with the eastern boundary along the Atlantic Coast extending westward to the Mississippi River. Canada remains with Britain while Louisiana and Florida are ceded to Spain.[8]

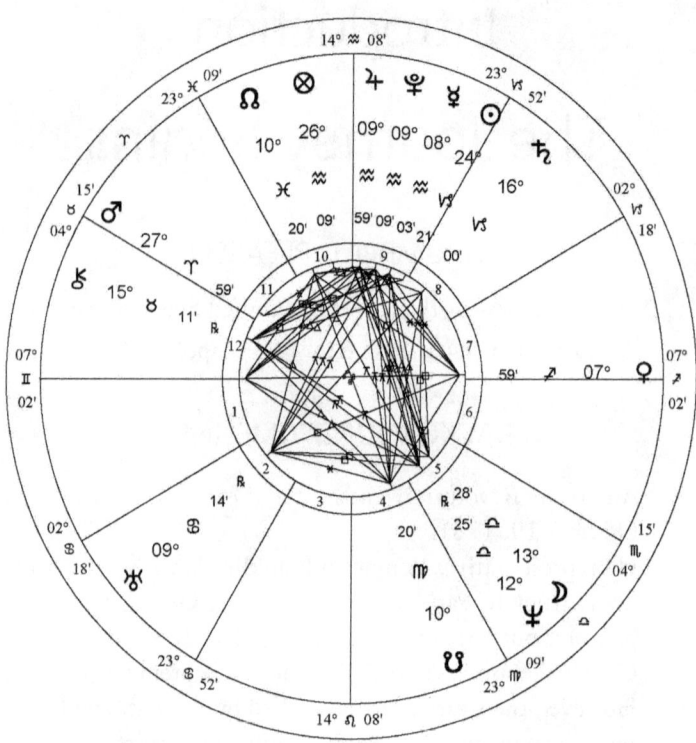

New Natal Chart for the United States Treaty of Paris
January 14, 1784, 1:31 PM LMT; Annapolis, Maryland

DISCUSSION OF MAJOR CONFIGURATIONS IN THE CHART

Grand Air Trine

The Grand Air Trine in the Fire Houses of the first, fifth, and ninth houses presents a dynamic energy flow which "symbolizes the essential quality of our innermost sense of self, as well as indicating our general approach to life itself."[9] The first, fifth, and ninth houses are "identity houses," from being to becoming, where we start and what we reach for. Air and Fire suggest ideas put into action, a sense of humor and optimism, inspiration, and the drive to realize them. Gemini provides adaptability, Libra the need for cooperation and justice, Aquarius is associated with the search for freedom as well as the need for connection to the

xiv An Astrological Journey Of The United States

larger group. Five planets plus the Ascendant and at least seven houses are drawn into the whole picture, making it extremely complicated.

Planets involved in the Grand Trine include the Moon conjunct Neptune in the fifth house, in addition to Mercury, Jupiter, and Pluto in the ninth house. Mercury is the Lord of the chart and its placement in the ninth suggests our origins as immigrants, emphasized by the Sun (ruler of the fourth house – our "roots"), also in the ninth. Mercury is exalted in Aquarius, bringing logic and intuition together to give us a highly original way of thinking and expressing ourselves (which we often hang onto stubbornly). On the other side, Mercury conjuncts Pluto, giving us strong opinions that are also openly expressed. Jupiter in Aquarius is high-minded but its conjunction to Pluto indicates a "dark side" or shadow. Conjunction of Moon with Neptune indicates the high vision of the people who came here but includes the negative qualities of a tendency to idolize some people and a vulnerability to duplicity.

The Yod

The Yod configuration is very important for understanding the problems related to our history. This "Finger of God" or "Destiny", as it's often called, may help clarify issues plaguing America since its birth. "If a child with a yod or an unaspected planet is born, he or she will express from day one, in some way or other, the unspoken, repressed, or unbalanced theme of generations." Such individuals are "giving form to the 'shadow-side' of their parent(s)."[10]

The six planets forming the Yod along with the houses they rule address the unresolved collective unconscious issues of our national character. These factors surface periodically, trying to get our attention. Perhaps a small amount of growth occurs before they are swept back into the dark corners, but they are not fully resolved. Their continued presence leads to restlessness, a search for a yet-undefined sense of self, and the insecurity that goes with it.

The diversity of beliefs, cultures, languages, ethnicities, and lifestyles brought to America by innumerable immigrants has precluded an easy definition of a national character. At one time, immigrants were expected to dissolve their heritage into a "melting pot" of a common "American" culture. Later, the analogy of a "salad bowl" allowed for each group to contribute its distinctive culture as a contribution into the mix. However, no "salad dressing" exists yet to unite those parts into a larger whole. This, I believe, is the goal for which we are searching. America, the "Great Experiment," is unique in this regard. No other country has had to contend with such a diverse influx of humanity.

The "American Dream" may be an expression of that goal, but it has not been clearly defined and has changed over time. For some it means freedom from oppression, for others it means new opportunities such as land ownership or business success, for still others such as slaves brought here against their wills, it signifies the equality promised in the Declaration of Independence.

The Yod ensures that various aspects of these repressed issues will continue to surface until they are resolved. For instance, the issue of slavery and racism has affected our attitude towards immigrants past and present. Despite the American vision of equality for all people, we ignored that concept when creating our Constitution. Slavery was disregarded, inevitably leading to the Civil War and the persistent racial conflicts affecting us today.

Only one opposition occurs in the chart and is part of the Yod. The "Axis of Awareness," the opposition between Saturn and Uranus, is the key to understanding another portion of the Yod's theme.[11] Like a tuning fork when activated, it sets off the differences between two types of government: authoritarian and democratic, initiating conflict among those preferring one or the other. This division has come to the fore in our own times, but it has been present since the beginning. Just as Pluto transited Capricorn into Aquarius before the Revolution, it is playing out today like an echo through time. At the beginning, it was the Tories who preferred the peace and order of the King, opposing the rebellious colonists who wanted independence and freedom with the right to make their own decisions. By whatever name they call themselves today- left and right, Red and Blue, Democrat and Republican, authoritarian and democratic- they still echo the re-emergent opposition and continue to represent the duality of our ascendant in Gemini (see below).

In keeping with the concept of the Axis of Awareness, note that Saturn plays the role of the conservatives: those who maintain the conventional customs and foundations of government, expecting obedience to the rules and laws that have been laid down. Saturn is in its dignity in Capricorn and its lesson in the eighth house is to learn how to share personal resources with others. One clings to these customs for fear of losing what one has, not realizing that we depend on others to share all resources.

A related lesson from Saturn is accepting the possibility of change- a possibility that induces great fear. Change may induce a fear of death, even though change often leads to a new birth. Look at the cost of human lives in the Civil War because of the South's need to maintain their status quo.

Opposing fear of change is Uranus, the disruptor, who demands reform, which usually stems from the people (Uranus in Cancer with the Moon in Libra always searching for justice and equality). Uranus in the second house also completes the imbalance in the Axis of Exchange. Americans have experienced times of prosperity but also times when the prosperity of most people disappears like the morning mist, creating protests and riots in its place. The power of Saturn is then required to crush the rebellion, again initiated from its fear of any change. Like a seesaw, "sometimes we're up and sometimes we're down." We have learned to live with this as if it is the only way open to us.

Gemini Ascendant

A study of the Gemini Ascendant and its ruler, Mercury (Greek Hermes) repeats the Yod's theme in the Axis of Awareness, in this case aristocrats vs. the common people. In mythology the Gemini twins, Castor and Pollux, were half-brothers, one mortal, the other immortal. When Castor was killed, Pollux offered Zeus half his immortality to his mortal brother so they could still be together. Zeus agreed and they spent half the year on Olympus and the other half on earth. The story of Hermes and Apollo echoes this theme. The god Apollo and the mortal Hermes maintained a rivalry, but when Hermes gave Apollo his lyre, the god was entranced by its music. Zeus was so pleased at the reconciliation that he made Hermes a demi-god who became the messenger of the gods. These myths demonstrate the conflict between the high and low born that is resolved by the sharing and cooperation of the two opposites, again reflecting the lesson of Saturn in the eighth house. The American colonists by the time of the Revolution did not want to be ruled over by British aristocracy but wanted an equal playing field.

Our Gemini Ascendant relates to an orientation towards youth. The fear of death and change discussed above is often avoided by the American focus on anything that extends our youth. The duality of Gemini also reflects the continued interplay between democracy and authoritarianism activated in the Yod.

A side note about Gemini is the fact that it rules the East coast of America along which the first colonies established themselves. Cancer rules the middle, the food belt, while Leo rules the West coast, once called the "Gold Coast".

Unaspected Sun-Mars Square

Two planets, the Sun and Mars, make only one aspect each, a square aspect between them, forming an unaspected "duet", which adds to problems concerning our national character. Take Mars in Aries in the eleventh house by itself. Being unaspected except for the square to the Sun, that martial energy can act in an "all or nothing" manner: present in excess when unnecessary, then disappearing when needed.[12] America has always prided itself on not being aggressive toward other countries unless provoked. Isolationists tried to keep us out of WWI and WWII until something provoked our anger. In WWI many thought it was the sinking of the *Lusitania*, but it was outrage at the discovery of a German plot to ally with Japan and Mexico and renew submarine warfare that precipitated US entry into the war.[13] In the case of WWII, it was the unprovoked attack on Pearl Harbor on December 7, 1941.

Being in an intercepted house, Mars' behavior may also be surreptitious by aiding a country in its own war if it suits our agenda. For example, consider our presence in South Korea and South Vietnam, as well as in Ukraine right now.

Examples of the martial energy of Mars disappearing when needed include our desertion of allies in South Vietnam, abandonment of the Kurds to Turkish forces in Syria, and the withdrawal from Afghanistan.

Examine the Sun in the ninth house. Planets in an unaspected duet may act alone or in concert. The Sun represents identity and sometimes the conscious ego. Since the Sun in this chart also represents the American president, we can say that each president brings their own identity and ego to leadership of the country. As the Commander-in-Chief, the president determines how that Mars energy will be used. The problem with this duet is that once a commitment is made, there's no giving up on it later, even if it was wrong. Vietnam provides an example: when citizens objected to the war, the US answered with complete denial.

In later chapters, we will explore historical events and who was president at the time. The identity of the president also impacts other countries' perception of the United States. The president must learn to relate to the power of his leadership, or it may be projected onto others.

The Sun in Capricorn ruled by Saturn in its dignity is conservative by nature but, being part of an unaspected duet, can be driven to the extremes of authoritarianism and resentment of those perceived to receive benefits without hard work. Though the Sun's placement in the ninth house should provide a measure of tolerance, its nature, as part of this duet, may lead to those extremes in times of need. For instance, during the Great Depression, the US government deported 1.8 million American citizens of Mexican descent because of panic over unemployment and the perception that these "immigrants" were stealing the very food from our mouths.[14]

Cardinal T-Square

The Cardinal T-square adds tension to the opposition from the square of both to the Moon in the fifth house in Libra. Since the Moon represents the people of America, we can see how they swing from one side to the other, depending on what the economy looks like and what politicians are offering us. The conjunction with Neptune makes us vulnerable to the best salesman before us and what the polls tell us. When the tension is too great, we can indulge in the many diversions of the fifth house including alcohol, drugs, sports, entertainments of all kinds, and the hero of the moment.

Sabian Symbols

For those who are interested in Sabian symbols, the eighth degree of Gemini has a symbol of "Aroused strikers surround a factory" with the keywords "Revolt against privileges."[15] Mercury at nine degrees of Aquarius has the symbol "A flag is seen turning into an eagle" with the keywords "Acting out of the vision."[16] These two symbols seem to be in keeping with the story of America which has yet to be totally fulfilled.

We might also add the fifteenth degree of Aquarius on the MC which I think tells us what is possible for America, the symbol being "Two lovebirds sitting on a fence singing happily." Rudhyar interprets this as representing two aspects of spiritual reality which have become united, the self and the ego. Such union is a blessing, "perhaps as a spiritual reward for long-sustained and well-done work." Also, "Inner happiness is seen to be the reward for all individuals who have made a valuable 'contribution' to their community or to humanity as a whole."[17] I interpret this to mean a sense of contentment rather than just happiness.

Chiron

Chiron in the US chart is at 15 Taurus and 11 posited in the twelfth house. "Chiron's primary themes are wounding and healing, taken in the broadest sense…"[18] Enlarging the meaning of Chiron in the US chart helps understand our wounds and how they express themselves. The position in Taurus defines a wound of deep insecurity coupled with a fear of losing safety and abundance. The search for security and safety is often sought through material values.[19] Thus, our wound is expressed in the materialism that has become so much a part of us.

The various issues brought by immigrants to this country define our collective unconsciousness while also representing our "wounds." Our ancestors migrated here to escape persecution, to pursue opportunities unavailable elsewhere, such as the ability to own land or start businesses, for a chance at a productive and happy life, or to seek untold profits. Prisoners were brought here, hoping for freedom and a new start. Slaves did not come freely but their descendants now hope for equality, a hope not yet fully realized.

Our Chiron in the twelfth house shows that we hide these wounds or project the associated fears onto others. For instance, the deep insecurity and fear of loss has led many times in our history to accusations of immigrants taking our jobs or even stealing the very bread from our mouths. Also, Chiron is square to the MC which tells us the issues affect most of the population and are played out on the public stage.

The best outlet for Chiron is in its trine to Saturn in the eighth house which illustrates the "American Dream" of work hard and play by the rules to achieve success, however one defines it. The reverse side views Saturn as the cause of repression. But ultimately, security and safety cannot be achieved with material goods. Our society requires an "awakening" to the fact that materialism does not satisfy our need for healing. What America needs is to show the world the true meaning of our motto "From Many, One." This entails full acceptance of differences, respect for each other, satisfaction of basic needs, and an education that reflects the Golden Rule- "Do not unto others what you do not want done unto you."

In this introduction, I have tried to present some of the relevant themes and issues of America rather than getting into the details of each planet, sign, and house. I leave that to the reader for further insight. The next two chapters give you the historical background of America's beginning before outlining the events that have served to contribute to its growth and development. Following chapters will be devoted to major American events and their ties to the new chart.

INTRODUCTION NOTES

1. https://american-history.net/war-of-independence/end-of-the-american-revolution/ *Accessed 11/19/2023*
2. https://www.history.com/topics/american-revolution/treaty-of-paris *Accessed 11/19/2023*
3. https://msa.maryland.gov/msa/educ/exhibits/treaty/treaty.html *Accessed 11/19/2023*
4. Ibid.
5. https://calvetconnect.blog/2021/01/14/treatyofparis/ *Accessed 6/21/2022*
6. *Journals of the Continental Congress, 1774-1789*, Volume XXVI January 1 – May 10, 1784, pp. 22-31. Available at: https://babel.hathitrust.org/cgi/pt?id=mdp.39015068547051&view=1up&seq=43 *Accessed 4/14/2022*
7. *The Maryland Gazette*, Annapolis, Maryland, article published 1/22/1783, pp. 2-3. Available at: www.newspapers.com/image/41044558 *Accessed 4/14/2022*
8. https://socratic.org/questions/how-did-the-treaty-of-paris-divide-land-in-north-america *Accessed 11/19/2023*
9. Arroyo, Stephan: *Astrology, Karma, and Transformation*; CRCS Publications; Davis, CA, 1978. pp. 220-221
10. Hamaker-Zondag, Karen: *The Yod Book*; Samuel Weisner, Inc., York Beach, ME, English Translation, 1998. p. 40
11. Kellogg, Joan: *The Yod: Its Esoteric Meaning*; American Federation of Astrologers, Tempe, AZ, 1989. p. 4
12. Hamaker-Zondag, Karen: *The Yod Book*; p. 24
13. www.britannica.com/event/Zimmermann-Telegram *Accessed 10/24/2022*
14. www.history.com/news/great-depression-repatriation-drives-mexico-deportation *Accessed 10/25/2022*
15. Rudhyar, Dane: *An Astrological Mandala*; Vintage Books, New York, 1974. pp. 94-95
16. Ibid. p. 254
17. Ibid. p. 258
18. Lass, Martin: *Chiron: Healing Body and Soul*; Llewellyn Publications, Woodbury, Minnesota, 2005. p. 2

19. Lass, Martin: *Musings of a Rogue Comet: Chiron, Planet of Healing*; Galactic Publications Nyack, New York, 2002. p. 299

Chapter One
Colonial Period

"We're Coming to America"
Neil Diamond

The early 1600s saw Western Europeans expanding world exploration in search of new lands, wealth, and trade. The Spanish had already settled in South America, Mexico, and southern parts of the future United States. Meanwhile, King James I granted a charter to the Virginia Company of London for the English settlement of Jamestown, Virginia in 1606.[1]

On May 14, 1607, the first hundred English colonists took up settlement on the banks of the James River, calling it Jamestown. In the first two years, they suffered from famine and disease as well as conflict with the local tribes of Native Americans, the Algonquians. In 1610, a new group arrived with supplies. Remember the story of John Rolfe's marriage to Pocahontas, daughter of Algonquian Chief Powhattan? That was followed by a period of peace in which the colony developed its first profitable crop, tobacco.[2]

The Pilgrims arrived on the Mayflower in 1620 in what is now called New England. Called Separatists, they were among the first religious groups who came to escape the Church of England. These Pilgrims were friendly toward the Native Americans who helped them survive the first year. The first Thanksgiving was a celebration of this event.[3]

The Puritans followed in 1630. They were much more dogmatic and soon dominated the Massachusetts Bay Colony, enforcing strict conformity in their religious beliefs and practices. Although migrating for religious freedom, they did not offer the same freedom to other religious groups. Their attitude of arrogance, superiority and aggression affected their treatment of Native Americans as "heathen savages."[4]

The Dutch sailed up the Hudson River in 1609, later building Fort Orange (now Albany) in 1614 to initiate trade with Native Americans. Some years later, families established the colony of New Netherland there. The Dutch West India Company followed, the Dutch government giving them exclusive trading rights. Twenty-four dollars, some trinkets, and knives were paid to the natives for the island of Manhattan. Peter Minuit became the first governor of the thriving settlement of New Netherland Amsterdam and a second settlement called Wiltwyck (now Kingston), where you can visit the old cemetery at the Dutch Reformed Church that holds the remains of ancestors of four American presidents, including the Roosevelts. To encourage immigration, the Dutch offered free land along the Hudson River.[5] In 1664, an English naval force arrived in New York Harbor and obtained the surrender of the Dutch in New Netherland, which then became New York. The Dutch were allowed to keep their land, language, and religion.[6]

The French established New France, a colony in what is now Canada, which eventually extended from the Gulf of St Lawrence, into the Great Lakes area, and along the Mississippi River to Louisiana.[7] French settlers escaping religious persecution in 1624 also came to the future states of New York, Massachusetts, Pennsylvania, and others.

The desire for religious freedom was a major impetus for American colonization. As we have noted, the Pilgrims and later the Puritans immigrated here to escape the Church of England. Because of the religious intolerance of the Puritans, other groups left the Massachusetts Bay Colony to establish their own settlements. Rhode Island was established in 1636 by Roger Williams, a Puritan who supported religious tolerance, after he was banished from the Massachusetts Bay Colony for religious conflicts.[8] The Religious Society of Friends (Quakers) found a home in Pennsylvania under the leadership of William Penn in 1682 where freedom of worship was allowed.[9] Groups of Amish settled in Pennsylvania[10] and Mennonites found a home in Germantown, Pennsylvania.[11]

The colony of Virginia was dominated by the Anglican church while Maryland was founded to be a refuge for Catholics.[12] New Jersey, Delaware, and the Carolinas were home to Protestants, Baptists, and Presbyterians.

Because King Louis XIV of France declared that Protestants (French Huguenots) must convert to Catholicism or leave the country, many came to America[13] and settled in New Paltz, New York, which is north of New York City. It was founded on land bought from a Native American tribe known as Esopus.[13] You can visit this historical town to see the stone houses built by 1678. The Huguenots also spread out to other colonies such as New York, Massachusetts, Pennsylvania, Virginia, and South Carolina.[15]

The first Jews, twenty-three of them, had originally settled in Dutch Brazil, but had to flee the Portuguese Inquisition after Portugal's conquest of Brazil.[16] Eventually, they made their way to the Dutch Colony of New Amsterdam in 1654. Not welcome at first, thanks to the colony's anti-Jewish governor, they won their right to settle, trade, worship, and own property.[17] When the British later took over, the rights of Jews were maintained after an appeal of Rabba Couty to the King's Council in England that established the Jews as British subjects. "This appears to be the first case in which a colonial grant of naturalization was recognized as valid."[18] By the start of the Revolution, the group had expanded into five communities: New York, Newport, Savannah, Charleston, and Philadelphia.[19]

Other groups came, although not by choice. During the early 1600s, England sent thousands of prisoners to America to be sold as workers on tobacco and grain farms or as soldiers in the time of battles such as the French and Indian War. Most of them were sent to Maryland and Virginia. Prisoners with skills could work in iron mining and ship building. By 1697, the colonies were refusing to accept prison ships, so the process was stopped temporarily. In 1718, Britain's Parliament passed the Transportation Act, subsidizing the shipment of convicts. Ultimately, more than 50,000 prisoners were sent to the colonies. In 1776, the last ship of prisoners was allowed to arrive. By then, many of the convicts had served their terms and either returned to England or remained to become honest citizens.[20]

A vital part of the colonial economy was the use of "indentured servants" who were contracted by landowners for a period of four to seven years in exchange for passage to America, board, and housing. Once the contract was fulfilled, the individual was often given "25 acres of land, a year's worth of corn, arms, a cow and new clothes." Treatment of this group was often harsh and brutal. Of all the immigrants to American colonies, indentured servants accounted for one-half to two-thirds of them.[21]

The slave trade had started with authorization of King Charles I of Spain in 1518 when many Africans were captured and sent to Spanish colonies in the Caribbean.[22] The first to arrive in the American mainland came to Jamestown in 1619. They worked in crop production and were probably treated as indentured servants.[23] As the cost of indentured servants and prison labor increased, plantation owners turned more and more to the purchase of slaves for workers. Laws supporting the institution of slavery increased during the 1600s, including a 1662 Virginia law establishing that children born to an enslaved mother would remain slaves, followed in the next two years by legalization of slavery in three colonies.[24] However, it wasn't until 1705 when the Virginia Slave Codes, "a series of laws that stripped away legal rights and legalized the barbaric and dehumanizing nature of slavery," firmly established the institution.[25] By 1790, the slave population had risen to almost 700,000, mostly in the colonies of Virginia, Maryland and the Carolinas.[26]

By 1700 the colonies contained 250,588 inhabitants, including slaves, that were scattered over a wide area.[27] Most of them were Protestants from England and Western Europe. The English had settled the East coast from Maine to Georgia while the Spanish were in Florida and the French were in the territory of Louisiana and parts of Canada.[28] The English language was used everywhere and by mid-1700s the word "American" was used on both sides of the Atlantic to describe the colonies.[29]

Why did all these immigrants find their way to America? What gave them the courage to face hardship and unknown risks to travel thousands of miles away from their homes? In Europe, America was looked upon as a "land of promise." As we have seen, political, religious, and economic motives contributed to the growing wave of immigrants. Poverty was a motivator. In Europe, where the Feudal Age was ending, the peasantry was not allowed to own land, and they saw an opportunity to do so in America. Another motivating factor was the potential economic profit for companies investing in the colonies. Other people, fleeing from religious persecution or oppression, sought freedom in America to preserve and practice their beliefs. As we have seen, in some places the same freedom was not permitted to others.

The unconscious baggage of beliefs brought by the colonists has impacted the American system to this day. One of the most rampant beliefs of the colonial period was the "civilizing mission," a concept that Western civilizations, being "superior" Christian nations, were obligated to impose their beliefs on what they considered primitive pagan cultures through colonization or even military means.[30] Defined later by

Rudyard Kipling's poem "The White Man's Burden," the philosophy "consisted of the 'Three C's of Colonialism: Civilization, Christianity, and Commerce.'" Indigenous peoples (non-white) were considered culturally inferior, and it was the responsibility of Western Civilization to bring to these "heathen savages" the light of Christianity, civilization, and commerce. The potential for commerce and natural resources gave the true impetus to colonization globally. If native peoples resisted, the colonists used force, saying these ignorant people should be grateful for their gift of Civilization.[31] This philosophy affected the colonists' attitudes towards Native Americans, Black slaves, and later towards other new immigrant groups, and remains part of our collective unconscious.

Another concept affecting colonial attitudes was obedience to the king. The hierarchical structure embedded in English society was evident in the early colonies but was less prominent. Events in England had changed the form of government from a monarchy to a constitutional monarchy. In 1688, Catholic James II was replaced by his Protestant daughter, Mary II and her husband William III of Orange. The two new Protestant rulers signed the Declaration of Rights, providing for free elections and freedom of speech. More power was given to Parliament. The changes had a strong effect on the colonies. Americans felt the rights enjoyed by British subjects were their rights as well.[32]

Of course, these rights applied only to men. Women's rights were not an issue in the early colonies. Women had no rights. They couldn't vote or hold property and were subject totally to their husbands' will and whim. America was a chauvinistic, patriarchal society as it had been in England and the European countries in general. Children were also subject to their father's domination, even when it came to the choice of a mate or a career.[33] It took a hundred years or more for this to gradually change.

The king, his lords and nobles lived in England but hereditary landed nobility had no place in America. The American landed gentry, being college educated, tended to move into seats of government and position because they had more free time. Other groups of lessening status formed the hierarchy, from professionals like doctors and lawyers, then traders and merchants, skilled workers and farmers, and then unskilled laborers.

A unique factor in America leading to rapid economic expansion was the "Puritan Ethic," which promoted the idea that one must work hard and follow the rules to be successful. A corollary to that equated wealth with the blessing of God.[34] This attitude contrasted with the European concept which placed people engaged in trades and other labor lower in the hierarchy. The nobility were the wealthy men of leisure whose obligation was to consume the goods produced by the workers; the latter could not hope to ascend to their level. Americans, however, could, with hard work, move upward and become men of leisure. The hope led to a vigorous work ethic resulting in aggressive economic expansion and westward expansion. Related to this and part of our ethos is the "American Dream" which symbolized the immigrants' hope of finding freedom and opportunity in the New World.

The American Dream "originated in colonial mystique regarding frontier life." [35] in the late 1700s. It is "the belief that anyone, regardless of where they were born or what class they were born into, can attain their own version of success in a society in which upward mobility is possible for everyone."[36] The dream is expressed in the promise given to us in the Declaration of Independence: "…all men are created equal, that they are endowed by their Creator with certain unalienable Rights, that among these are Life, Liberty and the pursuit of Happiness."[37]

Happiness is not guaranteed, only the pursuit of it. The promise of the American Dream creates expectations in its citizens which, if they fail, can lead to feelings of depression and hopelessness and sometimes to anger and violence. It can also lead to the use of drugs and alcohol. America's natal Moon is conjunct Neptune in the fifth house of pleasures which provides a channel for releasing the tension created by the Yod through the Grand Air trine. This conjunction is in Libra which dreams of fairness and justice.

As we shall see in later chapters, the American Dream has changed and evolved over time: post-WWII saw the return of emphasis on family, home, jobs, and consumerism; the '60s saw an emphasis on freedom and justice with protest movements against the Vietnam War and for minorities, women, gay rights, and civil rights, again, reflecting the conflict between Uranus and Saturn as the Axis of Awareness of the Yod in the American chart. The '80s saw the shift back to the materialism of money, fame, and power,[38] so beautifully portrayed by Oscar-winning actor, Michael Douglas in the 1987 film "Wall Street," written by Oliver Stone. In it, Gordon Gekko (Michael Douglas), declares that "…greed, for lack of a better word, is good." The movie is seen as "…an attack on the value of extreme competitiveness where ethics and the law are simply irrelevant."[39] (We could point out Mars square the Sun in the chart.) The

Great Recession of 2008, which produced a greater income gap, seemed to put an end to the American Dream for many,[40] as did the pandemic of the early '20s.

The relationship between the state and religion has been an issue affecting America since its very beginnings. In European countries such as England and France, a particular religion was closely aligned with the government. Immigrants seeking religious freedom, such as the Pilgrims fleeing the Church of England and the French Huguenots escaping forced conversion to Catholicism, carried these conflicts to the New World. Some colonies were more open to accepting various religions than others. As we have seen, the Puritan rule of the Massachusetts Bay Colony was strict and repressive, resulting in others fleeing elsewhere in America to seek their own religious freedom.

Our Founding Fathers saw the problems produced by the church-run state and tried to protect the country from that by including a Constitutional amendment guaranteeing freedom of religion. Despite this, the conflicts continue to this day, with some groups even calling for the United States to be declared a Christian nation. It should be noted that most of the Founding Fathers were Protestants, though of different denominations. However, many of them were influenced by a school of religious thought called Deism, which became popular as the Age of Reason (or Enlightenment) paralleled the settlement of the colonies in America. Although acceptance of a god as the "creator" was part of Deism, "God" was not defined as belonging to a particular religion, and it was human experience and rationality that should supersede religious dogma. Deistic beliefs also "advocated universal education, freedom of the press, and separation of church and state."[41] Its influence on the formation of the American state is significant.

An interesting historical point regarding separation of church and state is the Treaty of Tripoli. This document was negotiated by President George Washington with the Barbary Coast Muslim states of Tripoli, Morocco, and Tunis and signed by President John Adams. Article 11 of the treaty states: "As the Government of the United States of America is not, in any sense, founded on the Christian religion; as it has in itself no character of enmity against the laws, religion, or tranquility, of… (Muslims)…".[42] The document clarified the fact that the Founding Fathers were not interested in establishing a state religion; they were primarily concerned with religious freedom. "Ten years after the Constitutional Convention ended its work, the country assured the world that the

United States was a secular state, and its negotiations would adhere to the rule of law, not the dictates of the Christian faith."[43]

The conflict between Saturn and Uranus is even more visible today as division in the populace struggles with what form of government it really wants, democratic or authoritative, just as it did 250 years ago before the Revolution (as Pluto enters Aquarius). Since Saturn is also in Aquarius, there may be some hope that the issues portrayed in this book may come to some decisive conclusion in the decades to come.

CHAPTER ONE NOTES

1. www.history.com/topics/colonial-america/jamestown *Accessed 9/24/2022*
2. Ibid.
3. www.newsweek.com/whats-the-difference-between-pilgrim-and-puritan-397974 *Accessed 4/7/2022*
4. Ibid.
5. https://spartacus-educational.com/USAEholland.htm *Accessed 9/24/2022*
6. https://www.britannica.com/topic/American-colonies *Accessed 1/15/2024*
7. https://www.thecanadianencyclopedia.ca/en/article/new-france *Accessed 12/28/2023*
8. https://en.wikipedia.org/wiki/Colonial_history_of_the_United_States *Accessed 12/27/2023*
9. https://www.history.com/topics/immigration/history-of-quakerism *Accessed 5/3/2022*
10. Persecution, Division, and Opportunity: The Origins of the Old Order Amish | Pennsylvania Center for the Book (psu.edu) *Accessed 12/27/2023*
11. https://www.history.com/this-day-in-history/first-mennonites-arrive-in-america *Accessed 12/27/2023*
12. https://en.wikipedia.org/wiki/Colonial_history_of_the_United_States *Accessed 12/27/2023*
13. www.huguenotsocietyofamerica.org/history/huguenot-history/ *Accessed 5/3/2022*
14. https://en.wikipedia.org/wiki/New_Paltz,_New_York *Accessed 12/27/2023*
15. www.huguenotsocietyofamerica.org/history/huguenot-history/ *Accessed 5/3/2022*
16. https://en.wikipedia.org/wiki/Jewish_arrival_in_New_Amsterdam *Accessed 3/4/2024*
17. https://www.brandeis.edu/hornstein/sarna/contemporaryjewishlife/Archive/EvolvingAmericanJudaism.pdf *Accessed 5/3/2022*
18. https://en.wikipedia.org/wiki/History_of_the_Jews_in_Colonial_America *Accessed 12/23/2023*

19. https://www.brandeis.edu/hornstein/sarna/contemporaryjewishlife/Archive/EvolvingAmericanJudaism.pdf *Accessed 5/3/2022*
20. https://encyclopediavirginia.org/entries/convict-labor-during-the-colonial-period *Accessed 5/3/2022*
21. www.pbs.org/historydetectives/feature/indentured-servants-in-the-us *Accessed 5/3/2022*
22. https://www.history.com/news/transatlantic-slave-first-ships-details *Accessed 5/1/2022*
23. https://www.history.com/news/american-slavery-before-jamestown-1619 *Accessed 5/01/2022*
24. https://www.battlefields.org/learn/articles/slavery-colonial-america *Accessed 12/27/2023*
25. https://www.history.com/news/american-slavery-before-jamestown-1619 *Accessed 5/01/2022*
26. https://faculty.weber.edu/kmackay/statistics_on_slavery.htm *Accessed 12/27/2023*
27. https://en.wikipedia.org/wiki/List_of_colonial_and_pre-Federal_U.S._historical_population *Accessed 12/27/2023*
28. https://en.wikipedia.org/wiki/Colonial_history_of_the_United_States *Accessed 12/27/2023*
29. https://www.britannica.com/topic/American-colonies *Accessed 1/15/2024*
30. https://en.wikipedia.org/wiki/Civilizing_mission *Accessed 12/27/2023*
31. https://scholarblogs.emory.edu/violenceinafrica/sample-page/the-philosophy-of-colonialism-civilization-christianity-and-commerce/ *Accessed 9/24/2022*
32. https://history.com/topics/british-history//glorious-revolution *Accessed 9/27/2022*
33. Wood, Gordon S.: *The Radicalism of the American Revolution*; First Vintage Books Edition, NY, 1991. pp. 67-68
34. https://en.wikipedia.org/wiki/Protestant_work_ethic *Accessed 3/2/2024*
35. https://en.wikipedia.org/wiki/American_Dream *Accessed 12/27/2023*
36. https://www.investopedia.com/terms/a/american-dream.asp *Accessed 9/28/2022*

37. https://www.archives.gov/founding-docs/declaration-transcript *Accessed 9/28/2022*
38. https://realwealth.com/learn/what-is-the-american-dream-today/ *Accessed 9/29/2022*
39. https://en.wikipedia.org/wiki/Wall_Street_(1987_film) *Accessed 9/29/2022*
40. https://realwealth.com/learn/what-is-the-american-dream-today/ *Accessed 9/29/2022*
41. https://www.britannica.com/topic/The-Founding-Fathers-Deism-and-Christianity-1272214 *Accessed 9/29/2022*
42. https://en.wikipedia.org/wiki/Treaty_of_Tripoli *Accessed 9/30/22*
43. Lambert, Frank: T*he Founding Fathers and the Place of Religion in America;* Princeton University Press, Princeton, New Jersey, 2006. p.11

Chapter Two

From Rage to Revolt

"I was born in America"
Bruce Springsteen

The colonial population had increased to 1,170,760 by 1750,[1] bringing many changes. Although the English constitutional monarchy provided an example of republican values to the colonies, Americans did not have much understanding of a central government. Each colony followed its own ways.[2] Their appointed royal governors didn't have titles, wealth, or the tools of power.[3] The influence of an established church and a social hierarchy to maintain the divide between superiors and inferiors was also absent.[4]

Mobility was upward since most men could secure their own land and become rich enough to buy the luxury items that formerly only aristocrats could afford.[5] "Two-thirds of the white colonial population owned land compared with only one-fifth of the English population." This independence allowed many of the colonists to buy their way into the "gentry," assuring connections to commercial, banking, and political institutions. No central authority existed to rein in the growth of "republicanism" amongst the colonies.[6]

The keyword for this period was mobility. The burgeoning population increased the pressures of overcrowding, resulting in movement to more open space.[7] The number of transient emigrants going from job to job and from town to town rose. The percentage of poor increased, further straining the social system. Those who tried to rule found it difficult to enforce their authority.[8]

While many prosperous colonists became engaged in pursuing wealth, formal church attendance declined. Many under the influence of the

Enlightenment turned away from religious beliefs to concepts of reason, science, and personal morality. In response, the movement called the Great Awakening, stirred in every colony by transiting preachers of Calvinism, began in the 1730s and had great influence for the two decades that followed. Jonathan Edwards' 1741 sermon, "Sinners in the Hands of an Angry God," shocked the colonies in New England. As it spread through the rest of the colonies with preachers such as George Whitfield, new churches which conflicted with other churches were created.[9] "Edwards' message centered on the idea that humans were sinners, God was an angry judge and individuals needed to ask for forgiveness. He also preached justification by faith alone."[10] A sinner could only be saved from hell by salvation. This movement "reinvigorated religion in America at a time when it was steadily declining and introduced ideas that would penetrate into American culture for many years to come."[11] In today's America, it is still a powerful force affecting modern politics.

Meanwhile, concepts of the Enlightenment reached America from Europe, where they were magnified, combined with Native American sources, and transformed into a homegrown version. Philosophical and scientific thought moved away from the emphasis of religion toward the importance of human rationality, introducing new concepts of democracy, freedom, educational reform, and political ideals that had a profound effect on our Founding Fathers.[12]

The works of Enlightenment thinkers such as John Locke, Rousseau, and Voltaire were inserted into the curricula of American colleges such as Yale, the College of William and Mary, and Harvard. Such works influenced the thinking of Benjamin Franklin, John Adams, Thomas Jefferson, Alexander Hamilton,[13] and especially James Madison who attended the College of New Jersey (now Princeton), the "most politically radical college in the country."[14] "Politically, the age is distinguished by an emphasis on equality under the law, economic liberty, republicanism and religious tolerance, as clearly expressed in the United States Declaration of Independence."[15]

Enlightenment had other significant effects. "Attempts to reconcile science and religion sometimes resulted in a rejection of prophecy, miracle, and revealed religion, resulting in an inclination toward Deism among some major political leaders of the age."[16] Deism presented an alternative view, one that emphasized human rationality and experience over religious dogma.[17] It espoused the idea of a single creator god that had set the universe in motion under nature's laws, leaving it alone thereafter to function without the need for a deity to intercede in human concerns. "The evidence of a creator is discernible through human reason and logic and has nothing to do with any scriptural authority, revelation, or miraculous events. For Deists, God does not intervene in human affairs."[18]

Deism influenced the thinking of our Founding Fathers and influenced the move towards independence. "It stood for rational inquiry, for skepticism about dogma and mystery, and for religious toleration. Many of its adherents advocated universal education, freedom of the press, and separation of church and state. If the nation owes much to the Judeo-Christian tradition, it is also indebted to Deism, a movement of reason and equality that influenced the Founding Fathers to embrace liberal political ideals remarkable for their time."[19]

Classical education that included the study of Greek and Roman culture greatly shaped the Founding Fathers' views on the structure of governments, particularly democracies and republics. Roman writers presented republican ideals such as virtue, truth, and disinterested public leadership. "Virtue" meant the ability for leaders to govern by putting the public good above their own selfish interests[20] which, in this case, "…could be found only in a republic of equal, active, and independent citizens. To be completely virtuous citizens, men—never women, because it was assumed they were never independent—had to be free from dependence and from the petty interests of the marketplace. Any loss of independence and virtue was corruption."[21] Disinterest meant not being corrupted by private profit.

By 1756, England and France declared war on each other.[22] Americans took part in the conflict because the French were making incursions into their land. Some Indian tribes fought for the French, while the Iroquois nation of tribes joined the British and Americans.[23] This French and Indian war ended in 1763 with a treaty between England, France, and Spain. "France ceded her Canadian claims to England, as well as Louisiana east of the Mississippi R., excluding New Orleans, and Spain gave up Florida for return of Cuba and Philippines."[24]

The war left England depleted of funds and set off land fever in the colonists who saw opportunities to spread into new lands west of the Appalachian Mountains to the Mississippi.[25] Trade between the colonies increased and so did entrepreneurship as farm families turned to manufacturing goods that could be sold for profit. America had become a consumer nation.[26] The vigorous societal and economic growth encouraged increased feelings of independence in the colonists. A monarch was now considered more of a father figure who needed to respect the needs of his children (subjects), rather than demand complete obedience. "Idolatry to Monarchs, and servility to Aristocratical Pride" said John Adams in the summer of 1776, "was never so totally eradicated from so many Minds in so short a Time."[27]

What happened in this "short time" from 1760 to 1776 was a series of British Parliament Acts attempting to collect taxes from the colonists to pay for debts incurred during the French and Indian War. The acts affected colonial trade and were deeply resented as "taxation without representation."[28] For example, the Tea Act of 1773, "designed to save East India Co. from bankruptcy by remitting all British duties on tea while retaining tax on tea exported to America" resulted in a British monopoly that undersold colonial competition and almost eliminated the American business. The Tea Act precipitated the American revolt known as the Boston Tea Party.[29]

The negative impact on the colonial economy increased Americans' rage to the point that the severing of all relationships with England was considered.[30] Their appeals to Parliament went unheard, and on May 17, 1774, Rhode Island issued the first call for an intercolonial congress. Soon other colonies joined in. September 5, 1774 was the day the "1st Continental Congress met in Philadelphia with all of 13 colonies but Georgia represented."[31] They adopted a Declaration of Rights that included "rights to life, liberty, and property."[32]

King George III, angered by his rebellious colonists, sent British reinforcements to Boston. The Battle of Lexington in April of 1775 in Massachusetts in which eight of sixty colonialists were killed[33] began the conflict we all know as the Revolutionary War. In June, George Washington accepted the role of supreme commander of the Continental Army.[34]

The Declaration of Independence, which many astrologers use as the birth of the United States, was drafted by Thomas Jefferson in June of 1776. Copies were sent to all the colonies, and it was adopted July 4, 1776. By August 2, all members of congress had signed it. However, the signers' names were not made public for over six months for fear that this "treasonable act" could result in their deaths if the quest for independence failed. On September 9, 1776, the Continental Congress replaced the words "United Colonies" with the words "United States."[35]

The war continued for 8 long years. The British commander Cornwallis finally surrendered at Yorktown in October 1781, essentially ending the war in America, but American independence was not officially recognized by the British until the Treaty of Paris in 1783.[36] As we have noted, the Treaty was ratified by the United States in January 1784, marking the birthdate of the new nation.

By 1780, the population had increased to almost 3,000,000 colonists.[37] The war was close to ending, but no plans had been made for the aftermath. The colonies had agreed to the Articles of Confederation, written in 1777 because of wartime urgency, but they did not come into force until March 1, 1781. The Articles allowed limited central government authority,[38] but the independence and sovereignty of the states were the primary concerns. However, the central government was so limited that it was essentially rendered ineffective. The states continued their separate policies until the weaknesses became obvious.

A signal event exposing the problems was Shays' Rebellion, taking place in 1787 in Massachusetts. Revolutionary War soldiers who had become farmers had not received adequate compensation for their wartime service. They struggled to maintain their farms while paying off debts and taxes. Boston authorities foreclosed on their farms and began arresting them. Proposals for peaceful settlement of these issues were not heeded, eventually leading to a military confrontation.[39] Faced with an armed rebellion, Boston authorities called militias from neighboring states to help but received none. "Many sympathized with the Shaysite grievances and would not take arms as militiamen to suppress their neighbors, but they also deplored the insurgent attack on government and refused to join the rebellion."[40] Shays' Rebellion stimulated the debate regarding states' rights versus a strong federal government when a new Constitution was discussed to replace the Articles of Confederation.

Activity in democratically elected state legislatures magnified the perceived inefficiency of the Articles. James Madison, the father of the Constitution, was appalled by the endless discussions, pressure to make legislation "popular," and the prevalence of private and local interests that he observed in the state assemblies. He began to fear what democracy in America could entail.[41] "Democracy was no solution to the problem; democracy was the problem."[42]

In May 1787, state delegates met to revise the Articles of Confederation but instead they drew up a new Constitution to replace them.[43] The conflict between Federalists and antifederalists had begun, with states' rights versus central government control still a persistent battle today.

Paralleling that argument was the states' "right" to maintain the institution of slavery. Many Northern states abolished slavery between 1774 and 1804, but the South considered it an economically vital institution and continued it.[44] These differences became an issue at the Constitutional Congress and were put aside for the sake of ratification. However, the question of slavery would rear its head again, eventually leading to a civil war.

This important congressional session will be discussed in the next chapter.

CHAPTER TWO NOTES

1. List of colonial and pre-Federal U.S. historical population - Wikipedia *Accessed 12/27/2023*
2. Wood, Gordon S.: *The Radicalism of the American Revolution*; First Vintage Books Edition, NY, 1991. pp.. 139-142
3. Ibid. p. 140
4. Ibid. pp. 139-142
5. Ibid. pp. 144, 169-170
6. Ibid. p. 155
7. Ibid. pp. 159-160
8. Ibid. p. 163
9. https://thehistoryjunkie.com/first-great-awakening-facts *Accessed 11/5/2022*
10. https://www.history.com/topics/european-history/great-awakening *Accessed 11/5/2022*
11. https://thehistoryjunkie.com/first-great-awakening-facts *Accessed 11/5/2022*
12. https://en.wikipedia.org/wiki/American_Enlightenment *Accessed 10/31/2022*
13. Ibid.
14. Ricks, Thomas E.: *First Principles*; Harper Collins Publishers, New York, NY, 2020. pp. XXI-XXII, 9
15. https://en.wikipedia.org/wiki/American_Enlightenment *Accessed 10/31/2022*
16. Ibid.
17. https://www.britannica.com/topic/The-Founding-Fathers-Deism-and-Christianity-1272214 *Accessed 4/27/2022*
18. https://study.com/learn/lesson/deism-founding-fathers.html *Accessed 11/1/2022*
19. https://www.britannica.com/topic/The-Founding-Fathers-Deism-and-Christianity-1272214 *Accessed 4/27/2022*
20. Wood, Gordon S.: *The Radicalism of the American Revolution*; pp. 130-132
21. Ibid. p. 132

22. Carruth, Gorton, & Associates, Ed. *The Encyclopedia of American Facts & Dates*, 7th Edition; Thomas T. Crowell, Publishers, NY 1956. p. 70
23. https://en.wikipedia.org/wiki/French_and_Indian_War Accessed 2/27/2024
24. Carruth, Gorton, & Associates, Ed. *The Encyclopedia of American Facts & Dates*, p. 74
25. https://openstax.org/books/us-history/pages/5-1-confronting-the-national-debt-the-aftermath-of-the-french-and-indian-war Accessed 2/27/2024
26. Wood, Gordon S.: *The Radicalism of the American Revolution*; pp. 169-175
27. Butterfield, Lyman H. et al, Eds.: *Adams Family Correspondence, Volume 2;* The Belknap Press, Cambridge, Mass.,1963. p. 74 (Letter from John Adams to his wife Abigail Adams, July 3,1776)
28. Acts of the American Revolution - History of Massachusetts Blog Accessed 3/6/2024
29. Carruth, Gorton, & Associates, Ed. *The Encyclopedia of American Facts & Dates*, p. 80
30. Acts of the American Revolution - History of Massachusetts Blog Accessed 3/6/2024
31. Carruth, Gorton, & Associates, Ed. *The Encyclopedia of American Facts & Dates*, pp. 80, 82
32. Ibid. p. 82
33. Ibid. pp. 82, 84
34. Ibid. p. 84
35. Ibid. p. 88
36. https://en.wikipedia.org/wiki/American_Revolutionary_War Accessed 3/7/2024
37. List of colonial and pre-Federal U.S. historical population - Wikipedia Accessed 12/27/2023
38. https://www.history.com/topics/early-us/articles-of-confederation Accessed 3/4/2024
39. https://www.history.com/topics/early-us/shays-rebellion Accessed 11/5/2022

40. Beeman, Richard; Botein, Stephen; Carter, Edward C. II, Eds.: *Beyond Confederation – Origins of the Constitution and American National Identity*; University of North Carolina Press, Chapel Hill, NC, 1987. p. 115
41. Ibid. pp. 72-74
42. Ibid. p. 75
43. Fortenbaugh, Robert: *The Nine Capitals of the United States;* Maple Press Co., York, Pennsylvania, 1948. p. 76
44. https://www.history.com/topics/black-history/slavery *Accessed 3/4/2024*

Chapter Three

We the People of the United States

"People Have the Power"
Patti Smith

Shays' Rebellion showed the populace that the Articles of Confederation were not strong enough to confront the problems of the time. A conference at Annapolis in September 1786 was arranged to "consider the many problems of the commerce of the entire country." However, a quorum was not established and the delegates that showed scheduled another convention for May 1787 in Philadelphia. Here they could discuss a new constitution more adequate for the country's needs. Congress approved the meeting but specified it be held only "for the sole and express purpose of amending the Articles of Confederation and reporting action to Congress." However, delegates met secretly, George Washington presiding, drafting a new constitution despite Congress's instructions.[1]

For several months, the delegates made speeches, debated, and argued until it became clear that two opposing factions existed: the Federalists, led by James Madison, and those that were opposed to a strong federal government, called anti-federalists. The Founding Fathers' vision was of a republican government led by intelligent, well-educated men of "virtue" and "disinterestedness" that could govern for the sake of the whole community without a motivation of profit and gain. On the other side, revolutionaries that had fought for freedom from monarchial and aristocratic influences feared that a president could just as easily become a tyrant, taking away their rights and freedom as well as imposing a new form of aristocracy above the people. The state legislatures had made popular those who were not educated visionaries of the gentry but who had other ideas such as liberty and equality, competitiveness, and individualism. "By the early nineteenth century, America had already emerged as the most egalitarian, most materialistic, most individualistic – and evangelical Christian – society in Western history."[2]

In the end, both sides won because the Federalists got their constitution and those opposed would get amendments which would guarantee their liberty. Although a republic was the Constitution's proposed type of government in the sense that the population retained control and government positions would not be inherited, Madison claimed it "was of a 'mixed nature' and 'unprecedented' in the history of the world." It had components of both state and federal control, based on governing by both state and national representatives, all ultimately selected by the people.[3]

The next great hurdle was getting the required nine of thirteen states to ratify the Constitution to establish its legitimacy. This did not happen until New Hampshire signed for ratification at Concord on June 21, 1788, giving the needed vote. The official start of the new government was March 4, 1789. The remaining states fell in line and joined the Union. The new ten amendments we call the Bill of Rights were incorporated into the Constitution between 1789 and 1791.[4] Washington was inaugurated on March 30, 1789, with John Adams as Vice President.

At this important time in our history, a bargain was made that ensured continuation of slavery. Despite objections of many delegates, the Constitution tends to favor slavery, including five provisions explicitly sanctioning the practice. However, the word "slavery" appears in the Constitution only once- in the amendment ultimately abolishing that institution. "The Northern delegates to the 1787 Convention believed the word 'slave' would 'stain' the Constitution." Thus, labels such as "other persons" or "such persons" or "person held to service or labor" are employed. "As long as they were assured of protection for their institution, the Southerners at the Convention were willing to do without the word 'slave.'"[5]

Examine the comparison chart of the ratification chart with the US chart. I used a noon chart because they met at different times. You will notice Jupiter (constitutions) is conjunct the US Uranus (the change from the Articles of Confederation) as well as the Sun, and trine Saturn

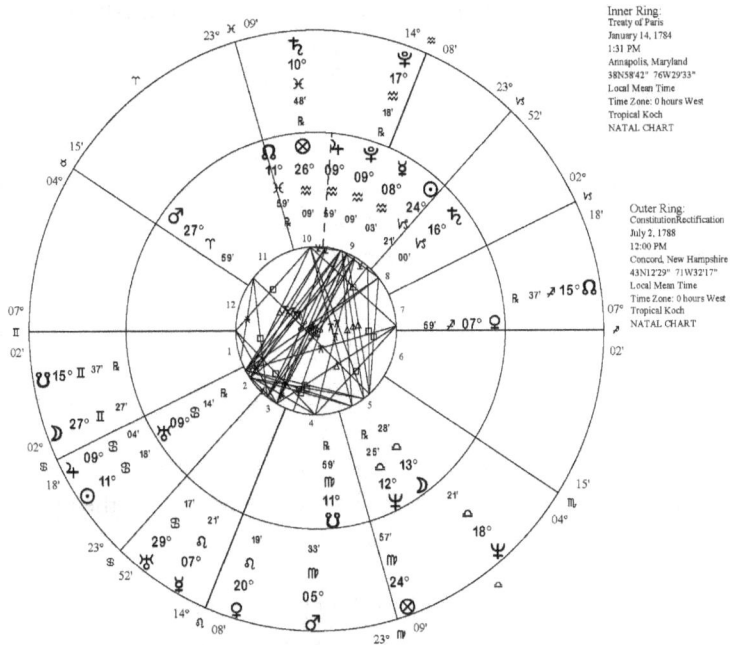

Figure 3-1
Comparison Chart of the Treaty of Paris and The Ratification of the U.S. Constitution

(Authority) in the tenth house conjunct the US North Node. The Moon in the first house has trined both Pluto on the Midheaven (transformation) with Neptune (vision) to indicate they have accepted the new republic. The adjustment in the wording of slavery made to the Southern states is shown by the inconjunct between Saturn in Pisces to Mercury in Leo in the third house.

An interesting historical fact concerns the contribution to the Constitution from the Iroquois Confederacy of Nations. This Native American league made up of five (later six) tribes living in New York was founded between 1142 and 1450. It was a fully functioning democracy that interested some of the Founding Fathers like Benjamin Franklin and George Washington. "The government structure of the Iroquois Confederacy is a democracy based around three branches of government. First, chiefs are chosen from each clan to represent the tribe in the confederacy. Second, all major legislation had to be voted across the whole of the confederacy. Third, the women of the Iroquois Confederacy could demote the chiefs providing a valuable balance."[6]

The American government waited for the two hundredth-year anniversary of our Constitution to recognize the contribution made by the Iroquois Confederacy. On October 21, 1988, Congressional Resolution 331 was issued to acknowledge "the contribution made by the Iroquois Confederacy and other Indian Nations to the formation and development of the United States" and "Whereas the original framers of the Constitution, including, most notably George Washington and Benjamin Franklin, are known to have greatly admired the concepts of the Six Nations of the Iroquois Confederacy;" and also, " Whereas the confederation of the original Thirteen Colonies into one republic was influenced by the political system developed by the Iroquois Confederacy as were many of the democratic principles which were incorporated into the Constitution itself;" and, finally, in recognition of America's need to maintain good faith with the tribes, "...to uphold its legal and moral obligation for the benefit of all its citizens so that they and their posterity may also continue to enjoy the rights they have enshrined in the United States Constitution for time immemorial."[7]

It took more than 100 years for the United States to allow women to have an integral part in the voting process. It is interesting to me that America delayed 200 years in recognizing the contributions of the Iroquois Confederacy to our Constitution, when at that time they were considered "heathen savages" who nevertheless, ironically, were able to include women in their government.

CHAPTER THREE NOTES

1. Fortenbaugh, Robert: *The Nine Capitals of the United States*; Maple Press Co., York, Pennsylvania, 1948. pp. 75-76
2. Wood, Gordon S.: *The Radicalism of the American Revolution*; First Vintage Books Edition, N.Y., 1993. p. 280
3. Maier, Pauline: *Ratification*; Simon & Shuster, New York, NY, 2010. p. 269
4. https://history.com/this-day-in-history/u-s-constitution-ratified *Accessed 11/14/2022*
5. Beeman, Richard; Botein, Stephen; & Carter, Edward C., Editors: *Beyond Confederation: Origins of the Constitution and American National Identity*; University of N. Carolina Press, 1987. In Finkelman, Paul: *Slavery and the Constitutional Convention: Making a Covenant with Death*. pp. 188-225
6. https://thehistoryace.com/the-3-branch-government-structure-of-the-iroquois-confederacy/ *Accessed 11/20/2022*
7. https://www.govtrack.us/congress/bills/100/hconres331/text *Accessed 11/20/2022*

Chapter Four

The First Federal Congress Meets

"Better World A-Coming"
Woody Guthrie

March 4, 1789 was the date set for the first federal Congress to meet in New York City. However, events did not proceed as expected, perhaps due to the Mercury retrograde that day.

"The guns boomed again at noon on March 4 to signal the opening of Congress. Senators and congressmen gathered in the glamorous chambers that Peter L'Enfant was building for them only to discover to their deep embarrassment that both houses fell far short of the quorum required to do business."[1]

Most of the expected delegates, it seemed, were too busy with local matters or personal concerns, such as planting crops, to attend. Each day the delegates already present entered Federal Hall with high hopes, only to be disappointed again at the lack of quorum. Then, gathering at local coffeehouses and taverns, they debated possibilities for the new capital's location rather than considering potential state affairs.[2]

On the first day of April, the House achieved a quorum (Mercury being direct). The Senate finally convened with a quorum on April 5th. Finally, the new Congress could begin setting up the newly established government.[3] (Whew!) This day being the start of business, I used the chart for April 5, 1789 at 11:00 AM, the hour being the most common opening time for Congressional sessions.

Whether the new government would function at all was an open question. The difficulties trying to unite such greatly disparate regions, personalities, and belief systems were immense. No country had ever attempted such a task. As James Madison, the man most critical in guiding the First Congress along the new road, stated: "We are in a wilderness without a single footstep to guide us."[4]

The first order of business required all members to take an oath to the Constitution. Many had previously rejected the Constitution and assurance of their loyalty was desired. Apparently, this did not present a problem. Next came the counting of electoral ballots for president and vice president. George Washington won the Presidency unanimously, as expected. John Adams received the plurality for Vice President.[5]

ACTIONS OF FIRST CONGRESS [6, 7]

- Washington inaugurated on April 30, 1789.
- Washington given the title of President of the United States on May 14, 1789.
- Creation of the Cabinet, allowing, after some debate, the President the power to hire and fire his appointees.
- Revenue bills debated and adopted by July 1789, after which Congress adjourned to join the Independence Day celebrations on July 4.
- John Jay appointed the Chief Justice of the Supreme Court.
- The State Department set up with Thomas Jefferson as Secretary of State.
- The Treasury Department set up with Alexander Hamilton as Secretary of Treasury.
- The Ten Amendments (Bill of Rights) ratified and added to the Constitution in December 1792.

Many other events occurred that cannot be covered here. Read about them in books such as *The First Congress* by Fergus M. Bordewich.

The First Congress was the most critical in our history. It was responsible for organizing the entire system of government we have. The work encompassed two years while an engaged population followed the process through multiple newspapers. The location of the capital city was selected but the building was not completed until 1800. During the First Congress, officials persisted in their work despite the difficulties attending sessions far from home, where living expenses were considerable

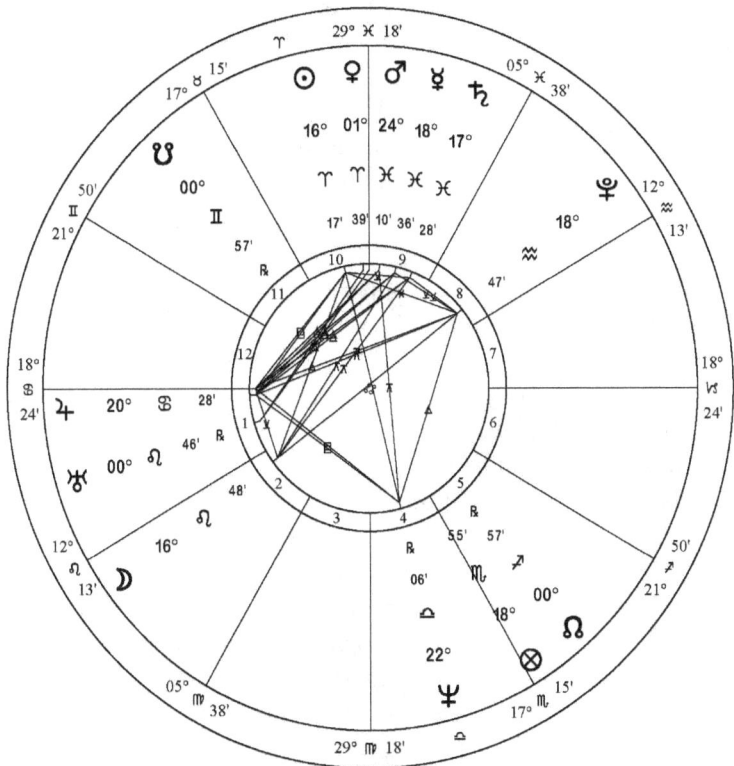

Figure 4-1
First Meeting of Senate Quorum
April 5, 1789, 11:00 AM
New York, New York

and their only income was six dollars a day. The determination and sacrifice displayed by these men to complete this great task are admirable.

The first chart to be examined is the day the Senate achieved a quorum, allowing the business of organizing the government to proceed. The date was April 5, 1789 at 11:00 AM in New York City. Notice first the stellium of planets in the ninth and tenth houses, both tied together by Pisces ruling them (long term vision, republics) and connected to eight houses in the chart.

The Venus that rules the legislators (11th house) is in Aries (beginnings) in the tenth house (government). Even though they were there to cooperate, each delegate had their own view which would lead to conflicts. The Federalists wanted a strong central government while others

The First Federal Congress Meets 31

were more concerned about states' rights.

Although the public adored their new President, they were suspicious that subsequent presidents could have too much power (being commander-in-chief as well as controlling the Treasury Department) with Pluto in the 8th house. James Madison tried to reassure them, pointing out the fact that since it required millions of votes to elect a president, a "vicious character" could never be selected and dictatorship would be a virtual impossibility.[8]

Neptune in the fourth house opposing the Sun illustrates the uncertainty George Washington felt about creating the role of president and the office of the executive branch. "I walk on untrodden ground," he wrote. "There is scarcely any action [I may take] whose motives may not be subject to double interpretation. There is scarcely any part of my conduct which may not hereafter be drawn into precedent."[9]

The Neptune-Sun opposition also relates to financial problems facing the new nation. After the Revolution, the country was facing bankruptcy. Debts from the war pressed on Congress as well as the states. Alexander Hamilton's proposal of a new national bank heightened the continual conflict between states' rights and federal rights, financiers and merchants vs farmers and plantation owners, and North vs South. People feared a national bank would supplant state banks. For once, the strong Federalist James Madison found himself opposed to Hamilton. The bill for the plan's adoption was debated for some time, but eventually it passed and was signed into law by George Washington on February 25, 1791. Hamilton's system allowed the bank to act as a fiscal agent for the new government. It could issue banknotes, collect tax revenues, make loans, pay government bills, extend credit, and promote commerce.[10] It is interesting to note that Hamilton has a stellium in Capricorn with his Sun, Moon, Venus, and Saturn falling in the eighth house (finances) in the US chart.

Jupiter in the first house is exalted in Cancer, illustrating the legislators' hard work in service to the people. Its trine to Saturn indicates the results of their work would have a long life. The trine of Uranus in the first house to Venus in the tenth demonstrates the newness of their undertaking which became known as "the Great Experiment."

The First Congress concluded its third and final session with an outpouring of legislation that was completed by candlelight March 3, 1791.[11] Much relieved but satisfied, the delegates were happy to return home. One Representative summed up events: "On a basis of what we have done, and in the manner it has been done in the course of two years – I think we may return to our Countries without a Blush."[12]

The activities of the First Congress were closely followed by Americans through newspaper reports avidly discussed by persons both literate and illiterate. People realized they were not just state citizens, but now citizens of a new nation. The common people would control their own governance.[13] But, as one European observer noted, "'These rebel colonists are on their way to become one of the most powerful of nations. We shall one day see them the astonishment of Europe; and if they do not actually dictate laws to the two worlds, at least, they will be their example.'" He added, "'Only let the Americans be wise.'"[14]

The one thing I would add to this interpretation is the Sabian Symbol for the Midheaven of 29 degrees of Pisces: "Light breaking into many colors as it passes through a prism."[15] An echo of E Pluribus Unum, "from the Many, One," which is the fundamental lesson America must eventually fulfill.

I hope to satisfy your curiosity by adding the charts of the two men who contributed to this Federal Congress and the establishment of our government: James Madison and Alexander Hamilton. See what connections they have to the two charts presented in this chapter.

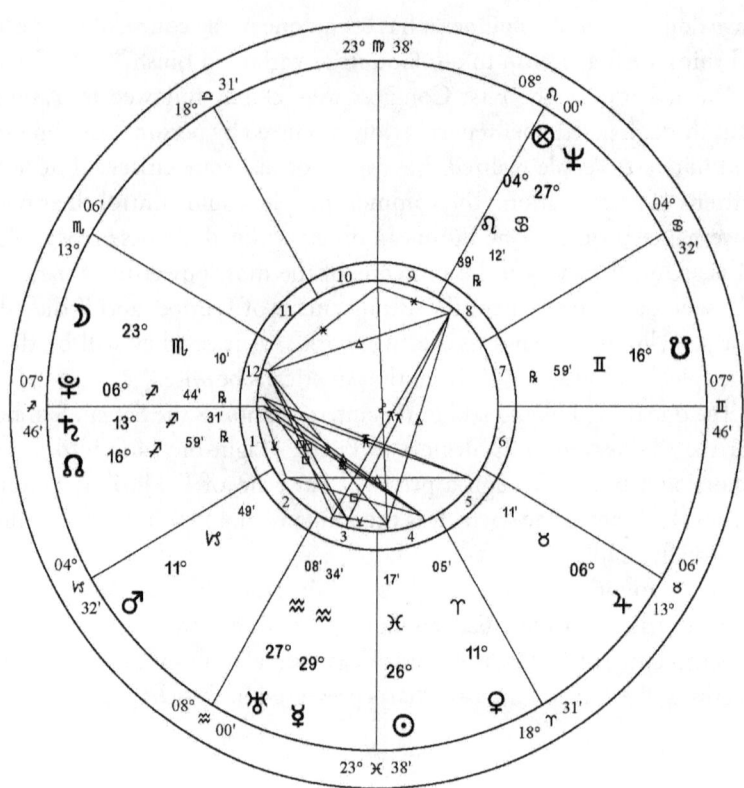

Figure 4-3
James Madison Natal Chart
March 16, 1751, 11:59 PM
Port Conway, Virginia

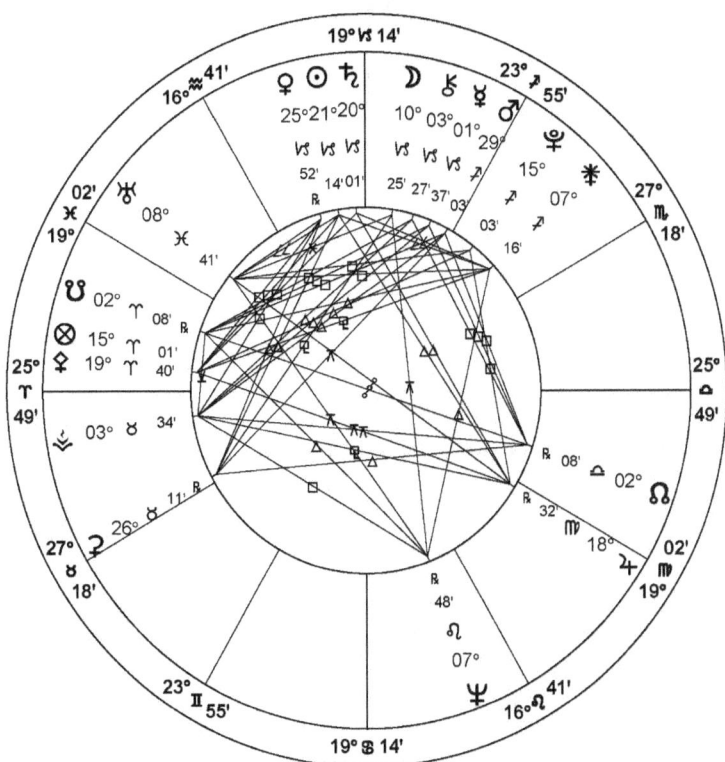

Figure 4-4
Alexander Hamilton Natal Chart
January 11, 1755, 12:00 PM
St. Croix, Virgin Islands

CHAPTER FOUR NOTES

1. Bordewich, Fergus M.: *The First Congress*, Simon & Shuster Paperbacks, NY, 2016. pp. 27-28
2. Ibid. pp. 29-30
3. Ibid. pp. 30-32
4. Ibid. p. 5
5. Ibid. p. 32
6. Gorton, Carruth, & Associates, Eds: *The Encyclopedia of American Facts and Dates*, 7th Edition; Thomas T. Crowell, Publishers, 1956. p. 100
7. Bordewich, Fergus M.: *The First Congress*.
8. Ibid. p. 97
9. Ibid. p. 36
10. https://www.philadelphiafed.org/-/media/frbp/assets/institutional/education/publications/the-first-bank-of-the-united-states.pdf *Accessed 4/22/2023*
11. Bordewich, Fergus M.: *The First Congress*, p. 301
12. Ibid. p. 303
13. Ibid. p. 307
14. Ibid. p. 313
15. Rudhyar, Dane. *An Astrological Mandala*; Vintage Books, New York, 1974. p. 287

Chapter Five

Westward Expansion

"From sea to shining sea"
"America the Beautiful"

The idea of "Manifest Destiny" was that territorial expansion from the Atlantic to Pacific was inevitable for white Americans and divinely inspired. The early settlers considered themselves superior beings tasked with enlightening primitive people of other races, and they felt justified in expelling Native Americans and other groups from land they believed destined to be theirs.[1]

The concept encouraged the rapid westward spread of settlers already eager to conquer new lands. Although not universally accepted and frequently debated, it resulted in five major increases in territory. These included the Louisiana Purchase in 1803, the addition of Florida in 1819, annexation of Texas in 1845, establishment of the Oregon Territory in 1848, and the Gadsden Purchase in 1853.

The rapid expansion created problems that are still with us. Whether slavery should be allowed in the new territories was bitterly debated and eventually led to the Civil War. Repercussions from that war continue to plague us. Memories of the brutal treatment Native Americans received disturb the American collective unconscious. Conflict between state and federal rights persists today.

The Louisiana Purchase constituted the first application of Manifest Destiny. The territory, owned by France, stretched from New Orleans to Canada and comprised 828,000 square miles. Napoleon offered it for sale to finance his war with England. President Jefferson sent representatives James Monroe and Robert Livingstone to negotiate with Napoleon's representatives. The treaty was signed on May 2, 1803, and

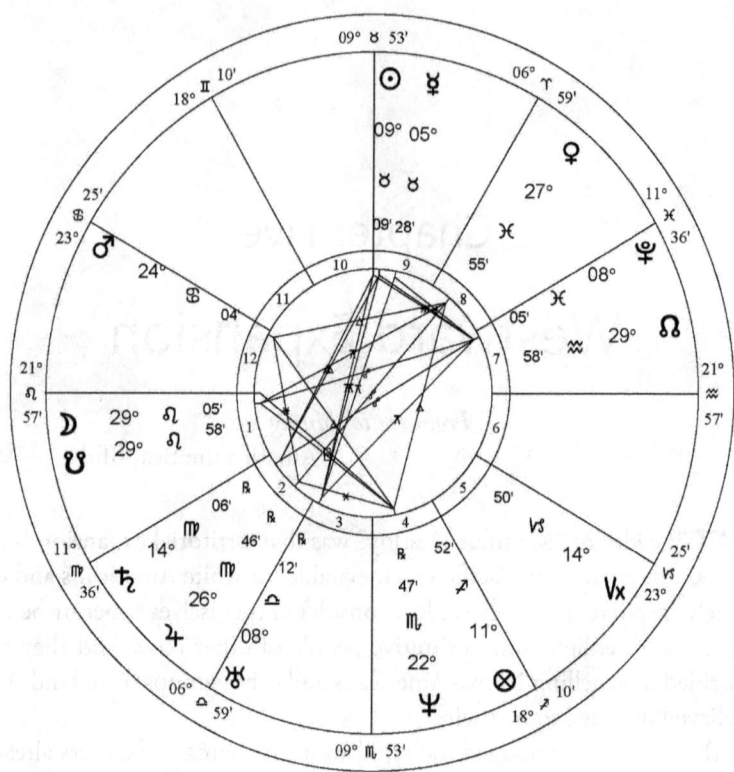

Figure 5-1
Louisiana Purchase Natal Chart
April 30, 1803, 12:00 PM
Paris, France

the documents were sent to the United States. The Senate ratified it October 1803, and the United States paid France eleven million dollars for Louisiana. This act doubled the territory of the United States.[2]

President Jefferson appointed Meriwether Lewis to explore the new territory. With his co-leader, William Clark, they led an expedition covering the lands west of the Mississippi River, returning in the fall of 1806 after nearly two years of exploration. During their journey of more than 8000 miles, the explorers catalogued numerous plant and animal specimens, gathered geographical information, created charts, and established friendly connections with many Native American tribes.[3] Successful achievements of the expedition included establishment of the fur trade among the Natives of the interior, letting foreign fur traders know that this was now US territory with exclusive trading rights, and claiming the Pacific West, which "convinced Americans that the Oregon region should be theirs."[4]

The chart shows the treaty (Jupiter) and Uranus (ruler of the seventh house of foreign relationships) in the second house (financial resources). Venus (ruler of the tenth house, heads of state, also ruler of national resources, Taurus) lies in the eighth house, (international finances). The Venus in Pisces is ruled by Neptune in the fourth house (land) indicating the purchase of the Louisiana Territory, which was largely unknown and unexplored. Mars in Cancer in eleventh house (Congress) makes a Grand Trine with Venus and Neptune. Fifteen states were eventually carved from this land: Louisiana (1812), Missouri (1821), Arkansas (1836), Iowa (1846), Texas (1845), Minnesota (1858), Kansas (1861), Nebraska (1867), Colorado (1876), Montana (1889), Wyoming (1890), and Oklahoma (1907).

Florida became part of America with the Adams-Onis Treaty of 1819. This followed the second of two military victories that made a hero of Andrew Jackson, catapulting him to the Presidency ten years later. Although Spain held Florida at that time, it did little to prevent Seminole Indians from raiding nearby American settlements in Georgia.[5] Jackson led the fight to defeat the Native Americans, drove out the Spanish, then seized Florida, almost precipitating a war with Spain.[6] John Quincy Adams, Secretary of State under President James Monroe, signed a treaty with Spain ceding Florida to the US. The United States did not have to purchase it but did agree to "pay legal claims of American citizens against Spain to a maximum of $5 million."[7]

The next great western expansion took place under President James Knox Polk who campaigned on the promise to expand US territory into Texas and Oregon; a lesser-known president, perhaps, but one who fulfilled his campaign promises in a single term. Texas had declared its independence from Mexico in 1836 after the battle for the Alamo, remaining an independent republic for ten years. President John Tyler created a treaty of annexation in 1844, eventually getting it passed and signed at the end of his term in March 1845 as Polk was coming into office. Polk encouraged Texas to accept the agreement, Texas ratified it, and Polk signed it, making Texas the 28th state on December 29, 1845.[8, 9]

Disagreements about permitting slavery in new territories were frequent during expansion and came to a head with Texas. If Texas was permitted slavery, it would upset the balance of states with and without it. In 1846 congressman David Wilmot introduced the Wilmot Proviso, a law that would prevent slavery in any territory acquired from Mexico. Several attempts to pass it failed.[10] Conflicts continued, eventually leading to the Civil War and the consequent issues affecting us today.

Despite the admission of Texas to the Union, border disputes continued with Mexico. Troops from both countries were sent into the affected areas because of claims of "aggressive intrusion". War was declared by Congress on May 13, 1846 at President Polk's urging. It took two years of fighting before a peace treaty was signed on February 2, 1848, making the Rio Grande River the southern boundary of Texas and ceding California and New Mexico to the United States.[11] The US also received Arizona, Utah, Wyoming, and part of Colorado in return for 15 million dollars and appropriation of Mexican debt.[12]

Meanwhile, the Oregon Territory, which been held in joint occupation with Britain for decades, became Polk's next goal for expansion. This area included the current states of Oregon, Washington, and Idaho and extended into what is now Canada.[13] The slogan, "fifty-four forty or fight!" had been promoted by Polk's supporters and helped him land the presidency. Fur from the Oregon Territory had become a profitable trade item between China and American merchants, and waterways in that area represented "the only link between American shipping and the Pacific trade."[14] Since Britain was dealing with the Irish potato famine and Polk was busy with the Mexican American War, diplomacy eventually won. Britain agreed to boundaries at the 49th parallel, which today divides the US and Canada, and both countries received the desired waterway access to the Pacific.[15, 16]

I used the natal chart for the beginning of the Mexican American War with an assumed time of 1:13 PM since Congress usually met by noon. Pluto was transiting at 25 Aries 04, setting off the unaspected duet of Mars square the Sun in the US chart. The opposition between Venus in the seventh house to US Neptune in the first house describes the so-called intrusion. Jupiter in the ninth house trines the US Sun which rules the fourth house in the US chart showing the expansion of our territory.

The last purchase to complete the continental US map was the Gadsden Purchase in 1853. The area occupied southern Arizona and southwest New Mexico and was also owned by Mexico. The US wanted to run a railroad along a deep southern route, extending from New Orleans to Los Angeles. The agreement also further defined the US-

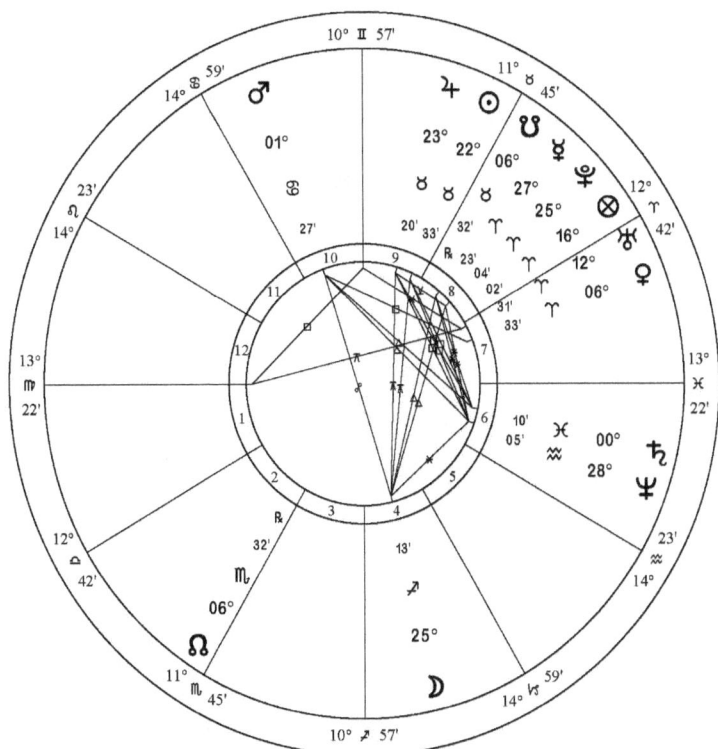

Figure 5-2
War with Mexico Natal Chart
May 13, 1846, 1:13 PM
Washington D.C.

Mexico border.[17]

I have included the chart for James Knox Polk. His Ascendant is conjunct the US Sun at 24 Capricorn which rules the fourth house (land). Add a conjunction to Jupiter for expansion. We should be grateful to Thomas Jefferson and James K. Polk for having the foresight to expand our nation to what it is today.

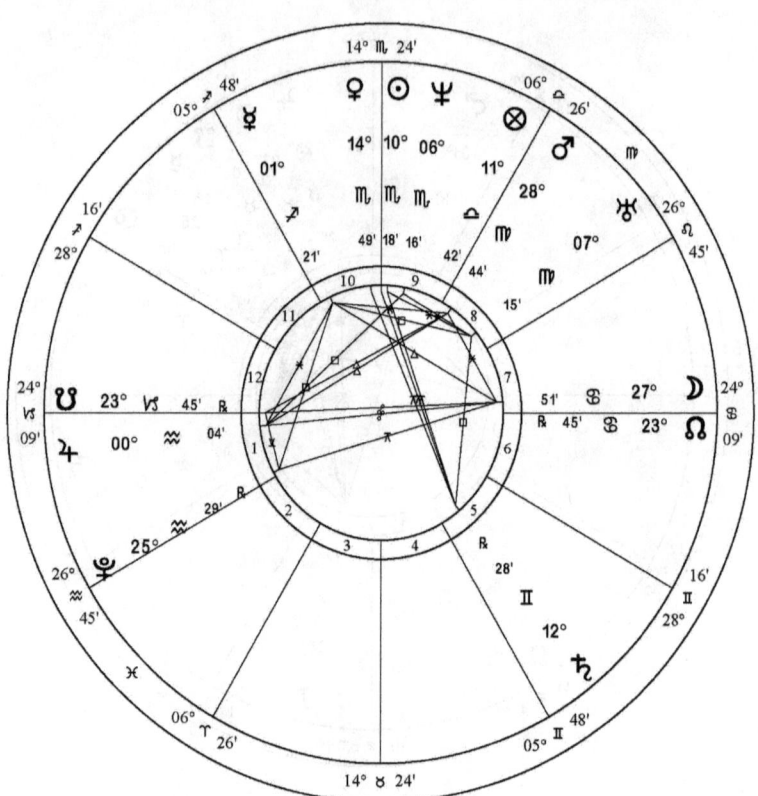

Figure 5-3: Natal chart for James K. Polk
November 2, 1795, 12:00 PM
Pineville, N. Carolina

CHAPTER FIVE NOTES

1. https://www.worldhistoryedu.com/manifest-destiny-meaning-facts/ *Accessed 11/29/2022*
2. https://www.history.com/topics/19th-century/louisiana-purchase *Accessed 11/29/2022*
3. https://www.history.com/topics/19th-century/lewis-and-clark *Accessed 11/29/2022*
4. https://www.newworldexploration.com/explorers-tales-blog/archives/04-2016   Accessed 11/29/2022
5. https://en.wikipedia.org/wiki/Adams-Onis_Treaty *Accessed 12/2/2022*
6. Remini, Robert V: *The Revolutionary Age of Andrew Jackson.* Harper and Row, 1976. p.25
7. https://en.wikipedia.org/wiki/Adams-Onis_Treaty *Accessed 12/2/2022*
8. https://www.history.com/this-day-in-history/us-congress-declares-war-on-mexico   *Accessed 12/2/2022*
9. Fehrenbach, T.R. *Lone Star; a History of Texas and the Texans.* New York, Macmillan (1968). p. 267
10. Wilmot Proviso | Encyclopedia.com   Accessed 4/27/2023
11. https://www.history.com/this-day-in-history/us-congress-declares-war-on-mexico   *Accessed 12/2/2022*
12. Fehrenbach, T.R. *Lone Star; a History of Texas and the Texans.* p. 272
13. Castor, Henry. *Fifty-four forty or Fight! A Showdown between America and England Settles the Oregon Question.* Franklin Watts, Inc. (1970). p. 5
14. https://worldhistory.US/american-history/the-oregon-territory-dispute-settled-in-the-polk-administration.php *Accessed 12/2/2022*
15. Ibid.
16. Castor, Henry. Fifty-four forty or Fight! *A Showdown between America and England Settles the Oregon Question.* p. 46
17. https://www.historytoday.com/archive/gadsden-purchase *Accessed 4/27/2023*

Chapter Six

The Jackson Era

"Democracy is coming to the U.S.A."
Leonard Cohen

President Andrew Jackson's 1829 inauguration marked the beginning of a new political era. The Founding Fathers perceived government as necessarily led by educated upper class men who could better direct the masses in appropriate management of society. But by Jackson's time, the country had expanded westward considerably, people were eagerly pursuing material success, and most (white) men over 21 years of age had achieved voting rights and were democratically managing local governments. They felt that the proper place of national government was only to ensure that no one group got unfair advantage over another, and otherwise stay out of private business.[1]

Jackson is considered the "maker of the modern presidency."[2] During his time, the Democratic Party was born, and the two-party system became entrenched. Direct appeals to the voters became the modus operandi in selecting a president.[3] Jackson was the first president rising from poverty even though practically illiterate. He eventually became one of the largest Tennessee landowners but maintained an antipathy towards wealthy people.[4] He stood for the common man (white men only) against the despised elites, and had a cabinet composed of mostly businessmen, political cronies, and regular citizens. He thought that "the nation had been corrupted by 'special privilege'" and that reform could only occur when majority rule was accepted using the democratic process.[5]

Parallel to Jackson's era, the Romantic Age began, which emphasized emotion rather than reason and focused on so-called heroes or otherwise exceptional people as the new leaders.⁶ Who better than "Old Hickory" to represent the transfer of the political power center to the West? He was the popular hero in the Battle of New Orleans in the War of 1812, and his exploits fighting the Seminole Indian tribe eventually led to the annexation of Florida.⁷

Jackson had a particular prejudice against Native Americans. He con-

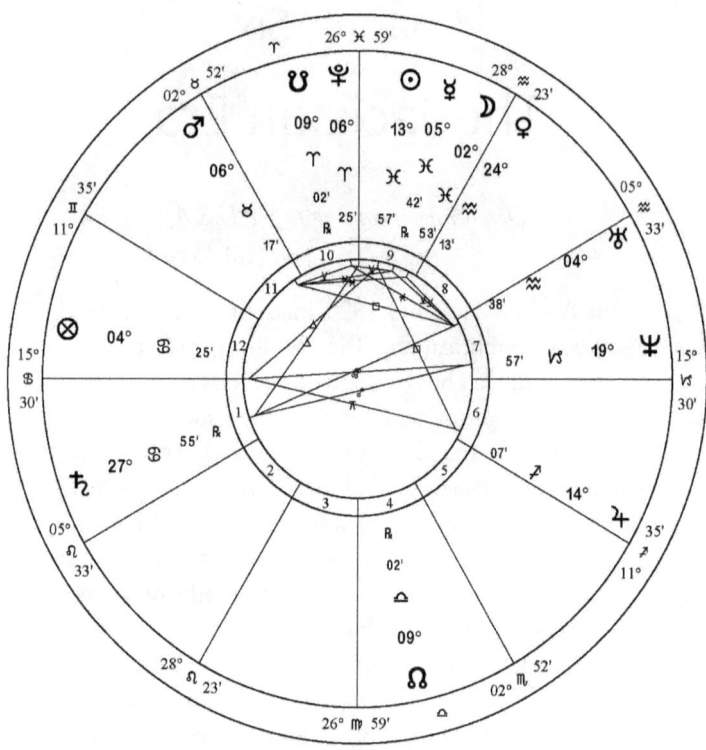

Figure 6-1
Andrew Jackson Inaugural Chart
March 4, 1829, 1:00 PM, Washington DC

sidered them inferior and did not believe the tribes could be assimilated into white culture. This justified his passing of the Indian Removal Act of 1830 which required Native Americans to trade their own lands for places farther west. The policy resulted in the infamous "Trail of Tears" when 15,000 Cherokees, despite a guaranteed treaty with the US, were forced to leave their land in Georgia and move west of Arkansas.⁸ Despite his bias, Jackson accepted a Native American infant into his care who had recently been orphaned in an attack ordered by Jackson himself. He named the child Lyncoya.⁹ Jackson did not do this because of guilt for having killed the boy's parents, but rather because the infant's situation recalled his own difficult childhood.¹⁰ He wanted Lyncoya to attend the US Military Academy at West Point as had he, but Lyncoya was denied entrance because of his race. He died of tuberculosis when he was 16 years old.

The chart of Jackson's inaugural echoes the conflicts of his own chart, Pisces Sun (democracy, empathy towards common man) versus Aries (combative, militant nature), reflected in his being the first president elected because of direct appeals to the general population.¹¹

Jackson's inaugural party was also a first. More than 20,000 citizens, politicians, and celebrities flocked to the White House, resulting in a "boisterous mob scene" at that usually dignified building.¹² Venus (social events) conjunct the Moon (the people) with the Sun (president) trining the Ascendant (ruled by the Moon). Pluto on the Midheaven ruling the fifth house of amusements indicates a "good time was held by all."

As a side note, Jackson was the first president someone tried to assassinate. On January 30, 1835, as he left a congressional funeral at the Capitol building, Jackson was approached by an unemployed painter who shot at him. Fortunately, the gun misfired.¹³ Furious, Jackson used his cane to wallop his attacker several times before Davy Crockett took the man down.

Jackson's popularity after two terms was even greater than upon entering the Presidency, and his success confirmed the new democracy's effectiveness. His "birth in humble circumstances, experience on the frontier, evidence of being close to the mass of people, a devotion to democracy" with the possible addition of heroic military feats became the qualities pursued by future presidential candidates.¹⁴

In the comparison chart below you can see the connection of Jackson to the US chart, especially his Uranus conjunct the US Mars and setting off the unaspected duet. He made his name as a war hero for fighting in the War of 1812 as well as an "Indian fighter."

His Pluto is conjunct the US Saturn in the eighth house, setting off the opposition to the US Uranus. In his first term, Jackson attempted to disband the Second National Bank which he felt was run by northern industrial and urban elites who were biased against common Americans. He vetoed the Senate's bill to renew the bank's charter. The bank's future

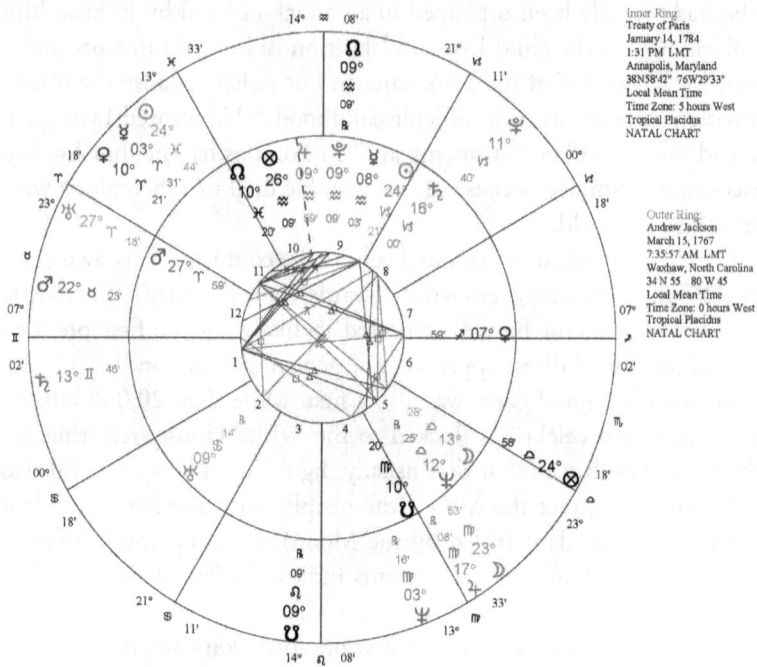

Figure 6-2
Andrew Jackson Natal Chart / USA Chart Biwheel

became the focus of his campaign for a second term. Upon winning the election, feeling he had been given a mandate, Jackson redistributed federal funds to state banks on September 30, 1833. In 1834, Congress censured Jackson for abuse of his presidential power.[15]

His North Node is tied to the Aquarian planets in the Yod pattern, emphasizing the issues of white supremacy and states' rights versus federal rights, as well as the wealth gap between the "elites" and the "common folk." His Saturn in the first house is trine the US Moon/Neptune conjunction, the vision of equality of all people expressed in the Declaration of Independence.

CHAPTER SIX NOTES

1. Remini, Robert V: *The Revolutionary Age of Andrew Jackson.* Harper and Row, 1976. pp. 4, 15
2. https://www.britannica.com/biography/Andrew-Jackson/Jacksonian-Democracy   *Accessed 12/2/2022*
3. https://www.britannica.com/biography/Andrew-Jackson   *Accessed 12/2/2022*
4. https://www.britannica.com/biography/Andrew-Jackson/Jacksonian-Democracy   *Accessed 12/2/2022*
5. https://www.ushistory.org/us/23f.asp   *Accessed 12/2/2022*
6. https://britannica.com/art/Romanticism   *Accessed 12/3/2022*
7. Remini, Robert V: *The Revolutionary Age of Andrew Jackson.* pp. 24-25
8. https://www.britannica.com/biography/Andrew-Jackson/Jacksonian-Democracy   *Accessed 12/2/2022*
9. https://www.grunge.com/927983/lyncoya-the-tragic-story-of-andrew-jacksons-adopted-creek-son/   *Accessed 12/3/2022*
10. Ibid
11. https://www.britannica.com/biography/Andrew-Jackson   *Accessed 12/2/2022*
12. https://www.history.com/this-day-in-history/jackson-holds-open-house-at-the-white-house   *Accessed 12/7/2022*
13. https://www.history.com/this-day-in-history/andrew-jackson-narrowly-escapes-assassination   *Accessed 12/8/2022*
14. https://britannica.com/biography/Andrew-Jackson/Jacksonian-Democracy   *Accessed 12/2/2022*
15. https://www.history.com/this-day-in-history/andrew-jackson-shuts-down-second-bank-of-the-u-s   *Accessed 12/8/2022*

Chapter Seven

The March of the Women

"You Don't Own Me!"
Lesley Gore

Women's rights have been an issue since America became a nation. In the early colonies, their rights were limited. Women could not vote, could not own property in their own names, could not work except as servants, and were totally subject to the husband's authority. Basically, women completely depended on others for their survival.

However, women did not fully accept this situation. In a letter dated March 31, 1776, Abigail Adams (wife of John Adams and future First Lady) told her husband: "I long to hear that you have declared an independency. And, by the way, in the new code of laws which I suppose it will be necessary for you to make, I desire you would remember the ladies and be more generous and favorable to them than your ancestors. Do not put such unlimited power into the hands of husbands. Remember, all men would be tyrants if they could. If particular care and attention is not paid to the ladies, we are determined to foment a rebellion, and will not hold ourselves bound by any laws in which we have no voice or representation."[1]

The rebellion has persisted throughout our history and has surfaced again recently due to a Supreme Court decision. A brief timeline follows.[2]

- 1769: Colonies continue the English system, forbidding women to own property or retain their own earnings.
- 1777: All states pass laws eliminating women's voting rights.

- 1839: Mississippi is the first state allowing women to hold property in their own names with spousal permission.
- 1848: At Seneca Falls, New York, a women's rights convention creates the "Declaration of Sentiments," a document asserting equality of women.
- 1866: Fourteenth Amendment passed by Congress with citizens and voters defined as males.
- 1872: Female federal employees guaranteed equal pay for equal work.
- 1890: Wyoming is the first state to grant women the right to vote.
- 1900: All states had passed legislation allowing married women to retain their own wages and to own their own property.
- 1920: Nineteenth Amendment grants voting rights to women.
- 1933: President Franklin Roosevelt appoints Frances Perkins as Secretary of Labor, making her the first female Cabinet member.
- 1963: The Equal Pay Act passed by Congress.
- 1964: Title VII of the Civil Rights Act passed, prohibiting sex discrimination in employment, and the Equal Employment Opportunity Commission is created.
- 1973: Supreme Court ruling in Roe v. Wade makes abortion legal.
- 1981: Sandra Day O'Connor becomes first female Supreme Court Justice.
- 1992: Record numbers of women are elected to Congress.
- 2007: Nancy Pelosi becomes first female Speaker of the House.
- 2016: Hillary Clinton becomes the first woman to secure the presidential nomination of a major party.
- 2022: Supreme Court overturns Roe v. Wade.

The convention at Seneca Falls, New York in 1848 was an historical first meeting of both men and women to draft resolutions pertaining to women's rights. It was planned by five women involved in the movements for women's rights, temperance, and abolition of slavery: Elizabeth Cady Stanton, Lucretia Mott, Martha Wright, Jane Hunt,

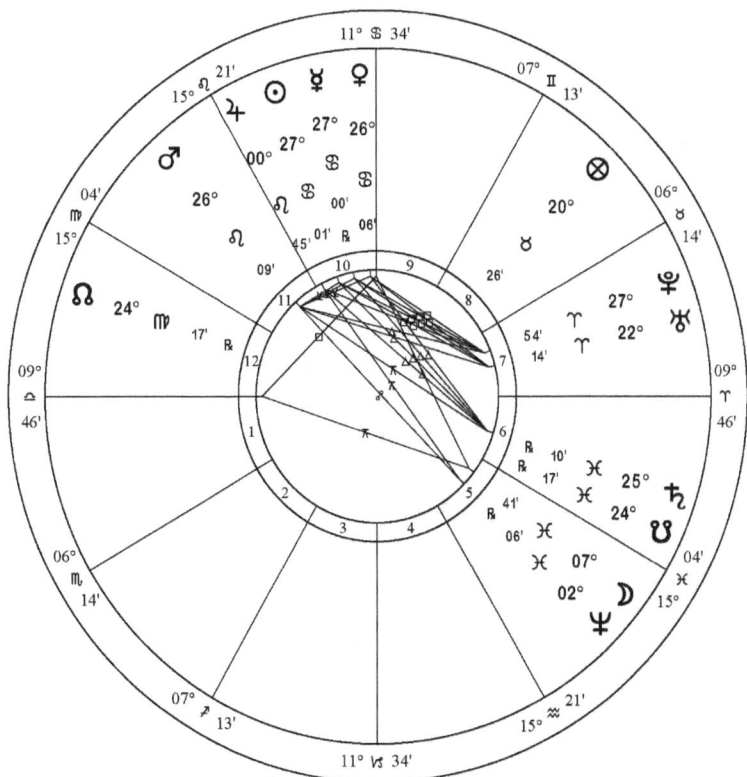

Figure 7-1
Seneca Falls Convention
July 19, 1848, 11:00 AM; Seneca Falls, New York

and Mary M'Clintock. They met at the Wesleyan Methodist Chapel at 11:00 AM on July 19, 1848. Mrs. Stanton opened the meeting:

> "We are assembled to protest against a form of government, existing without the consent of the governed – to declare our right to be as man is free, to be represented in the government which we are taxed to support, to have such disgraceful laws as give man the power to chastise and imprison his wife, to take the wages which she earns, the property which she inherits, and, in case of separation, the children of her love."[3]

One outstanding speaker was Frederick Douglass who supported the Declaration and wrote positively about it in his abolitionist publication *The North Star*. Most newspapers were not in favor.[4] Horace Greely had the only paper that took the meeting seriously. It would take women until 1920 before the 19th Amendment gave women the vote.[5]

In the above chart of the Seneca Falls Convention, women in general (Venus) are making a declaration (Mercury) openly demanding that their rights be recognized, (tenth house). Venus rules the Ascendant as well as the eighth house (transformation). The seventh house (women's conditions in the country) contains Pluto and Uranus in Aries, demanding change and freedom, trine to Mars in the eleventh house (wishes and goals). Pluto, ruler of the 2nd House, wants a transformation in the nation's values related to women's conditions.

Abortion rights were not an issue at this time. Children were born with the help of doctors and midwives, and abortion was generally tolerated. However, in the 1860s, the male-dominated medical profession, supported by some religious groups, began a campaign to outlaw abortion and phase out the female-dominated profession of midwives. By 1910, abortion was illegal in every state except in rare cases approved by physicians themselves.[6] Their views gradually changed when complications related to illegal abortions became frequent.

The 1960s saw the rise of people who were active protesters against the nonlegal status of abortion. It wasn't until 1973 that the Supreme Court made a ruling in the case of Roe versus Wade legalizing abortion. The decision came down on January 22, 1973.[7]

It is interesting to note that in the chart of the Roe v. Wade decision, we also have Uranus and Pluto in the seventh house (conditions of women of the nation, generally) but this time in Libra ruled by Venus in the tenth house (status) in Law (Jupiter ruling both ninth and tenth houses). Uranus, ruler of the twelfth house (illegalities) is now in the open (seventh house) for women of the nation and legalized.

On June 24, 2022, all that struggle was reversed when the Supreme Court at about 10 a.m. overruled the Roe vs Wade decision, sending it back to the states for them to decide. The controversy of federal versus states' rights has resurfaced again in conjunction with women's rights and "the rights to privacy" of the 14th Amendment.[8]

In this chart, we find the Moon, ruler of the twelfth house, (illegalities) conjunct Uranus (abortion), ruler of the seventh house (women conditions, in general) in the ninth house of law and courts.

In comparing the event chart to the US chart, one can see that the Moon conjunct Uranus is now in the twelfth house of the US and abortion is now illegal. The Moon is also square to the US chart's

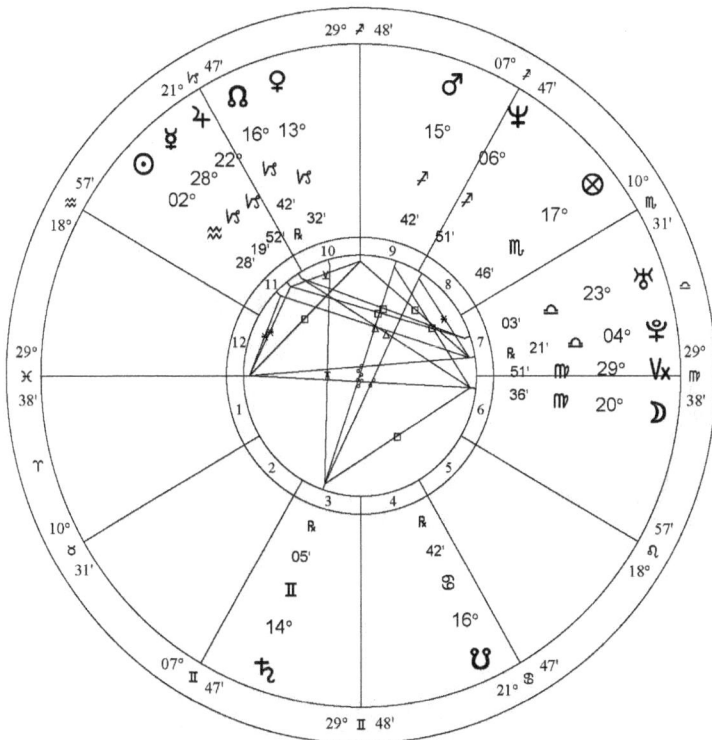

Figure 7-2
"Roe" Supreme Court Ruling Chart
January 22, 1973, 10:00 AM, Washington D.C.

Aquarian stellium setting off the issues of the Yod. Jupiter sets off the Venus section of the Yod, bringing an angry response of women to this decision. The Sun in the event chart sets off the Axis of Awareness by its conjunction to the US Uranus highlighting the issue of conflict of status quo (Saturn) against reform (Uranus). In this case, the mass of the public (fourth house) opposes the government (Saturn in Capricorn).

The issue of women's rights is before us again and requires a solution. As Uranus makes its journey across the Ascendant, as it did when the US declared independence, we are likely to see another movement in our country related to these issues we've never truly settled for over 200 years.

The March Of The Women

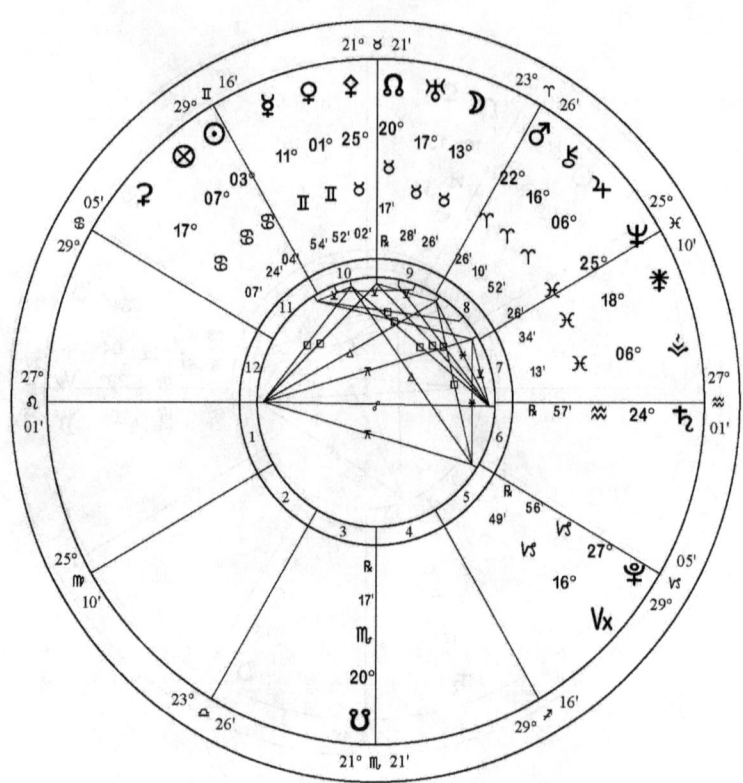

Figure 7-3
Roe vs Wade Overturned Natal Chart
June 24, 2022, 10:13 AM, Washington D.C.

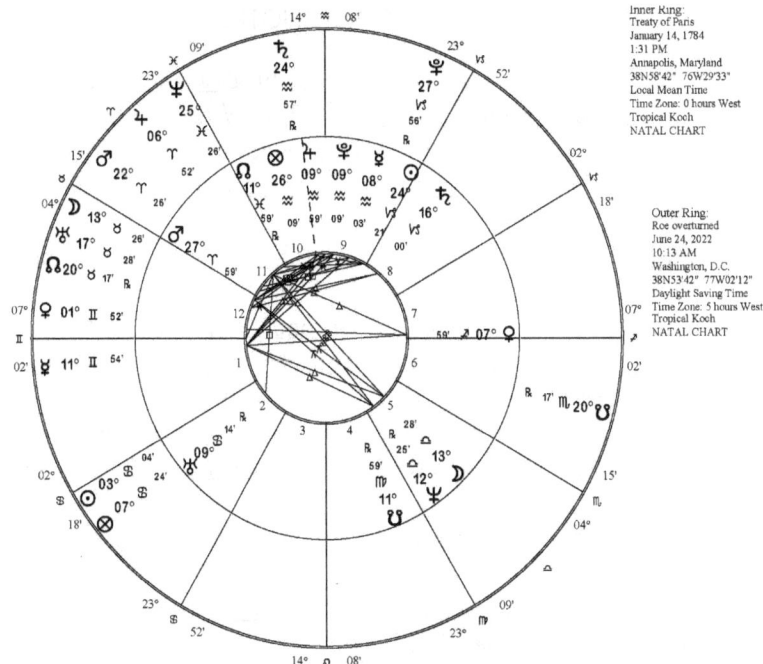

Figure 7-4
Roe vs Wade Overturned / US Chart Biwheel

CHAPTER SEVEN NOTES

1. www.history.com/this-day-in-history/abigail-adams-urges-husband-to-remember-the-ladies   *Accessed 12/9/2022*
2. https://www.usnews.com/news/the-report/articles/2017-01-20/timeline-the-womens-rights-movement-in-the-us   *Accessed 12/8/2022*
3. https://history.com/topics/womensrights/seneca-falls-convention   *Accessed 12/10/2022*
4. https://senecafallscoverage.tumblr.com/   *Accessed 4/28/2023*
5. https://history.com/topics/womensrights/seneca-falls-convention   *Accessed 12/10/2022*
6. https://plannedparenthoodaction.org/issues/abortion/abortion-central-history-reproductive-health-care-america   *Accessed 6/6/2022*
7. https://www.history.com/topics/womens-history/roe-v-wade   *Accessed 4/28/2023*
8. https://cbsnews.com/philadelphia/news/roe-v-wade-supreme-court-ruling   *Accessed 12/12/2022*

Chapter Eight

The Issue of Immigration

> *"My family's been having trouble with immigrants ever since they came to this country!"*
> Senator Rawkins in *Finian's Rainbow*

In a nation created by immigrants, why would immigration become an issue? Although today the emphasis is on "illegal" immigration, past laws concentrated on defining which immigrants could attain citizenship. For instance, the Naturalization Act of 1790 was the first law to describe those eligible for US citizenship: "…any free white person of 'good character', who has been living in the United States for two years or longer…"[1]

IMMIGRATION TIME LINE[1]

- Steerage Act of 1819: Called for ships carrying immigrants to the US to maintain better conditions and for captains to provide passenger demographic information, resulting in the first federal records to assess ethnic composition of US immigrants.

- 1850s: Continuous inflow of Chinese immigrants seeking work in gold mines, garment factories, railroad building, and agriculture. Their success resulted in growing anti-Chinese sentiment as white workers began blaming them for low wages.

- 1875: Supreme Court granted the power to create and enforce immigration laws to the Federal Government.

- 1880 to 1920: Immigration boom comprising greater than 20 million immigrants, primarily from Central, Eastern, and Southern Europe.

- Chinese Exclusion Act of 1882: Prevented Chinese immigrants from US entry. First act placing broad restrictions on selected immigrant groups. Formally ended with the McCarran-Walter Act in 1952.

- Immigration Act of 1891: Additional groups blocked from immigration to US, including felons, diseased persons, polygamists, and others. Creation of a federal office to manage immigration enforcement plus an officer corps stationed at principal ports of entry.

- January 1892: Ellis Island became the first immigration port.

- Immigration Act of 1917: Established literacy requirements for new immigrants and restricted immigration from most Asian countries.

- May 1924: Immigration Act of 1924 established nationality quotas to reduce immigration into the US. Asian immigrants were excluded, and those from Northern and Western Europe favored.

Immigration itself did not become a crime until 1929 when Senator Coleman Blease, a white supremacist from South Carolina, introduced the Undesirable Aliens Act. Persons not entering the country through an official entry point, where fees and testing were required, became subject to criminal prosecution.[2] The first offense was a misdemeanor that could result in imprisonment up to a year. For deported persons returning illegally, the crime was considered a felony with two years' imprisonment and a fine up to 1000 dollars.[3] The act has affected subsequent American immigration policy until today, focusing on illegal immigration as a criminal rather than as a labor issue.[4]

Change in immigration policy was greatly influenced by eugenics, a pseudoscientific theory that became popular in America during the 1920s. Writers like Dr. Harry Laughlin presented the idea that those who were not "Nordic" were inferior people.[5] In a report to Congress, Laughlin claimed that "the 'bad blood' of inferior racial groups was a threat to the country, and 'immigration control' was the greatest instrument which the Federal Government can use in promoting race conservation of the Nation."[6]

One of the most influential eugenics groups, the Immigration Restriction League, lobbied Congress for more restrictive immigration laws.[7]

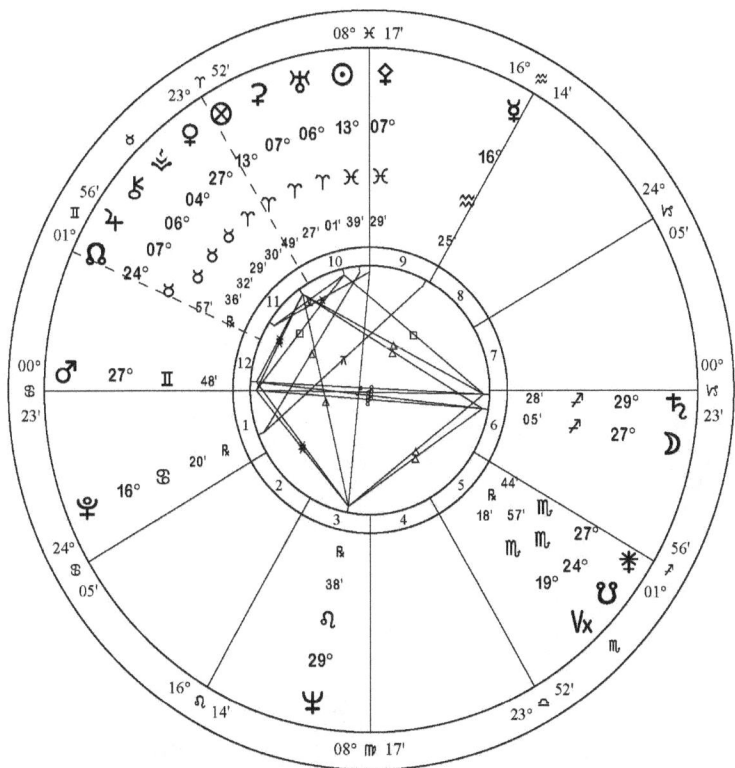

Figure 8-1
Undesirable Aliens Act Natal Chart
March 4, 1929, 12:00 PM, Washington D.C.

Similar groups "that demonized all immigrants from anywhere other than favored European countries" included white lawmakers known as "Nativists."[8] Representative John C. Box, who believed immigration law should be designed for "the protection of American racial stock from further degradation or change through mongrelization" joined Senator Blease to pass the restrictions.[9]

Sound familiar? These beliefs incorporate the idea of the "white man's burden," initiated in the colonialism period and persisting in the collective unconscious.

Eugenics was the idea that people should be selectively bred to improve human genetics. It was considered an intellectually respectable science and was taught in universities like Harvard and Stanford. Madison Grant's *The Passing of the Great Race* was the most famous American work

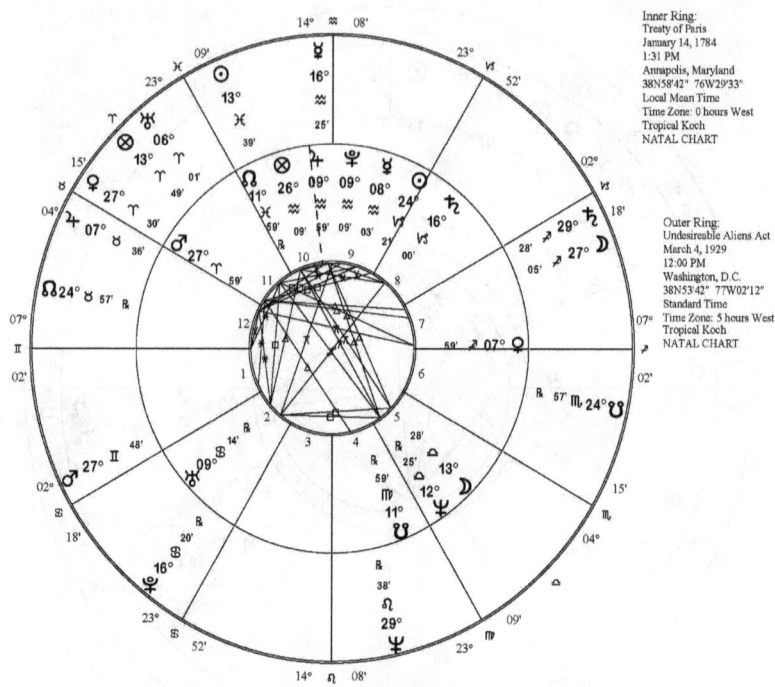

Figure 8-2
Undesirable Aliens Act / USA Chart Biwheel

on eugenics and had a great influence in the attempts to limit non-white immigration.[10] Followers still exist today who espouse similar paranoid fantasies such as "Replacement Theory." This conspiracy theory alleges "that left-leaning domestic or international elites, on their own initiative or under the directions of Jewish co-conspirators, are attempting to replace white people with nonwhite (i.e., Black, Hispanic, Asian, or Arab) immigrants" in Western countries that are primarily white. Because of supposedly higher birth rates, the fear is that non-whites eventually will "take control over national political and economic institutions" in what is termed "white genocide."[11]

Echoes of Hitler's Nazi Germany! It is no wonder that intimidation and violence against these groups have risen in the last few years.

Above is the chart for the Undesirable Aliens Act which is still in effect today. I used a noon chart because I could not get the exact time. The Act was signed into law on March 4, 1929 at the end of the 70th Congress.[12]

Comparing the chart to the US chart, most notable is the exact opposition of Pluto to the US Saturn, setting off the Axis of Awareness of the Yod and the issues of the collective unconscious. The State (Saturn) projects on to these workers symbolic Pluto images of disease, abnormalities, corruption, etc. to justify its change of policy.

A few months after passage of the act, Wall Street crashed and the Great Depression began. As unemployment became severe during the Hoover administration, repatriation drives rounding up Mexican Americans- including those born in the US- for deportation began under the slogan "American jobs for real Americans." No immigrant protection groups existed at this time to come to their aid.[13] The State itself was tainted by the corruption of Pluto as the program was largely unconstitutional and not based on any law or executive order.

Congress has done little to improve the situation since then, and fear of immigrants has become a political tool to get elected.

CHAPTER EIGHT NOTES

1. https://www.history.com/topics/immigration/immigration-united-states-timeline *Accessed 11/8/2022*
2. https://history.com/news/illegal-border-crossing-usa-mexico-section-1325 *Accessed 12/17/2022*
3. https://immigrationhistory.org/item/undesirable-aliens-act-of-1929-bleases-law *Accessed 12/17/2022*
4. https://www.zocalopublicsquare.org/2018/11/27/1929-law-turned-undocumented-entry-crime/ideas/essay/ *Accessed 5/4/2023*
5. https://papers.ssrn.com/sol3/papers.cfm?abstract_id=3827488 p. 1064 *Accessed 5/4/2023*
6. https://elpasomatters.org/2021/11/09/opinion-challenging-the-racist-underpinnings-of-laws-criminalizing-undocumented-immigration/ *Accessed 12/17/2022*
7. https://papers.ssrn.com/sol3/papers.cfm?abstract_id=3827488 p. 1061 *Accessed 5/4/2023*
8. https://racism.org/articles/citizenship-rights/immigration-race-and-racism/9559-racial-animus?start=1 *Accessed 12/17/2022*
9. https://www.digitalhistory.uh.edu/disp_textbook.cfm?smtID=3&psid=594 *Accessed 5/4/23*
10. https://papers.ssrn.com/sol3/papers.cfm?abstract_id=3827488 pp. 1059-1060 *Accessed 5/4/2023*
11. https://www.britannica.com/topic/replacement-theory *Accessed 12/18/2022*
12. US Senate Historical Office (by email) 12/19/2022
13. https://www.history.com/news/great-depression-repatriation-drives-mexico-deportation *Accessed 12/17/2022*

Chapter Nine

The Civil War

"As he died to make men holy, let us die to make men free…"
"The Battle Hymn of the Republic" by Julia Ward Howe

By 1861, the issue of slavery came to a head. The conflict between the industrialized North and the agricultural South was basically an economic one. It also highlighted the argument of states' rights versus the federal government. Compromises between slave and free states attempted over the decades had mostly failed.

The wave of hostility peaked with the election of Abraham Lincoln "who declared 'I believe this government cannot endure permanently half slave and half free.'" South Carolina quickly seceded from the United States, followed by six other states. The Confederate States of America was established, with Jefferson Davis elected its leader. Confederate forces began to seize federal forts in the South.[1]

Fort Sumter was a fortress standing on an island. It controlled entrance to Charleston Harbor in South Carolina. The newly elected President Lincoln informed South Carolina delegates that he intended to replenish needed supplies to the fort. This was interpreted as war, and when the fort commander refused to evacuate, the Confederacy Cabinet and President Davis decided to strike.[2]

On April 12, 1861, at 4:30 AM, Confederate mortar shots exploded over Fort Sumter. After about 36 hours of battle, the commander surrendered the fort to the Confederates. The attack marked the official start of the American Civil War- a war lasting four years. More than 620,000 Americans lost their lives in the fight. Almost 4 million slaves were freed.[3]

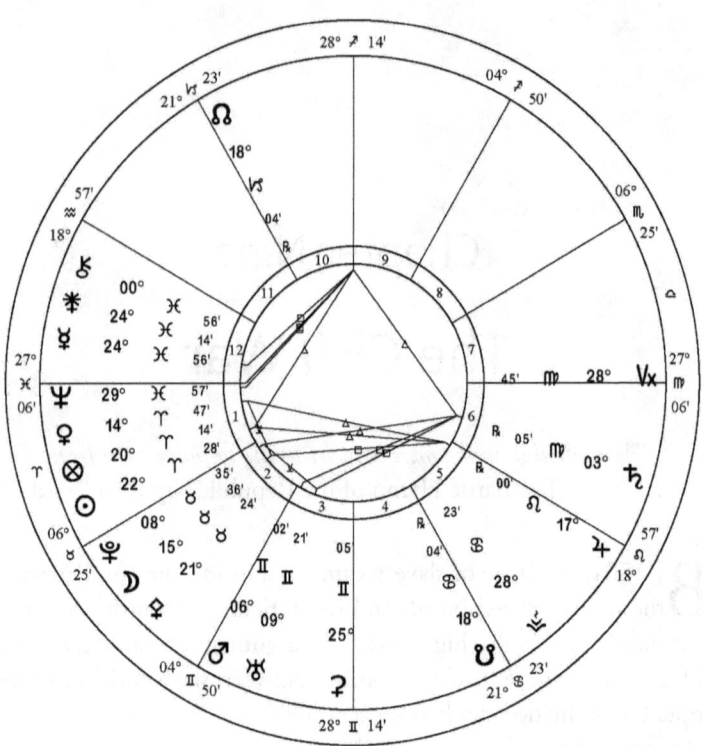

Figure 9-1
Start of Civil War
April 12, 1861, 4:30 AM, Charleston, South Carolina

It is not my intent to write a narrative about the entire Civil War. Let us examine the chart marking the Civil War's beginning and compare it to the US chart, noting connections between them. You can also examine Lincoln's natal chart and the chart for his assassination which started a new post-bellum period. The time used is the hour at which Fort Sumter was attacked, considered historically the beginning of the Civil War.[4]

What can this chart tell us about ourselves as a nation? Let us begin with the ascendant of Pisces, ruled by Neptune in the first house of the people at 29 degrees Pisces (reminding us of the US motto "from Many, One"). But the ruler of the seventh house (unions) is Mercury, now in the twelfth house of secret enemies. Mercury also rules the third (siblings) and fourth houses (land) which tells what the conflict is about. Mars and Uranus in the third show us that this is a confrontation between fellow countrymen that will inevitably lead to the Civil War.

What I consider most interesting is the opposition between Chiron and Saturn which contains the rest of the planets. Chiron is both in Pisces and the twelfth house which highlights the theme of victimization and persecution. The Confederacy feels victimized by the Federal government whom they perceive as taking away their states' rights (slavery is not the problem- the Romans had slaves, didn't they?). The government, playing the "rescuer" role, feels victimized by the Confederacy as wanting to destroy the Union. Standing between are the slaves who have been victimized since the country's very beginning.

The Saturn opposition is a particularly difficult aspect as it holds the people in the same place over time. It reminds us that we avoid the real issue by blaming the victim and denying our own role as persecutors. At the same time, Mars is in square aspect to both, creating a T-square, building frustration and tension until the inevitable explosion erupts into the violence of the Civil War. The hate and fear released by Mars and Saturn has undermined our values (second house) with unconscious guilt (Pluto) that the people (Moon) continue to carry into the future (our Karmic baggage).

TIME LINE OF US SLAVERY UP TO THE CIVIL WAR [5]

- 1619: First slave ship arrives at Jamestown, Virginia.
- 1787: Slavery is tacitly acknowledged in new US Constitution, in which each enslaved individual is considered three-fifths of a person in determining taxation and congressional representation.
- 1808: Congress outlaws the African slave trade, but domestic trade continues, tripling over the next 50 years.
- 1831: The Nat Turner slave rebellion is used as evidence that Black people are "inherently inferior barbarians" and should be contained in slavery.
- 1857: The US Supreme Court decides against the slave Dred Scott who had sued for his freedom, declaring that people of African descent are not citizens and thus had no legal standing to sue. Additionally, the federal government is declared to have no authority to regulate slavery in its states or territories.[6]
- 1830-1860: Abolitionist Movement grows in strength and opposition.
- 1860: The number of slaves reaches almost 4 million, more than

50 percent residing in the cotton-producing states of the South.

- 1862: Lincoln signs the Emancipation Proclamation, setting slaves "forever free."

The Civil War and its aftermath left wounds in the collective that still have not been healed. Descendants from those slaves have had to continuously fight for every little piece of progress in their rights to be equal, as promised in the Declaration of Independence. Protest movements like the Civil Rights Movement and Black Lives Matter appear to remind us of this unresolved issue. But protests bring backlashes. The Ku Klux Klan was founded in 1865 to resist "…the Republican Party's Reconstruction-era policies aimed at establishing political and economic equality for Black Americans."[7]

In 1915, the Ku Klux Klan was revived by white Protestant nativists near Atlanta, Georgia. However, the organization's new targets included not only Black people, but also foreigners, Jews, Roman Catholics, and organized labor. The immigration surge America experienced in the early 20th century stoked the growing hostility.[8]

In May of 1922, the Danville Daily Messenger of Kentucky published a speech by Dr. C. Lewis Fowler on "America for Americans Only," supporting the KKK as "red-blooded citizens…that it will give acceptance to the things that are purely American." The term WASP (white Anglo-Saxon Protestants) was born with Fowler's call to "direct the entire white, Anglo-Saxon protestant native born manhood" to protect the principals of liberty handed down from the Founding Fathers.[9]

Many Americans hoped that the election to the presidency of a Black American, Barack Obama, in 2008, would represent a resolution to this issue. However, a backlash was precipitated, leading to the Trump era of division. The KKK may be less prominent, but its new expression may be found with the white supremacy militia groups that stormed our Capitol on January 6th. The hatred and fear that brought us to the Civil War has resurged in America where violence to any group (other than WASP) has risen over the last few years.

A "caste" system (like the one which existed in India for some time) has developed and should be brought to our awareness. In our case it acts silently. "No one escapes exposure to its message that one set of people is presumed to be inherently smarter, more capable, and more deserving than other groups deemed lower. This program has been installed into the subconscious of every one of us. And, high or low, without intervention or reprogramming, we act out the script we were handed."[10]

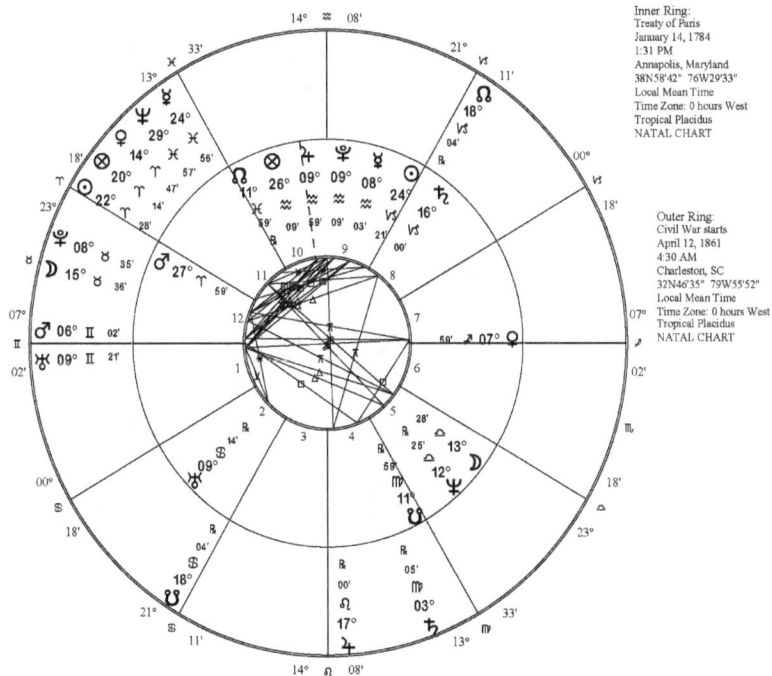

Figure 9-2
Start of the Civil War / US Natal Chart Biwheel

Look at the chart of the Civil War and how it has affected our country. Notice the conjunction of Pluto (rules sixth house of "inferiors") with the Moon (the people) lies in the twelfth house of the unconscious. The Venus that rules it is in the eleventh house of groups squaring our Saturn (repression) that rules the ninth house of immigrants. Mercury, which rules the country, is conjunct Neptune in Pisces which blinds the purpose (eleventh house) of our motto, From Many, One. The powerful conjunction of Mars with Uranus straddles our ascendant, bringing the truth of this issue to our conscious awareness (trines the Aquarius stellium in the Grand Air trine with Moon conjunct Neptune in the fifth house which affects our identity as a country). The North Node in Capricorn is conjunct our Saturn and trine to the Moon in Taurus, reminding us of the Karmic baggage we have brought with us from the past and an opportunity to move forward which eventually fails.

In the following comparison chart of Lincoln and the US, you can see the strong ties between them, most notably Lincoln's Pluto/Mercury conjunction to the US North Node. He certainly brought a major trans-

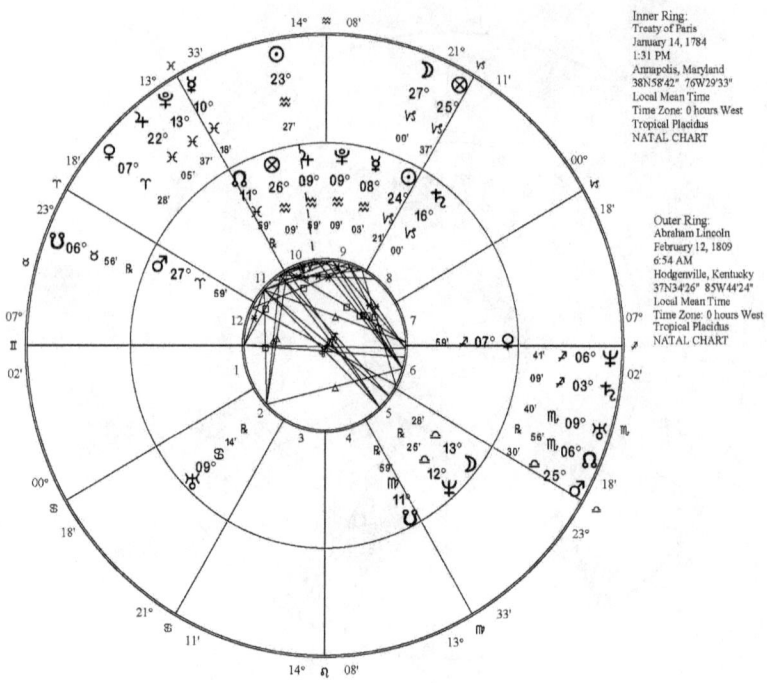

Figure 9-3
Abraham Lincoln Natal Chart / US Chart Biwheel

formation in our history that moved us into a whole new era. His Moon is conjunct the US Sun, setting off the unaspected duet of Sun and Mars, reinforced by his Mars in Libra making a T-square to it, indicating the coming conflict.

His Sun and Ascendant fall in the tenth house of the US chart, illustrating the strength of his authority and purpose as well as the Aquarian bond to our nation. One cannot think about Lincoln without the Emancipation (freedom) Proclamation. His Uranus in Scorpio makes a Grand trine with our Uranus in Cancer and the US North Node. The Venus in both charts is in exact trine while Neptune, his hope of "a new birth of freedom," remains with us yet to be fulfilled.

The last chart to examine is of Lincoln's assassination, the first assassination in US history.

Comparing it with the US chart, the Yod is set off in several places and so is the unaspected duet of Sun square Mars. Transiting Saturn makes an exact opposition to US Mars which is conjunct the Sun of the assass

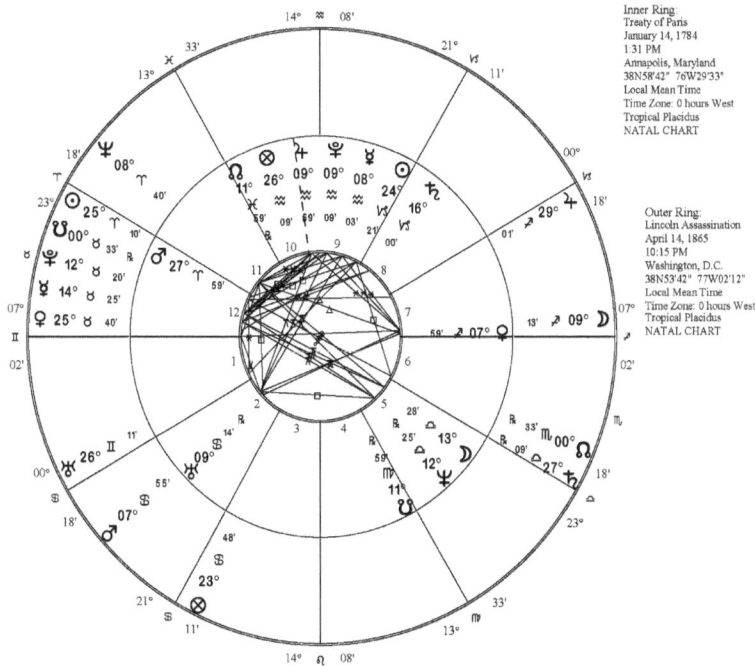

Figure 9-4
Abraham Lincoln's Assassination / US Chart Biwheel

-ination chart and both squared by the US natal Sun. The transiting Moon is conjunct the US Venus in the house of enemies, both ruled by Jupiter also in the seventh house directly opposite Uranus. Most importantly, transiting Mars is conjuncting Uranus, the action point of the Yod's Axis of Awareness. The hidden enemy was John Wilkes Booth, an actor, in Ford's Theater, represented by Mercury, ruler of the fifth house placed in the twelfth house conjunct Pluto (revenge). Attempts to assassinate Vice President Johnson and Secretary of War Stanton were, however, not successful. The conspiracy hoped to create chaos in the executive branch. Ironically, Lincoln that very morning had signed legislation creating the Secret Service.

By setting off Uranus (change), the Axis of Awareness simultaneously sets off Saturn in Capricorn (repression). Even though the freed slaves enjoyed a few benefits, even being elected to Congress, this period did not last long, with the rise of the Klan, "Jim Crow" laws, segregation, and the silent caste system still present today. In the last few years, it has risen to such new heights of violence and become so openly embraced by conspiracy theorists, it calls for a radical renewal of empathy among our citizens and a return to the vision of Lincoln and the Founding Fathers of "a government of the people, by the people and for the people".

> This is just to explain why the period goes after the quotes, and will be removed for printing:
>
> >>If the sentence ends with a parenthetical citation (like in academic papers), the period goes after the citation, not inside the quotation marks. <<

CHAPTER NINE NOTES

1. https://battlefields.org/learn/civil-war/battles/fort-sumter *Accessed 12/28/2022*
2. Ibid.
3. Ibid.
4. https://en.wikipedia.org/wiki/American_Civil_War *Accessed 12/15/2023*
5. https://history.com/topics/black-history/slavery *Accessed 12/31/2022*
6. https://www.history.com/topics/black-history/dred-scott-case *Accessed 12/31/22*
7. https://www.history.com/topics/19th-century/ku-klux-klan#the-ku-klux-klan-and-the-end-of-reconstruction *Accessed 12/30/2022*
8. Ibid.
9. *Danville Daily Messenger,* Boyle County, Kentucky, article published 5/1/1922. Available at https://newspapers.com/image/237442304/ *Accessed 12/31/2022*
10. Wilkerson, Isabel: *Caste, the Origin of Our Discontents*, Random House LLC. New York, 2022. p. 384

Chapter Ten

The American Labor Movement

"Oh, you can't scare me, I'm sticking to the union…"
"Union Maid" by Woody Guthrie and Millard Lampell

The journey of the Labor Movement has been long, sometimes bloody, and hard fought. Workers initially had no control over their wages, hours, or the safety of their working conditions. Because so many laborers were available, they could be easily replaced; thus, they had to accept any conditions to survive. Gradually, workers found they had more power as a group to bargain for improvements in their lives.

The first unions were like guilds formed by groups of workers in the same trade, such as carpenters or tailors. They faced a lot of opposition from hostile employers and strikebreakers. The courts often looked on the concept of collective bargaining as illegal. Labor legislation might be helpful or restrictive, depending on the views of Congress or the President during any given administration.

Advances in production affected the labor market. Worldwide changes in the manufacture of goods occurred during the Second Industrial Age in the 1830s. The agricultural economy transformed into one of machine manufacturing and industry. New energy sources such as coal, electricity, and steam were sought, and new basic materials such as iron and steel were introduced. Energy-efficient inventions increased production while decreasing labor, and factory systems reorganized work functions to meet increased demands. Culture and society were transformed. The skills needed in the new industries allowed the workers to move from working with hand tools to becoming machine operators.[1]

Such massive alterations required numerous changes in how employers and workers interacted. Numerous events occurred throughout American history to effect these changes. The following timeline highlights important events that have shaped the labor movement. I must confess to some bias because my father was a labor organizer back in the day.

TIME LINE

- 1768: First recorded strike in New York by journeyman tailors protesting wage reductions.[2]
- 1794: Federal Society of Journeymen Cordwainers formed, establishing trade unions as a form of organization for American workers.[3]
- 1827: Local craft unions start uniting under a central body within cities.[4]
- 1845: Lowell Female Labor Reform Association begins public petitioning for a 10-hour workday.[5]
- 1852: Local unions of same trade become organized under national unions across US.[6]
- 1869: Noble and Holy Order of Knights of Labor becomes the first major American labor union.[7]
- 1886: American Federation of Labor (AFL) founded.[8]
- 1886: The Haymarket Riot occurs at a rally called by workers to protest police violence that had occurred at a labor strike the preceding day. As police tried to disperse the large crowd, an unknown person threw a bomb. Seven police officers were killed. Eight activists were convicted for the bombing despite the lack of evidence. Seven labor leaders were sentenced to death and one was imprisoned for 15 years.[9]
- 1894: The American Railway Union (ARU) supports a railroad boycott/strike that eventually became widespread and violent. The strike began on May 11 when railroad workers refused to work on trains containing Pullman cars after George Pullman, president of the Pullman Company, cut Pullman employee wages by 25% but refused to talk to them. Railroads were tied up or completely stopped. By June 30, over 125,000 workers were involved and showed their anger by setting fire to buildings and overturning

locomotives. Militia were sent by the Illinois governor. An injunction by President Cleveland was used for the first time to break a strike. He also sent federal troops to get the railroads moving again. Union labor leaders were arrested and eventually jailed. The strike was a failure. As an appeasing measure, Cleveland and the Congress created a national holiday, Labor Day, in honor of the Labor Movement.[10]

- 1905: Industrial Workers of the World ("Wobblies") founded because of workers' dissatisfaction with the work of AFL.[11]
- 1911: Triangle Shirtwaist factory fire in New York City kills 146 workers- the factory owners had locked the fire escape doors. Worker safety issues become a focal point for activists as a result.[12]
- 1914: Ludlow Massacre- United Mine Workers strike and the National Guard and local militia attack the miners' tent colony with machine guns, killing women and children.[13]
- 1916: The Adamson Act is the first federal law to regulate hours of workers, establishing an 8-hour workday.[14]
- 1935: National Labor Relations Act, also called the Wagner Act, passes under President Franklin D. Roosevelt, allowing employees to organize into unions.[15]
- 1938: Fair Labor Standards Act establishes the first minimum wage and the forty-hour work week.[16]
- 1947: Taft-Hartley Act restricts union activities by outlawing the closed shop, as well as permitting states to pass "right to work" legislation.[17]
- 1955: The AFL and CIO merge.[18]
- 1962: The United Steel Workers of America reach settlement with Kaiser Steel Corporation, allowing workers replaced by machines to keep full pay until retrained for a new job.[19]
- 1966: The United Farm Workers union is formed from the merging of Cesar Chavez's National Farm Workers Association and the Agricultural Workers Organizing Committee.[20]
- 1981: President Reagan breaks the Air Traffic Controllers' strike.[21]

An early example of union building occurred in Lowell, Massachusetts in 1834 in the textile mills, where young women came in droves

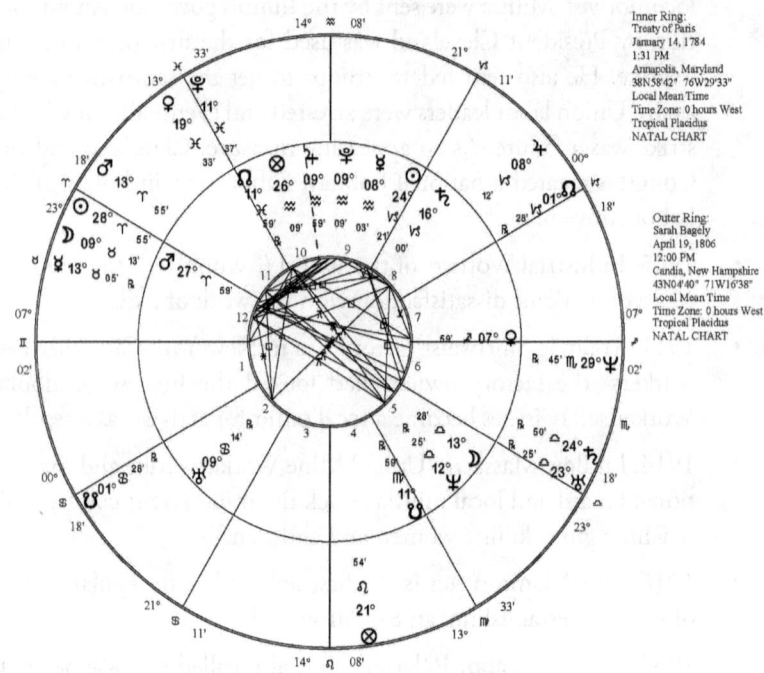

Figure 10-1
Natal Chart of Sara Bagley / US Chart Biwheel

to work thirteen-hour days and live in rooms the company provided. The workrooms were noisy, confining and lint-filled.[22] Sarah Bagley was one young woman who complained that they were "being abused and exploited by their male overseers."[23] The mill cut wages and increased production and the women went on strike. The strike was unsuccessful but repeated in 1836 with better organization. However, it too was unsuccessful. The women became politically active in the 1840s, taking their efforts to a new level.[24] Sarah and two other women demanded a ten-hour day, founding the Lowell Female Labor Reform Association, the first female union in America. Sarah went on to be a labor activist and became the first woman superintendent of a telegraph office.[25]

For Sarah I used a Noon chart, and you can see her connection to the US chart. Sarah was a simple farm girl who became the disrupter in the Lowell Mill and a leader of a strike- one of those unknown persons who necessarily moved the country forward in her own way. I find the most interesting tie is her Pluto conjunct the US North Node. Her strong Aries Sun conjuncts the US Mars which fires off the opposition of her

Saturn/Uranus conjunction. Her Taurus Moon/Mercury conjunction exactly sextiles the US Uranus in the second house, providing the tie to her skill in the telegraph office. Another thing to note is the Sabian Symbol of 12 degrees of Pisces on the US North Node: "In the sanctuary of an occult brotherhood, newly initiated members are being examined and their character tested." The individual must stand up to declare his beliefs as an integral part of the whole.[26]

In the whole history of the labor movement, one figure stands out because of her 60-year career as a labor activist. Mary Harris was born 5/1/1830 in County Cork, Ireland, immigrated to Canada to escape the Potato Famine, and eventually entered the United States. She married George Jones, an iron worker and strong union supporter in Memphis, Tennessee; they had four children.[27] In 1867, an outbreak of yellow fever claimed the lives of her husband and children. She returned to Chicago only to lose her home and belongings in the Chicago fire of 1871.[28]

Undaunted by tragedy, Mary Harris Jones spent the rest of her life fighting for the rights of workers and against child labor. She participated in some of the greatest strikes of the 19th and early 20th centuries, worked with the Knights of Labor,[29] helped establish the Industrial Workers of the World, and was involved with the Social Democratic Party. She called the United Mine Workers "her boys" and was named Mother Jones and the "Miners' Angel,"[30] but authorities called her "the most dangerous woman in the country."[31] Her last arrest occurred at the age of eighty-six.[32]

Mother Jones was involved in the anthracite coal miners' strike in 1902, one of the largest seen in the business. The miners had asked for reduced working hours, higher wages, and union recognition. J.P. Morgan, the owner, had brought in thousands of immigrant laborers to keep wages down. Threatened by a coal famine, President Theodore Roosevelt, in an unprecedented move, called in both sides for discussion. He promised to appoint a neutral fact-finding commission to investigate claims by both sides. The two parties agreed to abide by the commission's report.[33]

During the next few months, the commission visited coal mines and questioned many witnesses, including the United Mine Workers Union president, John Mitchell.[34] In her autobiography, Mother Jones quotes his statement to the commission: "For more than twenty years the anthracite miners have groaned under most intolerable and inhuman conditions. In a brotherhood of labor, they seek to remedy their wrongs."[35]

Clarence Darrow, the lawyer representing the union, closed his supporting arguments as follows: "This contest is one of the most important contests that have marked the progress of human liberty since the world began - one force pointing one way, another force the other. Every advantage that the human race has won has been at fearful cost. Every contest has been won by struggle. Some men must die that others may live. It has come to these poor miners to bear this cross, not for themselves- not that- but that the human race may be lifted up to a higher and broader plane than it has ever known before."³⁶

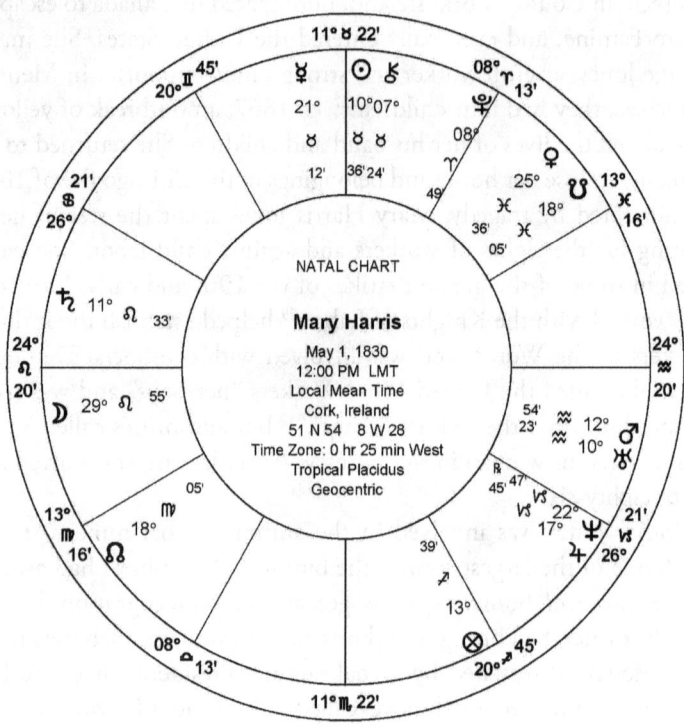

Figure 10-2
Mary Harris Jones Natal Chart
May 1, 1830, 12:00 PM, County Cork, Ireland

The strike was successful. As Mother Jones reported: "The commission found in favor of the miners in every one of their demands."³⁷

I used a noon chart for Mother Jones. Her birthday is uncertain, but it is known that her 100th birthday was celebrated on International Workers Day on May 1, 1930, so I used that date. The Mars conjunction to

Uranus in Aquarius tells us a lot about her radical life and it's tied to the US chart's stellium in Aquarius. The opposition to Saturn illustrates her struggle against the status quo just as the opposition of Saturn to Uranus in the US chart.

Cesar Chavez is another outstanding figure in the labor movement. He was born near Yuma, Arizona[38] to a poor immigrant family. He had little education but inherited strong beliefs from his Catholic mother.[39] Inspired by a priest, he read about Mahatma Gandhi's use of non-violent methods for defying oppressors. Gandhi's techniques became part of his toolbox as he rose steadily to be a labor organizer among migrant workers. Fred Ross of the Community Service Organization (CSO) taught him how to be an "effective organizer" so that he could "help Mexicans and Latinos improve their living conditions."[40]

Not satisfied with the CSO or the AFL-CIO, Chavez organized his own union, working sixteen-hour days talking to and recruiting farm workers.[41] On September 30, 1962, the National Farm Workers Association (NFWA) had its first convention in Fresno with 250 members.[42] During the grape boycott, the NFWA merged with the Agricultural Workers Organizing Committee to form the United Farm Workers.[43]

The grape boycott, lasting from 1965 to 1970, was one of the longest and most difficult strikes Chavez led. Filipino workers around Delano had gone on strike against the grape growers.[44] The NFWA joined the battle and the movement blossomed. Chavez called for a public boycott of grapes.[45] In March 1966 the protestors marched 300 miles from Delano to Sacramento to present their grievances to Governor Pat Brown.[46] This led to a contract with one grower,[47] but the battle continued. Further strikes ensued, and at times were violent. In 1968, Chavez began a hunger strike to quell the violence, a goal he achieved. The nationwide boycott on grapes encouraged by the movement was supported by millions of Americans.[48]

The strike ended in July 1970. The workers received a wage increase and an employee health and welfare fund. Chavez lauded the workers' commitment to nonviolence, their sacrifices, and the support of millions of Americans that had made the strike so powerful.[49] He died on April 23, 1993.[50] A year later, President Bill Clinton awarded him the Presidential Medal of Freedom.[51]

Chavez, like Sarah Bagley, has a tie to the US chart's North Node, moving America forward for better lives for its citizens. His Pluto conjuncts the US Uranus, setting off the opposition to Saturn, authority.

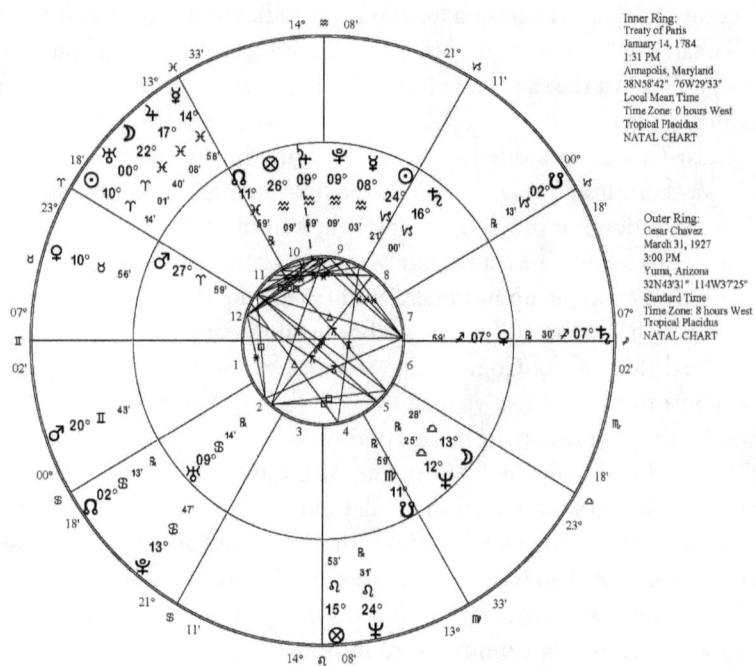

Figure 10-3
Cesar Chavez Natal Chart / US Chart Biwheel

Also, look at the exact conjunction of his Saturn to the US Venus, creating contracts between growers and immigrant workers. The stellium of Moon, Jupiter, and Mercury in Pisces in the US tenth house describes his compassion for others and the need to take action.

Labor union strength began declining around 1955. Although the National Labor Relations Act had allowed employees to unionize, it applied to individual firms and not the industry as a whole. Union organizers could not keep up with rapid job growth. An increase in imports led to reduction in American manufacturing and a shift to lower-paying jobs. Strikes became less effective as companies could more readily close factories or move them outside the US. Additionally, conservative attacks encouraged distrust of unions, while the criminal activities of some high-profile "labor bosses" further weakened public support. Some administrations were hostile to unions. The percentage of workers in unions has declined steadily.[52]

This has resulted in the wide income gap between groups as illustrated in the chart below.[53]

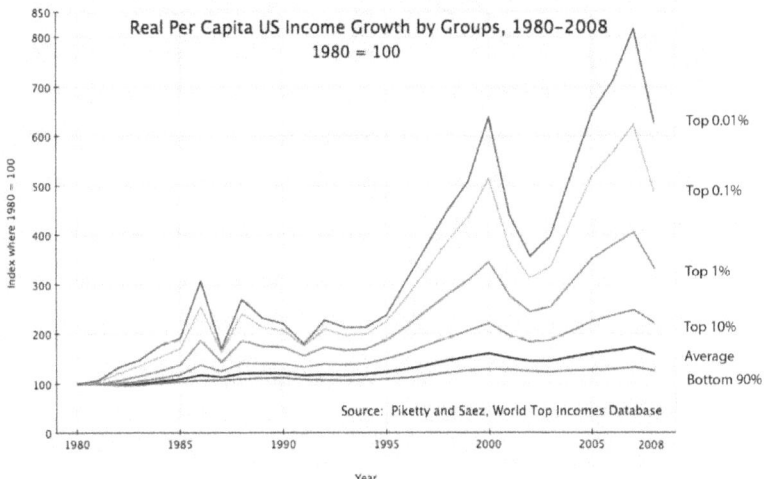

Figure 10-4
Real Per Capita Income Growth by Groups, 1980-2008

The "trickle down" economic policy of Ronald Reagan added to the income disparity until Americans were alerted to it by the "Occupy Wall Street" movement. In September 2011, young people declared "We are the 99%!" and began the occupation in New York City's financial district.[54] The movement decried the top 1% who owned a large portion of America's wealth, had half the stocks, bonds, and mutual funds, had less personal debt, and took home a tremendous portion of the national income. Their share was greater than at any other time since the 1920s, leaving the 99% behind.[55] The Occupy Wall Street movement's strong emphasis on income inequality introduced it into political discourse and inspired the fight for the fifteen-dollar minimum wage.[56]

Union growth and activity began increasing in 2016, primarily due to millennial workers. The number of strikes has risen considerably. Public sector union membership surpassed that of the private sector for the first time in 2009. Even so, a 2023 Oxfam study found the US to rank among the lowest in industrialized countries for labor protections and the right to unionize.[57]

The struggles continue today as the promise of "work hard, play by the rules, get ahead" seems to have disappeared. The people are under increasing stress while politicians and government seem helpless to change it. The early colonists sought freedom from a landed aristocracy. What happened?

CHAPTER TEN NOTES

1. https://www.britannica.com/technology/Industrial-Revolution *Accessed 12/3/2022*
2. https://www.history.com/topics/19th-century/labor *Accessed 12/15/2023*
3. Ibid.
4. Ibid.
5. https://www.nps.gov/lowe/learn/historyculture/lflra.htm *Accessed 12/15/2023*
6. https://www.history.com/topics/19th-century/labor *Accessed 12/15/2023*
7. https://www.thoughtco.com/knights-of-labor-1773905 *Accessed 12/15/2023*
8. https://en.wikipedia.org/wiki/American_Federation_of_Labor *Accessed 12/15/2023*
9. https://www.history.com/topics/19th-century/haymarket-riot *Accessed 12/15/2023*
10. https://www.britannica.com/event/Pullman-Strike *Accessed 1/19/2023*
11. https://en.wikipedia.org/wiki/Industrial_Workers_of_the_World *Accessed 12/15/2023*
12. https://aflcio.org/about-us/history/labor-history-events *Accessed 12/15/2023*
13. https://en.wikipedia.org/wiki/Ludlow_Massacre *Accessed 12/15/2023*
14. https://en.wikipedia.org/wiki/Adamson_Act *Accessed 12/15/23*
15. https://en.wikipedia.org/wiki/Labor_history_of_the_United_States *Accessed 12/15/2023*
16. https://en.wikipedia.org/wiki/Fair_Labor_Standards_Act_of_1938 Accessed 12/15/2023
17. https://en.wikipedia.org/wiki/Labor_history_of_the_United_States *Accessed 12/15/2023*
18. Ibid.
19. *The World Book Encyclopedia*, Vol. 12. World Book, Inc., Chicago, Illinois, 2009. pp. 13-14
20. https://ufw.org/research/history/ufw-history/ *Accessed 12/15/2023*
21. https://en.wikipedia.org/wiki/Labor_history_of_the_United_

States *Accessed 12/15/2023*
22. https://aflcio.org/about/history/labor-history-events/lowell-mill-women-form-union *Accessed 12/12/2022*
23. *The Lowell Sun*, Lowell, Massachusetts. Article published 7/4/1976. Available at https://www.newspapers.com/image/45856604/ *Accessed 1/11/2023*
24. https://aflcio.org/about/history/labor-history-events/lowell-mill-women-form-union *Accessed 12/12/2022*
25. *The Lowell Sun*, Lowell, Massachusetts. Accessed 1/11/2023
26. Rudhyar, Dane: *An Astrological Mandala*. Vintage Books, New York, 1974. p. 275
27. https://en.wikipedia.org/wiki/Mother_Jones *Accessed 12/16/2023*
28. Jones, Mary Harris: *Autobiography of Mother Jones*. Dover Publications, Inc., Mineola, NY, 2004. pp. 1-2
29. https://almanac.com/meet-mother-jones *Accessed 1/10/2023*
30. https://en.wikipedia.org/wiki/Mother_Jones *Accessed 12/16/2023*
31. Jones, Mary Harris: *Autobiography of Mother Jones*. p. 27
32. https://almanac.com/meet-mother-jones Accessed 1/10/2023
33. https://www.dol.gov/general/aboutdol/history/coalstrike Accessed 1/20/2023
34. Ibid.
35. Jones, Mary Harris: *Autobiography of Mother Jones*. p. 34
36. *Wilkes-Barre Semi-Weekly*, Wilkes-Barre, Pennsylvania. Article published 2/17/1903. Available at https://www.newspapers.com/newspage/390491489/ *Accessed 1/21/2023*
37. Jones, Mary Harris: *Autobiography of Mother Jones*. p, 34
38. Young, Jeff C.: *Cesar Chavez*. Morgan Reynolds Publishing, Greensboro, N. Carolina, 2007. p. 127
39. Ibid. p 23
40. Ibid. pp. 48-52
41. Ibid. pp. 68-70
42. Ibid. p. 72
43. https://ufw.org/research/history/ufw-history/ *Accessed 12/16/2023*
44. https://history.com/this-day-in-history/delano-grape-strike-begins-ufw *Accessed 1/20/2023*

45. https://ufw.org/research/history/ufw-history/ *Accessed 12/16/2023*
46. Young, Jeff C.: *Cesar Chavez.* pp. 96-97
47. Ibid. p. 104
48. https://ufw.org/1965-1970-delano-grape-strike-boycott/ *Accessed 12/16/2023*
49. Young, Jeff C.: *Cesar Chavez.* pp. 128-132
50. Ibid. p 144
51. Ibid. p. 11
52. https://en.wikipedia.org/wiki/Labor_history_of_the_United-States *Accessed 12/16/2023*
53. https://aneconomicsense.org/2012/07/11/taxes-as-a-share-of-income-are-the-lowest-in-decades-while-income-distribution-is-close-to-the-worst/ *Accessed 12/16/2023*
54. https://en.wikipedia.org/wiki/Occupy_Wall_Street *Accessed 12/16/2023*
55. https://americanprogressaction.org/article/the-99-percent-movement *Accessed 1/23/2023*
56. https://en.wikipedia.org/wiki/Occupy_Wall_Street *Accessed 12/16/2023*
57. https://en.wikipedia.org/wiki/Labor_history_of_the_United_States *Accessed 12/16/2023*

Chapter Eleven

World War I

"Over there, over there"
George M. Cohan

It was called "The Great War" because of its extent. Multiple European countries were involved, with battles fought not only in Europe, but also the Middle East, the Pacific, Africa, and Asia. It gave us new technology such as tanks and machine guns, mustard gas, trench warfare and airplane warfare, not to mention submarines and then the technology to counteract them.[1] In its wake more than 16 million people, including both civilians and soldiers, were left dead. After the carnage and destruction, seeds of hatred and resentment remained to later blossom into the next world war, so the Great War became World War I.[2]

Instability in the Balkans preceded World War I. Bosnia, Serbia, and Herzegovina were itching to get out from under the rule of the Austrian-Hungary Empire. When a Serbian nationalist assassinated the Archduke Franz Ferdinand (the next heir to the empire) and his wife Sophie in Sarajevo on June 28, 1914, events exploded. On July 28, 1914, Austria-Hungary declared war on Serbia, and like dominoes, within the week countries fell to support one side or the other. With the Allies stood France, Russia, Serbia, Belgium, Great Britain, Italy, and Japan; on the other side the Central Powers of Austria-Hungary, Germany, and the Ottoman Empire (Turkey) united.[3]

Where was the United States? Americans wished to avoid foreign conflict, and President Woodrow Wilson declared that the country would remain neutral. In fact, the motto of his second campaign was "He kept us out of war." But during his second term, a German submarine sunk the ship *Lusitania* near the Irish Coast, killing many Americans. Public

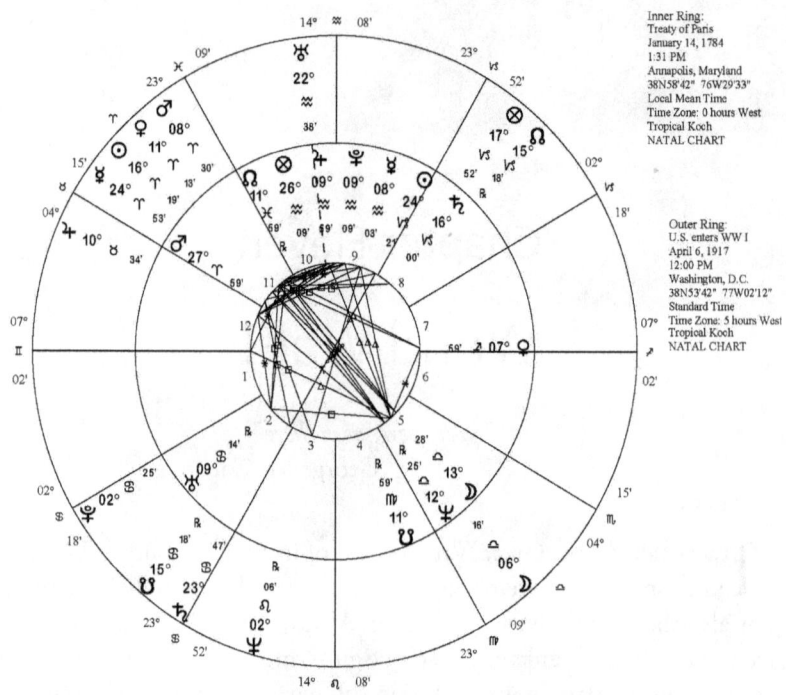

Figure 11-1
Declaration of World War I / US Natal Chart Biwheel

opinion changed. Although Germany promised not to use submarines against American ships, the guarantee was short-lived.

The nail in the coffin of American neutrality was struck by "The Zimmerman Telegram". Tracked by British intelligence who informed President Wilson, the document described an offer by Germany to Mexico to return lands they had ceded to the US in exchange for joining Germany in the war effort. On April 2, 1917, Wilson asked a joint session of Congress to declare war against Germany. On April 4, 1917, the US Senate voted its support, with the House agreeing two days later on April 6.[4]

Johnny got his gun and sailed across the Atlantic, bringing aid to a desperate ally, France, and remaining until the armistice on November 11, 1918. Examine the chart of the declaration of war compared to the US chart. Mercury in Aries (war) in the eleventh house (Congress) is the declaration that sets off the unaspected duet of the US Mars and the Sun as well as creating a T-square with transiting Saturn opposing the US Sun (President). I imagine this was a difficult decision for Wilson, a man devoted to peace. The transiting Sun that day makes a square aspect to the US Saturn in the eighth house, suggesting the heavy price the US will pay in terms of resources as well as human life.

The sacrifice of so many demanded a solution to possible future conflicts. In response to Wilson's Fourteen Points speech, the League of Nations was formed to promote global peace and international cooperation. The new idea was quickly embraced by most nations.[5]

Not so the United States. Despite Woodrow Wilson's support and 8000-mile trip in 22 days to promote the League to the public, Republicans demanded a return to isolationism while fiercely impugning Wilson's character. His wife, Edith, blamed them later for his near-fatal stroke on October 2, 1919.[6] He won the Nobel Peace Prize in 1919 for his efforts. The League of Nations continued until the start of World War II and later became the framework for the United Nations. Wilson was devastated by US refusal to participate in the League and lived the rest of his life in retirement until his death on February 3, 1924.[7]

I present two additional charts for you to examine because the people represented were very much a part of this time: one, a soldier and war hero, Sgt. Alvin York; and two, George M. Cohan, a songwriter.

For Sgt. York, I used a noon chart to compare with the US chart.

Sgt. Alvin C. York was the most decorated soldier of the Great War, considered a hero for his military action during the Meuse-Argonne offensive in France. His attack against a German machine gun nest resulted in the capture of over 100 enemies and 35 machine guns. At least 25 enemy soldiers were killed. He was awarded medals from France, Britain, Montenegro, and Italy,[8] and he received the Medal of Honor from the United States "for conspicuous gallantry and intrepidity above and beyond the call of duty..."[9]

But it was an article about York by George Pattullo in *The Saturday Evening Post* in 1919 that made York a hero to Americans. "The story of Alvin York seemed to captivate the American imagination and, in some way, reflect the collective psyche of the populace that was reluctant to enter the war, but once in it, was committed to winning it. He seemed to represent how Americans viewed themselves: pioneers, devout, patriots, slow to action but firm in resolve."[10]

From the Cumberland Valley of Tennessee, Alvin was the third of eleven children born to hard-working religious parents. He developed a strong bond with his father, a farmer and blacksmith, through their work and hunting together to support the family. But his father died in 1911, leaving him the responsibility as head of the household to support

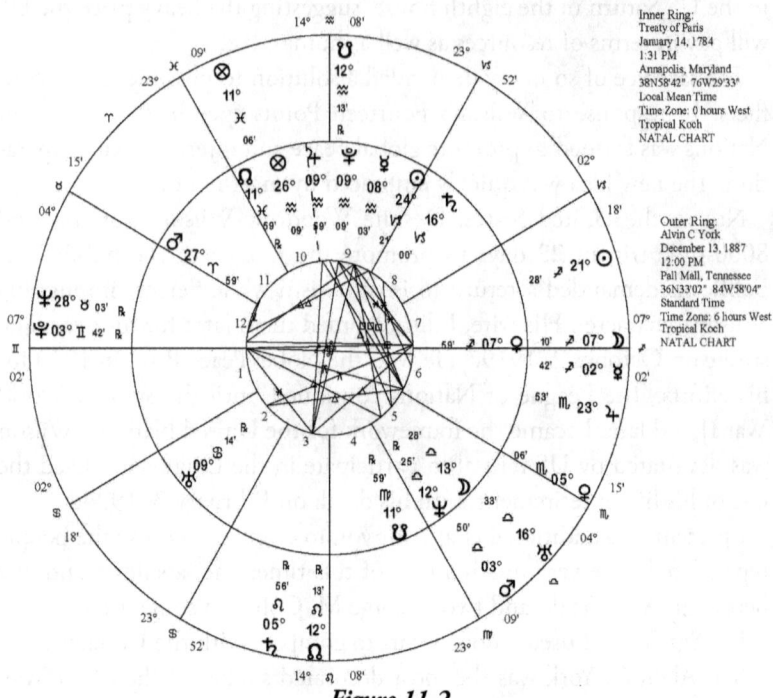

Figure 11-2
Sgt. York Natal Chart / US Natal Chart Biwheel

his mother and remaining siblings. Alvin was in his early twenties and the burden was a heavy one for him.[11]

Encouraged by young men around him, Alvin slid into self-destructive behavior that included drinking, smoking, gambling, cursing, and fighting, far from the examples of his religious parents. His mother waited patiently without admonishing his behavior but trying to lead him back to the right path.[12] Over time an inner moral conflict developed, intensified by his attraction to Gracie, a young woman he wanted to marry but who would never accept a "backslider" like him. As York himself put it, "I was fighting the thing inside of me and it was the worst fight I ever had."[13]

At the end of 1914, as Alvin struggled with his dilemma, he attended a week of revival meetings led by the Reverend Russell. He heard the words that changed his life during the final meeting. "I truly felt as though I had been borned again," he said as he was accepted into the Christian faith on January 1, 1915, finally at peace with himself and the world.[14]

Faith presented him with another dilemma when the US entered the Great War. As a religious pacifist, he was against killing, but as an American he wanted to fight for his country. His claim for a religious exemption was denied, so he entered army training. As the departure time to France approached, Alvin discussed his conflict with his commanding officers. They supplied biblical passages contradicting his arguments, and gave him leave home to consider the matter, allowing the possibility of a non-combative position if he could not come to terms with fighting.[15] During his leave, Alvin went to his favorite mountain place to fast and pray, returning with the conviction that it was right to go to war and he would be protected as long as he kept his faith.[16]

In examining his chart, you can see the important conjunction of Neptune and Pluto opposing his Moon, Mercury as well as Jupiter, which seems to account for the dilemmas he faced in his life. This opposition connects to the 1st-7th axis of the US chart and reflects the same dilemma in America. Since both Pluto and Neptune are the slowest moving planets, the effect of this pair was at work during most of Alvin's formative years. On the evening of January 1, 1915, when Alvin made his choice of his faith over his "sinful behavior," the planets had moved apart from each other enough to lessen the effect. In addition, his progressed chart shows transiting Venus conjunct his natal Moon and the transiting Moon and Jupiter were conjuncting his natal Mercury. His natal Mars was progressing toward a conjunction of his natal Uranus. This caused a complete turn-a-round in his life from then on. His exact trine between Mars and Pluto gave him immense courage during the battle in the Meuse-Argonne offensive, even though he felt he had done nothing more than any other soldier would have done.

Alvin lived an exemplary life after the war. He refused the wealth and fame he had earned, returning home to Gracie and his small community. However, his expanded world view motivated him to improve conditions around him. He devoted his time to bringing roads and schools to his isolated town, recognizing the need for the education that he had not received as a youth. He built a Bible school as well. As a second war with Germany approached, he spoke out against the isolationists. His life remains a model of what it means to be an American: honest, hardworking, tolerant, faithful, and patriotic.[17]

The second chart is that of George M. Cohan: singer, dancer, actor, producer, writer, and song writer. For half a century, he dominated the Broadway theater. He spent his early years with his parents and sister in

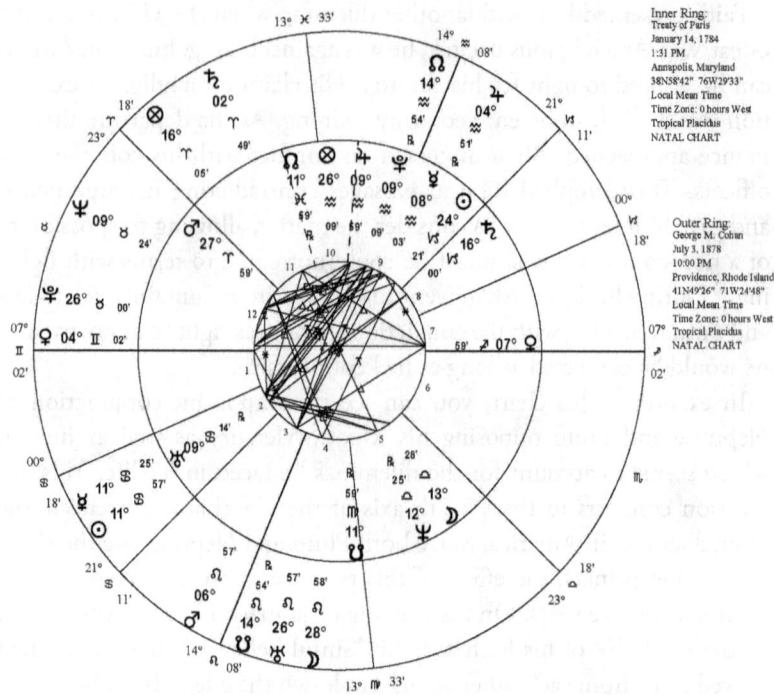

Figure 11-3
George M. Cohan Natal Chart / US Natal Chart

their vaudeville act "The Four Cohans."[18] Recognizing his early genius, his father made him manager of the company when he was 20.[19] But George was ambitious and was ready to move up to Broadway, where he was soon writer, lyricist, producer, and star of his own productions with his partner, Sam Harris.[20]

His North Node is exactly conjunct the US Midheaven. His Jupiter conjuncting the US chart ruler, Mercury, indicates his total identification with America and his fundamental patriotism, as he was known as the "Yankee Doodle Boy."[21] He is the only musician to have won the Congressional Gold Medal, presented to him by Franklin D. Roosevelt in 1940 for his song "Over There".[22] Like York, he did not believe he was entitled to such an honor because he was just "a hoofer." He is the only man of the theatre to have a statue in Times Square. Emblazoned on it is the title of his hit song, "Give My Regards to Broadway."[23]

CHAPTER ELEVEN NOTES

1. https://en.wikipedia.org/wiki/World_War_I   *Accessed 2/01/2023*
2. https://www.history.com/topics/world-war-i/world-war-i-history   *Accessed 2/01/2023*
3. Ibid.
4. https://www.history.com/topics/world-war-i/u-s-entry-into-world-war-i-1   *Accessed 1/24/2023*
5. https://www.history.com/topics/world-war-i/league-of-nations   *Accessed 6/13/2023*
6. https://www.history.com/this-day-in-history/woodrow-wilson-suffers-a-stroke   *Accessed 2/02/2023*
7. https://www.britannica.com/video/172722/overview-Woodrow-Wilson   *Accessed Transcript 2/02/2023*
8. https://en.wikipedia.org/wiki/Alvin_York   Accessed 6/12/2023
9. Mastriano, Douglas V.: *Alvin York*; University Press of Kentucky, 2014. Chapter 8.
10. Ibid. p. 145
11. Ibid. Chapter 2
12. Ibid. Chapter 1
13. Ibid. p. 17
14. Ibid. p. 21
15. Ibid. Chapter 3
16. Ibid. Chapter 3
17. https://en.wikipedia.org/wiki/Alvin_York   *Accessed 6/13/2023*
18. https://en.wikipedia.org/wiki/George_M._Cohan   *Accessed 6/13/2023*
19. Morehouse, Ward: *George M. Cohan: Prince of the American Theater*; J. B. Lippincott Co., New York, 1943. p. 17
20. Ibid. p. 19
21. Ibid. p. 15
22. https://en.wikipedia.org/wiki/George_M._Cohan   *Accessed 6/13/2023*
23. https://www.nycgovparks.org/parks/father-duffy-square/monuments/282   *Accessed 6/13/2023*

Chapter Twelve

Two Pandemics One Hundred Years Apart

*"Oh, when darkness comes, and pain is all around,
Like a Bridge Over Troubled Water, I will lay me down"*
Simon and Garfunkel

After the carnage of the Great War, humanity was struck with the most devastating pandemic in human history. It lasted two years and cost an estimated 20 to 50 million lives globally. The initial wave of influenza, known as Spanish flu, was relatively mild. The second wave, however, was much more lethal and developed into pneumonia followed by death in two days. The first case occurred in March of 1918. The pandemic ended in the summer of 1919.[1]

Whole families were wiped out, many widows and orphans left behind. Businesses were shut down, basic services were hindered, crops could not be harvested, and even the health departments were frequently closed and unable to answer questions about the disease. No drugs or

Figure 12-1 Three Waves of 1918 Pandemic of Spanish Flu[2]

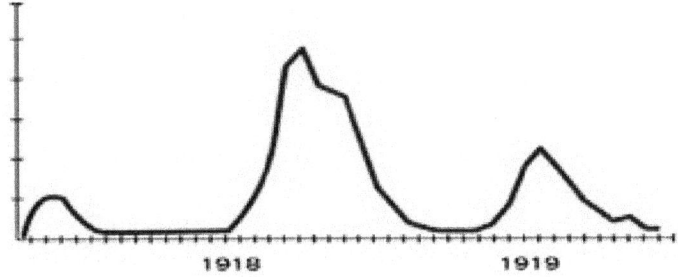

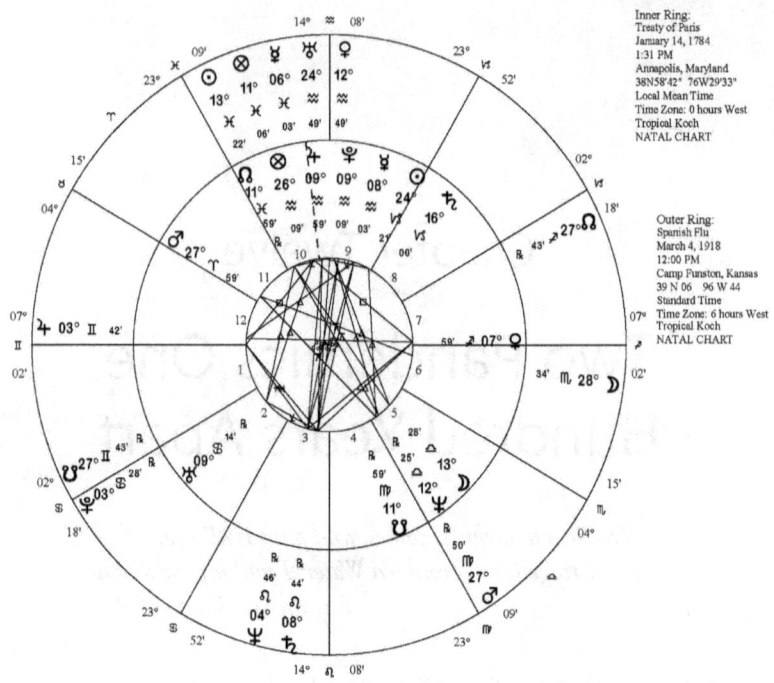

Figure 12-2
Spanish Flu Epidemic / US Chart Biwheel

vaccines existed. People wore masks and avoided shaking hands. Schools and theaters were closed.[3]

In the comparison chart of the flu pandemic and US chart, you see Neptune and Saturn conjunction is opposing the upper leg of the US Yod, the stellium in Aquarius which includes Pluto (diseases), Mercury (the nation), and Jupiter (global). Jupiter (expansion) is on the US Ascendant from the twelfth house. The Moon in Scorpio is in the US sixth house (health matters) which itself forms a Yod with its Mars and the US Mars in the eleventh house of "things out of control". Pluto in Cancer and the US second house indicates the economic problems facing the citizens. The pandemic chart has Uranus squaring the Scorpio Moon, describing the disruption in the life of the citizens.

The second pandemic started one hundred years later and was caused by a new coronavirus labeled COVID-19. A partial time line of this pandemic follows.[4]

- January 20, 2020: CDC reports the first case in Washington state.
- March 11, 2020: WHO declares COVID-19 a pandemic after

118,000 cases in 14 countries and 4291 deaths.
- March 15, 2020: States begin shutdowns to prevent the spread of COVID-19.
- April 30, 2020: President Trump launches Operation Warp Speed for rapid development of a vaccine.
- May 9, 2020: Unemployment in the US reaches almost 15 percent.
- August 2020: COVID-19 cases surpass 5.4 million in the US.
- October 2020: Food insecurity reaches 52 million people.
- Nov 16, 2020: Moderna reports its COVID vaccine is 95.4% effective.
- Nov 18, 2020: Pfizer-BioNTech reports its vaccine to be 95% effective.
- December 31, 2020: 2.8 million vaccine doses have been administered in the US.
- 2022: COVID and its mutations remain prevalent, creating a 25% increase in anxiety and depression worldwide.

Figure 12-3 Waves of COVID Pandemic USA 2020 to 2023[5]

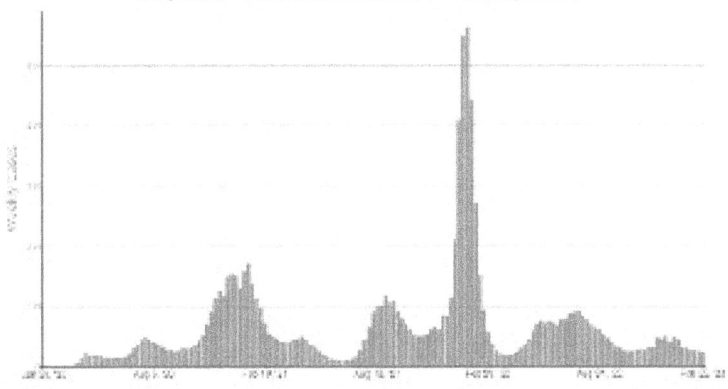

Unlike the Spanish flu pandemic, COVID-19 affected people from racial and ethnic minorities as well as those of lower economic status more severely. Rates of infection and death are higher in these groups. Discrimination reduces access to good health care, increases economic insecurity leading to inadequate nutrition, stress, and subsequent susceptibility to disease. The economic consequences of the pandemic itself also impact minorities, resulting in poorer outcomes.[6] CDC Director Dr Rochelle Walensky noted in an April 2021 statement that "...the

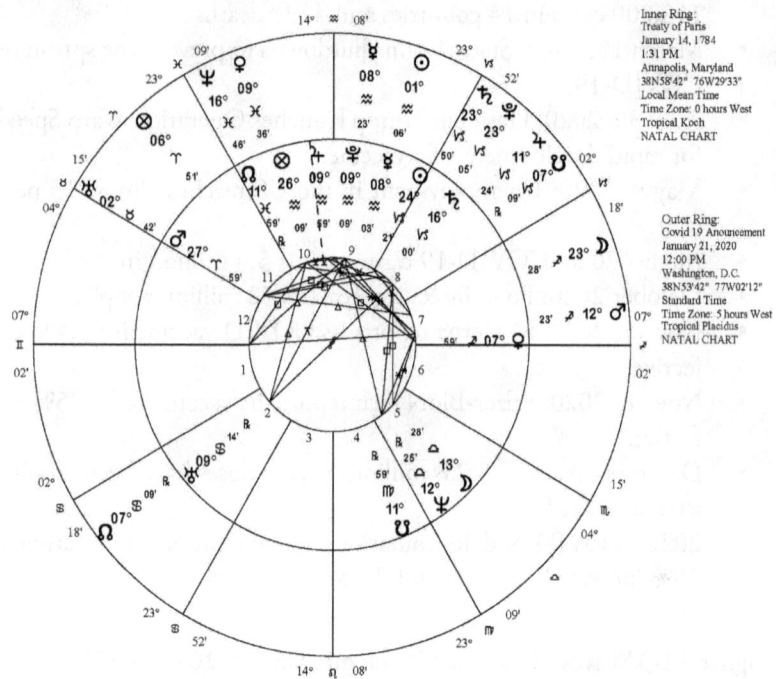

Figure 12-4
Covid 19 CDC Announcement / US Chart Biwheel

disparities seen over the past year were not a result of COVID-19. Instead, the pandemic illuminated inequities that have existed for generations and revealed for all of America a known, but often unaddressed, epidemic impacting public health: racism."[7]

Another critical difference between the two pandemics was the conflict about disease management, a particular issue in the US. Disagreement about public health policies such as shutdowns, mask-wearing, receiving vaccinations, and other government mandates divided the population, becoming "the latest frontier in the great American defense of freedom and liberty" — a dynamic seemingly unique to America.[8]

The conjunction of Pluto and Saturn in the eighth house of the US chart passing over the US Sun describes the restrictions (Saturn) caused by the new virus (COVID-19) which also squares the US chart Mars (conflict). Mercury in Aquarius has also returned to its natal place (the nation). The eighth house placement also points to the draining of resources as well as the conflict over them. Transiting Jupiter in Capricorn conjuncting the US Saturn further expanded the crisis.

By June 2022 the US recorded a total of 84 million infections and over 1 million deaths.[9] Perhaps many deaths would have been prevented if this crisis had not been made into political football. Politicizing the public health system may have serious consequences, as evidenced in the comparison of two pandemics that ravished America one hundred years apart.

CHAPTER TWELVE NOTES

1. https://www.britannica.com/event/influenza-pandemic-of-1918-1919 *Accessed 2/6/2023*
2. https://www.cdc.gov/flu/pandemic-resources/1918-commemoration/three-waves.htm *Accessed 2/6/2023*
3. www.history.com/topics/world-war-i/1918-flu-pandemic *Accessed 2/6/2023*
4. https://www.cdc.gov/museum/timeline/covid19.html *Accessed 2/15/2023*
5. https://www.cdc.gov/coronavirus/2019-ncov/covid-data/covid-view/index.html *Accessed 3/1/2023*
6. https://www.bbc.com/future/article/20200420-coronavirus-why-some-racial-groups-are-more-vulnerable *Accessed 2/22/2023*
7. https://www.cdc.gov/museum/timeline/covid19.html *Accessed 2/15/2023*
8. www.npr.org/2021/10/1046598351/the/political-fight-over-vaccine-mandates-deepen-despite-their-effectiveness *Accessed 2/13/2023*
9. https://www.cdc.gov/museum/timeline/covid19.html *Accessed 2/15/2023*

Chapter Thirteen

The Roaring Twenties

"Another season, another reason, for Makin' Whoopee"
Gus Hahn & Walter Donaldson

The decade of the 1920s started out with a bang called Prohibition. After a long, protracted conflict between the "wets" (mostly distillers, brewers, and saloons) and the "dries" (mostly women with male allies), the dreaded Volstead Act, prohibiting the making and selling of alcoholic spirits, went into effect on January 16, 1920. Weeks before, people stored up on any alcohol available, anticipating the upcoming shortage. By the way, the Act did NOT prohibit drinking alcohol!

American love of alcohol had its onset with the Puritans' arrival in the 1600s. Though the Puritans espoused many moral restrictions, abstinence from alcohol was not one of them. John Winthrop, the Puritan founder of the Massachusetts Bay Colony in 1630, traveled to America in a ship that carried more than ten thousand gallons of wine as well as considerably more beer than water.[1] Society, from the lowest workers to the highest of elites, drank from morning to night. By 1810, fourteen thousand distilleries existed, and adult Americans consumed roughly seven gallons of pure alcohol annually.[2]

Imagine the effect on families. Eventually, opposition to this "sinful" profligacy would arise. It took form as the Women's Christian Temperance Union, a group allied with men who had pledged abstinence, having recognized the danger from excessive drinking. The women's suffrage movement was intimately bound up with them, as women recognized having power at the ballot box was critical for achieving the goal of prohibition.[3] Realizing this as well, the booze business fought against women's voting rights.⁴ The battle resulted in two amendments to the Constitution, the 18th and 19th, providing the ban on alcohol in addition to granting the vote to women. (Wine was allowed for "sacramental purposes" only.⁵)

No more making whoopee!

Or so the temperance movement had hoped. However, rebellious Americans detest relinquishing their "rights" and quickly found ways to indulge their favorite pastime, drinking. And who could blame them! After a terrible war and a pandemic, they wanted to forget the past horrors by indulging in alcohol, jazz, drugs, cars, fashion, movies, and sports.

The new era provided the opportunity. It was a time like no other. Novel inventions like the automobile, the radio, the refrigerator, and the vacuum cleaner made life easier. An economic boom increased wealth and the desire to spend it. Women entered the work force in millions. They felt liberated and showed it, with the "flappers," bobbed hair, smoking, and freer sexuality. Movie stars like Charlie Chaplin, Greta Garbo and Rudolph Valentino were all the rage.⁶ In 1927 Babe Ruth hit 60 homers to help the NY Yankees win the baseball World Series⁷ and Charles Lindbergh flew across the Atlantic in the first nonstop flight between New York and Paris.⁸

Despite Prohibition, it was a time for making whoopee anywhere and anytime you could.

Examine the chart of the Volstead Act which became effective at midnight on January 16, 1920 and the US chart.

The main aspect bringing about change is Pluto making a slow journey through Cancer, passing over Uranus in the US chart, the Axis of Awareness of the Yod, and setting off a vibration of the Yod on the Uranus (change) in the second house (values) which continued to hum through this generation, overriding the Capricorn restrictions of Sun and Saturn. Transiting Uranus is squaring the Moon in Sagittarius, emphasizing the disruption and need for change, particularly for women. At the same time, Uranus trines the Mars in the fifth house, indicating all the new inventions of the period which brought about major change in mobility. Hop in your Ford Model-T or Model-A and explore this new world! The Yod's restlessness is released by an outlet through the Neptune/Moon conjunction in the fifth house of amusements.

But a dark side also exists. Pluto in the Yod mixes in crime and racism. An anti-communist scare along with anti-immigrant hysteria resulted

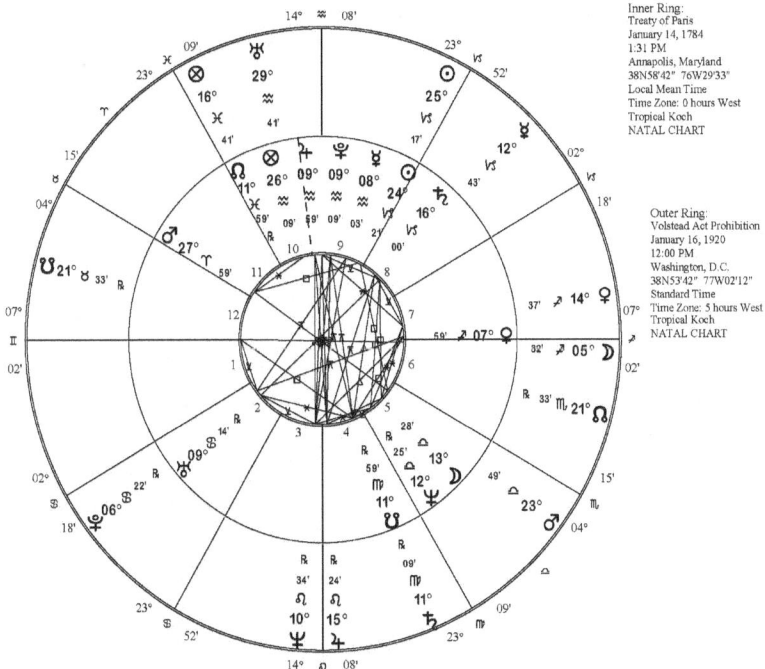

Figure 13-1
Volstead Act / US Chart Biwheel

in the National Origins Act of 1924, restrictive legislation that set immigration quotas favoring Northern Europeans while excluding Asians and Eastern Europeans.[9] Prohibition led to the emergence of organized crime,[10] and Ku Klux Klan membership increased to fight "Prohibition violators" it claimed were among southern and eastern European immigrants as well as Catholics.[11]

Significant social, economic, and political changes occurred in the 1920s. Rural Americans migrated to the cities, and Black Americans from the south to the north, changing the US demographics. The increasing prominence of Black culture, including jazz, blues music, and Black literature, disturbed some white Americans, resulting in millions becoming Ku Klux Klan members. They sought to reduce perceived disruption of the social hierarchy induced by the improvement in Black American status.[12]

In answer, the NAACP actively investigated voting restrictions, discriminatory housing practices, and mob violence. They supported an antilynching law, but it was defeated by Senate filibuster. The election of Oscar De Priest, the first Black congressman since Reconstruction, to the House of Representatives in 1928 was one milestone achieved by Black Americans in the 1920s.[13]

A sensational event that went global during this decade was the trial of Sacco and Vanzetti, two Italian-born anarchists convicted of killing a paymaster for a shoe company and his guard during a robbery in Massachusetts. Evidence of their guilt was lacking and protests both in Massachusetts and throughout the world demanded their release. Despite this, the state Supreme Court upheld the verdict and the Massachusetts governor denied clemency. They were executed on August 23, 1927.[14]

The so-called "trial of the century" occurred in 1925. The "Scopes Monkey Trial" began when well-known lawyer Clarence Darrow, ACLU member, agreed to defend a young science teacher, John Scopes, who violated a Tennessee bill that made the teaching of evolution in public schools illegal. Darrow considered the bill unconstitutional. The prosecution was directed by William Jennings Bryan, a three-time presidential nominee and anti-evolution advocate. This trial highlighted the controversy over evolution since the publication in 1859 of Charles Darwin's *On the Origin of Species*. The battle of these two great American orators was highlighted by the press. In the end, Scopes was pronounced guilty after nine minutes of jury deliberation and was fined $100.[15]

The first major scandal involving the US government was the Teapot Dome Scandal, occurring in the Warren Harding administration at the decade's start. Teapot Dome and two California sites contained considerable federal oil reserves that had been set aside for the US Navy.[16] Oil tycoons wanted to open these lands to commercial drilling. Harding's campaign manager's negotiations with such men eventually won Harding the presidency.[17] The plan was to have the president select a Cabinet Interior officer who would lease these reserves to the oilmen.[18]

Harding selected Albert Fall for the Interior Cabinet position.[19] Fall had the oil reserves transferred to Interior, and leased the drilling rights, without competitive bidding, to the oil tycoons.[20] He received considerable reimbursement from Sinclair, one of the oilmen.[21]

By April 1922, a Senate investigation was opened about the shady deals, continuing into the Coolidge administration after Harding died in office. Fall was eventually convicted of taking bribes. Sinclair fought his case to the Supreme Court, arguing that Congress did not have the power to do investigations of this type. He was unsuccessful.[22]

The Teapot Dome scandal was the most egregious episode of federal

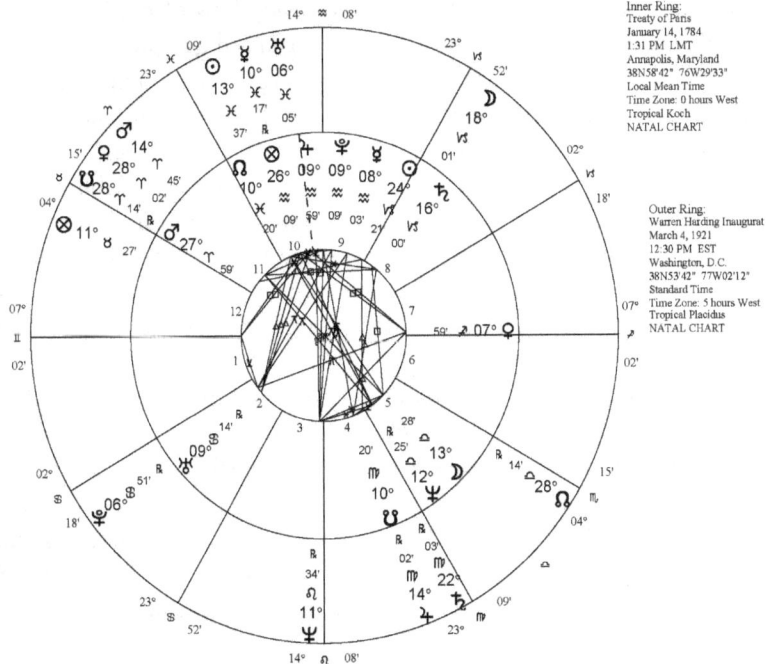

Figure 13-2
Warren G. Harding Inauguration / US Chart Biwheel

government corruption in US history prior to Watergate. It led to acknowledgement of Congressional power to investigate government corruption. And it was the first time that a high government official was convicted of and served time for a felony done while in office.[23]

The chart of President Harding's inauguration shows that his administration returned to a conservative Republican agenda. Big business saw reduced taxes for corporations and the wealthy, immigration was limited, and Congress passed protective tariffs. Although Harding was popular while in office, after his death on August 1, 1923, the Teapot Dome Scandal revealed the corruption going on among his cabinet members. His reputation was tarnished even though he himself may not have been directly involved.

Prohibition was a major factor in the development of organized crime. Prior to its passage, gangs of criminals ran small-time operations in local areas, but the subsequent huge enterprise managing illegal alcohol distribution and sales required extensive oversight and cooperation. Lawyers, accountants, money-laundering operations, security services, and more became necessary to maintain the steady flow of millions in income from illegal booze. Political bosses organized gangsters into paramilitary operations for this purpose. Criminal groups formed syndicates that cooperated in the business, and thus "syndicated" crime was born.[24]

Crime and corruption reigned in the city of Chicago where competing gangs battled for control of bootlegging, speakeasies, gambling, and prostitution. The violence culminated in a bloody confrontation called the St. Valentine's Day Massacre on February 14, 1929. Seven members of the "Bugs" Moran gang were shot down by men dressed as policemen. Although they were believed to be part of Al Capone's gang, it was never proved.[25]

The horror of automatic weapons like sub-machine guns described in the well-published newspaper accounts of the massacre brought more public awareness of gun issues, which will be further explored in later chapters.

A chart of the St. Valentine's Day Massacre is the next to be examined.

Here we see transiting Pluto making a long journey through the US Chart's second house of values, opposing its Natal Saturn, severely alter-

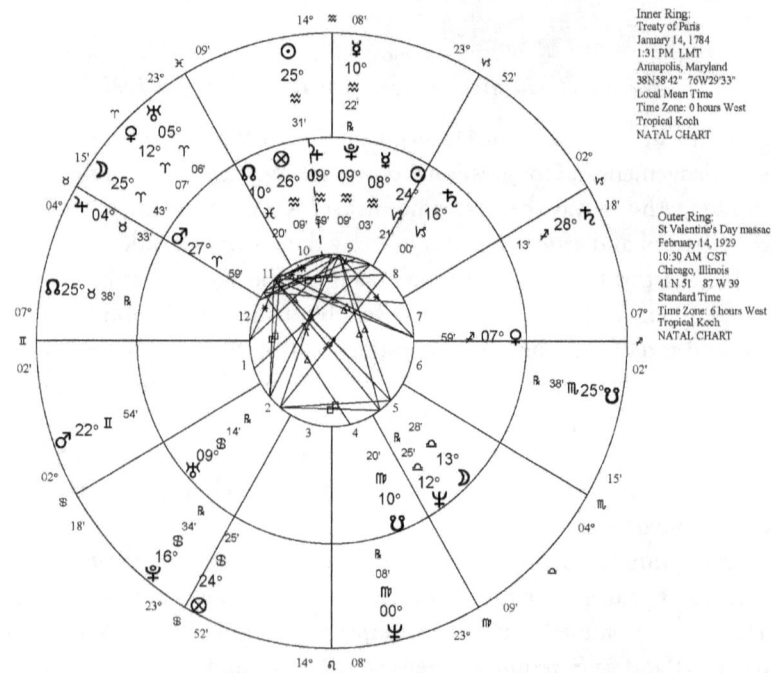

Figure 13-3
St Valentine's Day Massacre / US Chart Biwheel

ing the values and morals of the time and setting off the Yod's restlessness and search for answers. The amount of death occurring in WWI along with the global devastation of the Spanish flu caused many to question their former beliefs. The Saturn in the US chart is in the eighth house, showing the government repression of the American right to drink alcohol and releasing Pluto's rise of crime and illegal behavior of the populace. The Moon in Aries sets off the hostility between the public and authority by activating the unaspected duet of Mars and the Sun in the US chart.

What we see is not truly a physical war but rather a war of values. A good illustration of this conflict is presented in Somerset Maugham's 1946 novel (and later movie) *The Razor's Edge*. In this work, an American pilot traumatized by his experiences in WWI searches for meaning. His pursuit is contrasted with other characters who represent different moral positions. One character who lost her husband and child destroys herself with alcohol. Another character becomes obsessed with material values. The pilot's ex-girlfriend marries his friend because she is unable to understand his search for transcendental answers.

One of the worst episodes of US racial violence occurred during the Tulsa Race Massacre in May 1921. A confrontation in an elevator between a white female elevator operator and a Black teenager named Dick Rowland led to Rowland's arrest. Newspapers suggested he had sexually assaulted her. At the courthouse later, an angry white mob of 1500 confronted 75 armed Black men who had gathered to protect Rowland from a potential lynching.[26]

The outnumbered Blacks retreated to the Greenwood District, a primarily Black area with a successful business area known as "Black Wall Street." Fueled by rumors that Black residents were starting an insurrection, "thousands of white citizens poured into the Greenwood District, looting and burning homes and businesses over an area of 35 city blocks." It ended with the arrival of the National Guard and declaration of martial law.[27]

The event was deliberately covered up for decades. A commission in 2001 reported that 100 to 300 were killed, 8000 people made homeless. Buildings damaged or destroyed by fire included 1256 houses, a library, school, and hospital, as well as stores, churches, and other Black-owned businesses. Dick Rowland left town after all charges against him were dropped.[28]

In the chart below you see a Grand T-square between Uranus (riots)

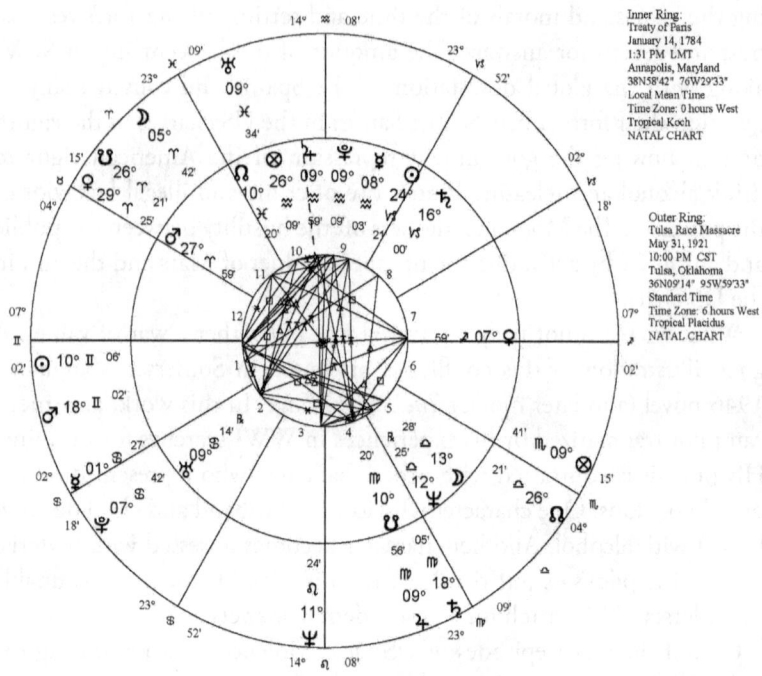

Figure 13-4
Tulsa Race Massacre / US Chart Biwheel

opposed to Jupiter (expansion) and both square to the Sun in the first house (the people), which all converge on the US Venus in the seventh house (open enemies). The rumors which started the riot are shown with Neptune in the third house (communications) opposing Mercury and Pluto in the US chart's Yod.

Many great events occurred during this era. One should mention the excellent literature produced by writers such as Sinclair Lewis, who won the Nobel Prize for literature in 1930, as well as Hemingway, Dos Pasos, and F. Scott Fitzgerald. Fitzgerald's chart is included as his written works reflect the era's moral attitudes along with that search for the American Dream.

Who better than Fitzgerald could present such an accurate picture of the Roaring Twenties with his Libra Sun, Venus, and Mercury in the fifth house of creativity of the US chart? The Moon in Taurus ruled by Venus in Libra reflects his connection to the US collective unconscious (twelfth house). His Mars conjunct Neptune in the first house of the US chart shows his identification with the problem of the era, alcohol,

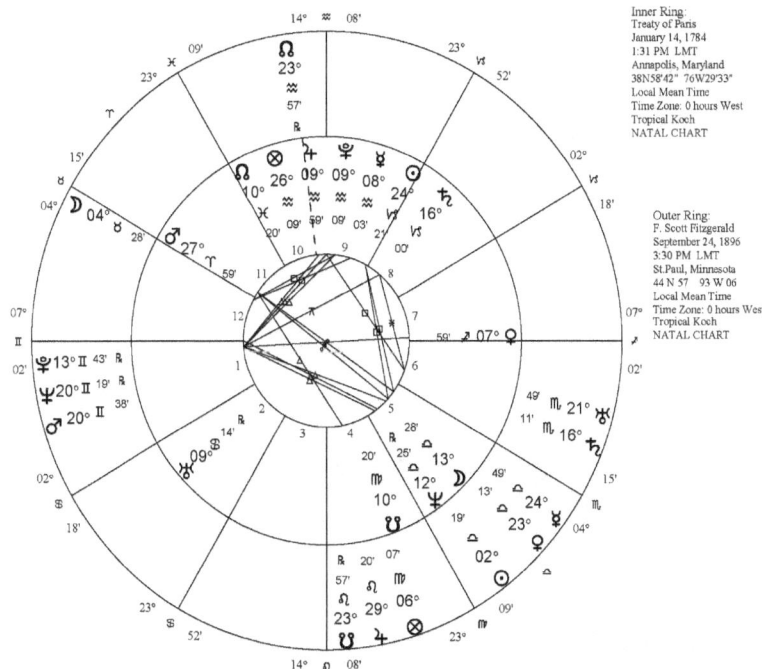

Figure 13-5
F. Scott Fitzgerald Natal Chart / US Chart Biwheel

and his victimization by it.

The '20s started with a bang and ended with another- the Wall Street Crash, Oct. 19, 1929- the beginning of the Depression.

CHAPTER THIRTEEN NOTES

1. Orkent, Daniel: *Last Call: The Rise and Fall of Prohibition*. Scribner, New York, NY, 2010. p.17
2. Ibid. p. 18
3. Ibid. pp. 24-29
4. Ibid. pp. 86-87
5. Ibid. p. 142
6. https://www.history.com/topics/roaring twenties/roaring-twenties-history
Accessed 8/12/2022
7. https://en.wikipedia.org/wiki/Babe_Ruth
Accessed 5/9/2023
8. https://www.britannica.com/biography/Charles-Lindbergh
Accessed 5/9/2023
9. https://www.history.com/topics/roaring twenties/roaring-twenties-history
Accessed 8/12/2022
10. https://www.history.com/news/prohibition-organized-crime-al-capone
Accessed 5/9/2023
11. https://www.history.com/news/kkk-terror-during-prohibition
Accessed 5/11/2023
12. https://www.history.com/topics/roaring twenties/roaring-twenties-history
Accessed 8/12/2022
13. Ibid.
14. https://www.history.com/this-day-in-history/sacco-and-vanzetti-executed
Accessed 2/16/2023
15. https://www.history.com/topics/roaring-twenties/scopes-trial
Accessed 2/20/2023
16. https://www.history.com/topics/roaring-twenties/teapot-dome-scandal

Accessed 5/11/2023

17. McCartney, Laton: *The Teapot Dome Scandal, How Big Oil Bought the Harding White House and Tried to Steal the Country*. Random House 2008. pp. 28-30

18. Ibid. pp. 18-19

19. Ibid. p. 56

20. https://www.history.com/topics/roaring-twenties/teapot-dome-scandal
Accessed 5/11/2023

21. McCartney, Laton: *The Teapot Dome Scandal, How Big Oil Bought the Harding White House and Tried to Steal the Country*. p. 111

22. https://www.history.com/topics/roaring-twenties/teapot-dome-scandal
Accessed 5/11/2023

23. Ibid.

24. https://www.history.com/news/prohibition-organized-crime-al-capone
Accessed 5/11/2023

25. https://www.history.com/topics/crime/saint-valentines-day-massacre
Accessed 2/20/2023

26. https://www.history.com/topics/roaring-twenties/tulsa-race-massacre
Accessed 5/13/2023

27. Ibid.

28. Ibid.

Chapter Fourteen

The Great Depression of 1930

"Brother, Can You Spare a Dime?"
Jay Gorey and Yip Harburg

The Wall Street Stock Market Crash on Black Tuesday, October 29, 1929, was the official beginning of the Great Depression. Some had anticipated a crash because of increasing stock prices and accelerating speculation between 1925 and 1929. Consumer demand had increased, but goods were often purchased using installment contracts, which meant ownership was postponed until the final payment. Ultimately, ordinary citizens lost their possessions as well as savings when the banks failed. Production declined and businesses collapsed.[1]

President Herbert Hoover vetoed several bills for relief of the growing recession. He signed the Reconstruction Finance Corporation Act which lent money to large institutions such as railroads and banks to prevent their failure. Little aid was provided to the average citizen, and resentment against the government and Hoover grew.[2]

Note in the following chart that Pluto making an opposition to both the Sun and Saturn (midpoint) turns everything related to the 2nd/8th houses upside down. Transiting Uranus is squaring itself in the US chart bringing rebellion from the people who had once trusted the bankers, business, and government officials but now turned against them.

The inequality between the haves and have-nots captured the populace's attention and spurred a demand for change. A Brookings Foundation report detailed the income disparity, noting that 59 percent of national wealth was owned by only 1 percent of the population, while 87 percent had only 8 percent, and some owned nothing. Many felt it

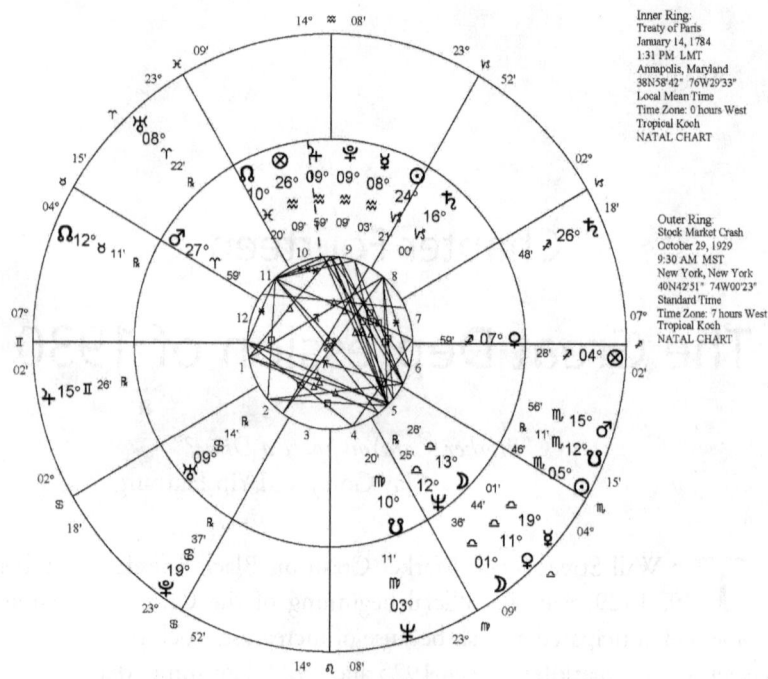

Figure 14-1
Stock Market Crash / US Chart Biwheel

was time for revolution.³

Violent incidents began. At the Ford factory in Detroit, an assembly of unemployed workers confronted the police and Ford guards. Four people died and many were wounded.⁴

In June 1932, approximately 11,000 WWI veterans marched on Washington DC demanding that their bonus, promised by law to be paid in 1945, be given now. Setting up camp along the Anacostia River, this "Bonus Expeditionary Force" waited in the Capitol Plaza for the Senate to approve the payment. It did not. They returned to the camp with their families while President Hoover, convinced that the march was organized by communists, refused to meet with them to discuss their demands. Instead, he sent General Douglas MacArthur with troops and weapons to clear the camps, which were then burned.⁵

In August, striking Iowa farmers fighting farm price collapse used roadblocks to prevent delivery of farm products. Many were arrested. The strike was called off after gunshots were fired at their camps.⁶

Such events alerted the nation to the increasingly disgruntled and hostile attitude of workers in America. Legislation forbidding "yellow-dog contracts," which had allowed employment only if workers promised not to join a union, was passed. The law eliminated one of the militant antiunion organization's most potent weapons.[7]

Attention turned away from Hoover and towards the popular governor of New York, Franklin Delano Roosevelt, who spoke of the "forgotten man at the bottom of the economic pyramid."[8] At the 1932 Democratic convention in Chicago, Roosevelt won the nomination for president and, untraditionally, personally went to accept the nomination with a shout of "I pledge you- I pledge myself to a new deal for the American people."[9]

The slogan of "New Deal" became the motto of Roosevelt's campaign and his administration. He defeated Hoover in a landslide, winning 42 of the 48 states, and gaining a Democratic Congress.[10] The next step would be to fulfill the promises made to a hopeful nation.

The US Nodes have seen a nodal return, indicating the end of a cycle and the beginning of a new one involving the 4th/10th axis. Neptune conjunct the South Node in the fourth house shows the confusion in the

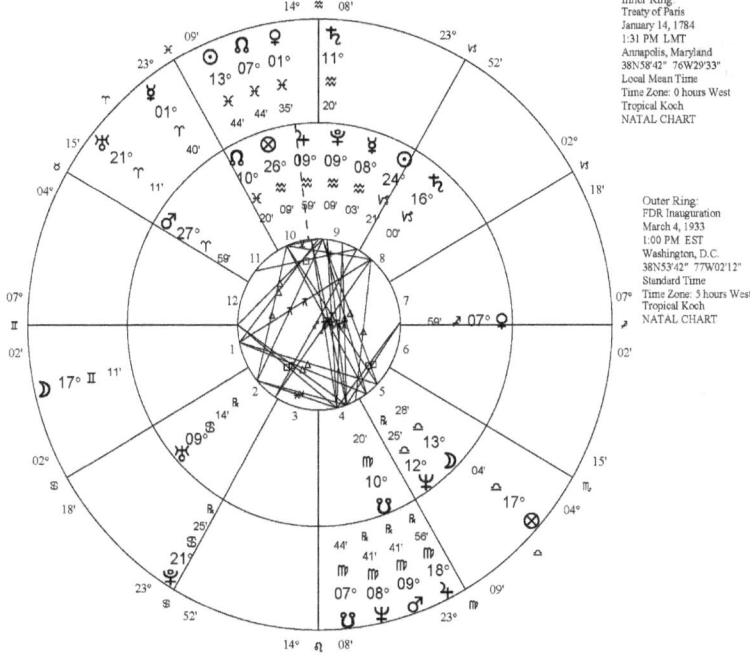

Figure 14-2
FDR Inauguration / US Chart Biwheel

country as well as the hostility of Mars in opposition to the government and president, the tenth house. Uranus is squaring the US Sun and Saturn, setting off a vibration in the US Yod, bringing to the fore the issues of the country's collective unconscious, the wealth gap, and the divisions in the country. It explains the many calls for a revolution.

Fourteen years prior, Saturn was transiting the US South Node, the beginning of Prohibition and the Roaring Twenties with its expansion of greed. In this chart, Saturn's transit of the US MC brings the risk of losing everything- the unhappy results of the previous careless boom. That materialism clashed with the American promise of "From Many, One" and "Justice for All." The nation demanded that these issues be addressed. The election of Franklin Roosevelt, as well as his three consecutive elections, provided the necessary changes, some of which have long been criticized as "socialism"- a complaint still heard today.

The Roosevelt administration's First One Hundred Days of Action set criteria for subsequent presidents who wished to attain the same distinguished bar.[11]

- The Emergency Banking Act allowed the Treasury Department to determine which banks could reopen. Their deposits were then ensured by the Federal Deposit Insurance Corporation, encouraging the public to start depositing their money again.

- FDR took US currency off the gold standard. Foreign investors had been demanding payment in gold rather than paper dollars, rapidly depleting Fort Knox reserves and potentially rendering the dollar worthless.

- The Volstead Act was amended to permit brewing of low-alcohol-content beer. Legal consumption was now allowed for the first time since 1920 in the hopes of improving public mood.

- The Works Progress Administration (WPA) reduced unemployment, assigning over 3.5 million workers to build highways, bridges, schools, airports, and other infrastructure.

- The Civilian Conservation Core (CCC) provided jobs for 2.5 million men aged 17 to 28. The workers received free medical care, work clothing, blankets, housing, and 30 dollars a month. City, state, and federal parks were improved with their hard work fighting fires, building trails and reservoirs, planting trees, and managing wildlife.

- The Federal Emergency Relief Administration gave the states money to supply food, shelter, and other necessities to people requiring immediate relief.
- The Rural Electrification Act brought electrification to rural areas, allowing communities to partner with government agencies to form networks of nonprofit electric cooperatives.
- Dust Bowl residents secured relief through programs such as the Drought Relief Service, the Federal Emergency Relief Administration, the CCC, WPA, and the Federal Surplus Relief Corporation.
- The National Industrial Recovery Act tried to balance the rights of workers and businesses. It promoted fair competition, industrial recovery, and employment through construction of public projects. It also provided the right to unionize and bargain collectively, free from employers' interference.

Although the New Deal agenda did not solve all problems, by 1934 the economy had turned around somewhat. Unemployment had fallen to 21.7 percent and the GNP had risen by 7.7 percent.[12] At the same time the public became hooked on the news. Americans eagerly followed the exploits of criminals such as John Dillinger and Bonnie and Clyde in newspapers and magazines, seeing them as heroes. Corruption grew amongst politicians and the police, and organized crime came into its own. Outlaw gangs engaged in kidnappings and robberies.[13]

Not all was bad in the 1930s. Some of the greatest movies were created during this era, including many wacky comedies by Laurel and Hardy. Charlie Chaplin's antics kept Americans laughing during the doom and gloom of the time. Comic strips and action heroes expanded with "Blondie" and "Superman." Entertainment aplenty existed to distract the public from their problems.

Radio blossomed, introducing great comedians such as Jack Benny, Fred Allen, Amos and Andy, as well as George Burns and Gracie Allen. One unique radio event to which people listened religiously was Roosevelt's "Fireside Chats." The chats reassured the population that the government was doing what it could to relieve their situation.[14] The weekly intimate talks made FDR so beloved that he was elected for four terms as President, the only occurrence in our history.

Being an Aquarian gives Roosevelt strong ties to the US chart, his Sun/Venus conjunction vibrates with the US Yod, but also gives impetus

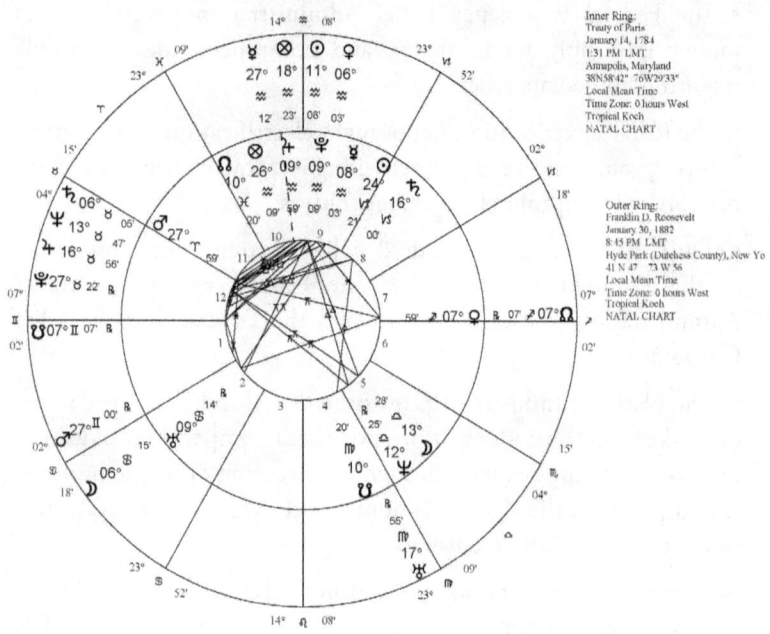

Figure 14-3
Franklin D. Roosevelt Natal Chart / US Chart Biwheel

to that Grand Air Trine of the US. The exact trine of his Jupiter to the US Saturn brings his long-term vision to the problems of the country's resources and makes a Grand Earth Trine to his Uranus (change) in the US chart's fourth house.

Change is also emphasized by his Cancer Moon conjunct the US Uranus, facing the great opposition of members of his own conservative class who decried his "socialistic" agenda. Such changes included the passage of Social Security to help the elderly. The 21st amendment repealed the Volstead Act and Prohibition in 1933. Americans returned to one of their favorite amusements, drinking, which allowed some escape from the dark mood of the Depression.

The labor situation improved under Roosevelt as unions grew and workers increased their rights to bargain collectively. In 1935, the National Labor Relations Act, known as the Wagner Act, spelled out restrictions on employers' ability to interfere with workers' rights to unionize. Membership in unions exploded thereafter.[15]

Although the economy seemed to be on the mend when the 1936 election rolled around, Roosevelt's New Deal agenda had stepped on a lot of conservative toes. During the Republican Convention in Cleveland, Herbert Hoover attacked the New Deal as the first stage of fascism. However, since Hoover was thought unelectable, the Republicans nominated Alfred M. Landon, a somewhat liberal Republican from Pennsylvania.[16] Harsh opposition and polls predicted an easy victory for Landon. In the surprising end, Roosevelt carried every state but two, winning by more than 10 million popular votes. The proportion of electoral votes he received was greater than any other presidential candidate since James Monroe.[17]

Despite improved workers' rights, corporations fought back, increasing hours while keeping wages low. The number of strikes exploded. The most notable strike was the United Auto Workers against General Motors in Flint, Michigan. The strike was unusual in that workers did not picket outside. Instead, they occupied the building in a "sit-down" strike, preventing further manufacturing in the plant.[18]

Workers were unhappy with the work pace demanded and the dangers incurred and frustrated with the company's policy of firing workers at will. When employees occupied the plant, General Motors retaliated by turning the heat off in freezing weather. Security guards and police fought the workers but lost "the battle of the running bulls." The Michigan Governor Frank Murphy, a labor fan, sent in the National Guard, not to disband workers, but rather to facilitate negotiations. The strike lasted 44 days, ending on February 11, 1937 with a win for the Union. Wages were raised and the company promised no reprisals on striking workers.[19]

In the chart, you can see Pluto (sixth house workers) opposing the company and the government authorities. The conjunction to the unaspected duet of Mars square Sun by transiting Uranus also creates a T-square with transiting Pluto. The conjunction to the unaspected duet of Mars square Sun by transiting Uranus also creates a T-square with the event chart Moon in the third house (messages) which also rules the second house of money while Pluto (the workers) oppose the Sun, (administration) and want the law changed (Mercury in the ninth house [status quo]). The Moon in Leo (the people) opposes the Aquarius stellium in the US ninth house.

The idea of the sit-down strike spread to other unions across the country as a useful tool for negotiating with companies. Union membership expanded quickly. Labor concerns were also reflected in the idea of fair pay, and in 1938 Congress passed the Fair Labor Standards Act which established the minimum wage.[20] The important shift in this era was

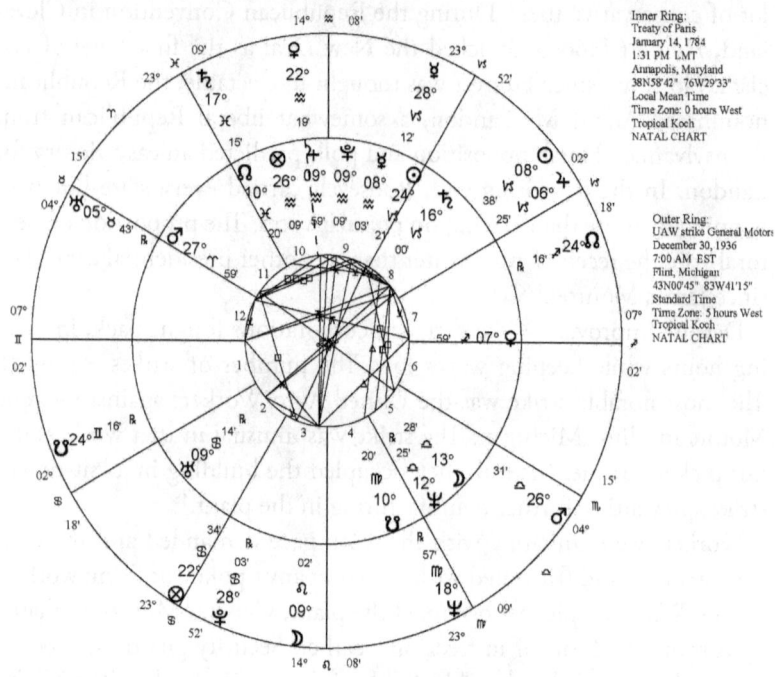

Figure 14-4
UAW Strike / US Chart Biwheel

that government became part of negotiating process between labor and industry.

Tensions grew globally during the Great Depression. Japan invaded China. Hitler's Nazi Party came into power in Germany and began expansion into other European countries. Italy invaded Ethiopia. It was obvious another war was brewing. The United States would require a strong leader for the 1940 election to see it through future conflicts. Although Roosevelt preferred retirement, he became the nominee to run against Wendell Willkie, the Republican. He won by nearly 5 million popular votes, taking 449 electoral votes to Willkie's 82.[21]

Americans had reiterated their desire for isolation from foreign wars. The Neutrality Act of 1935-1937 claimed a "policy of peace at any price," noting Americans' disillusionment with the last war and their fear of engaging in another.[22] Although the US maintained its isolation through most of the decade, great controversy reigned among political leaders. Meanwhile, the war progressed until it appeared that Great Britain remained the sole defender of democracy against fascism. Winston

Churchill appealed to Roosevelt. America would not engage militarily but could help in other ways, and Congress passed the Lend-Lease Act, sending military supplies to Britain and other allies. As Roosevelt noted in his fireside chat, "We must be the great arsenal of democracy."[23]

America's isolationist stance was to be transformed after a surprise event in Hawaii provoked our participation in World War II in 1941.

CHAPTER FOURTEEN NOTES

1. The World Book Encyclopedia, Vol. 8: *The Great Depression*; World Book, Inc, Chicago, Illinois, 2003. pp. 338-342
2. Ibid. p. 341
3. Daniels, Jonathan: *The Time Between the Wars – Armistice to Pearl Harbor*; Doubleday & Co., Inc., Garden City, New York, 1966. p. 194
4. Ibid. p. 191
5. Ibid. pp. 192-194
6. Ibid. pp. 196-197
7. Ibid. p. 197
8. Ibid. p. 213
9. Ibid. p. 218
10. 1932 United States presidential election - Wikipedia *Accessed 6/27/2023*
11. Press, Petra: *A Cultural History of the United States Through the Decades – The 1930s*; Lucent Books, Inc., San Diego, CA, 1999. pp. 14-16, 20-22, 24, 44-45, 48-49
12. Ibid. p. 112
13. Ibid. Chapter 4
14. Ibid. Chapter 5
15. Ibid. p. 49
16. Daniels, Jonathan: *The Time Between the Wars – Armistice to Pearl Harbor.* p. 273
17. Ibid. p. 275
18. https://www.history.com/news/flint-sit-down-strike-general-motors-uaw *Accessed 3/04/2023*
19. Ibid.
20. https://www.history.com/news/minimum-wage-america-timeline *Accessed 3/04/2023*
21. Roberts, Jeremy: *Franklin D. Roosevelt*; Lerner Publications Co., Minneapolis, MN, 2003. pp. 77-82

22. Daniels, Jonathan: *The Time Between the Wars – Armistice to Pearl Harbor*, Doubleday & Co. Inc., Garden City, New York, 1966. p. 312
23. Ibid. pp. 320-321

Chapter Fifteen

World War II and Its Aftermath

"Let's remember Pearl Harbor and go on to Victory."
Sammy Kaye

After its conquest of Poland in 1939, Germany invaded Denmark, Norway, Netherlands, and Belgium in early 1940. France surrendered in June 1940. The Battle of Britain and the London Blitz began. As the European war expanded, America maintained its isolation but continued to provide war materiel to Britain. But the isolationist cause had begun to weaken. By September, Roosevelt had signed an act requiring men twenty and over to register for a military draft. After his election for a third term, he established the Office of Production Management to regulate defense production. In 1941, the Office of Price Administration was created to develop wage and price controls.[1] The Pacific Fleet based in Honolulu, Hawaii was totally unprepared for the Japanese attack on December 7, 1941. The devastation was severe. Eighteen ships, including eight battleships, either sank or were seriously damaged, 118 planes were damaged, 1178 people were injured, and 2403 lost their lives.[2]

The Pearl Harbor attack launched America into World War II. The next day, President Roosevelt asked the Congress to declare war on Japan, which was done unanimously within the hour.[3] Two days later, Germany declared war on the US. In response, Congress and the Senate voted unanimously to declare war on Germany.[4] With both eastern and western fronts threatened, the nation feared invasion. The government needed to build an army and plan a wartime economy promptly.[5]

Note the chart below. Comparing the event taking place in Honolulu

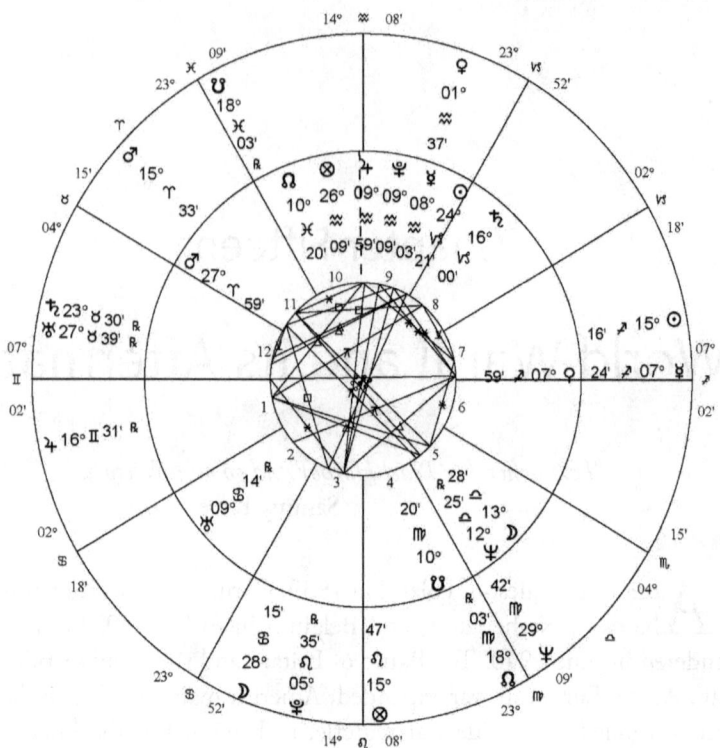

Figure 15-1
Inner wheel: US Chart / Treaty of Paris
Outer wheel: Pearl Harbor Day 12/7/1941, 7:48 AM, Honolulu, HI

with the US chart finds transiting Pluto opposing the ruler of the US chart, Mercury, when the secret plans of the Japanese become known to Americans. I was a teen sitting in a movie theatre when the usher announced that the Japanese had just bombed Pearl Harbor and we should all go home. I will never forget the fear and panic as we all exploded out of the theatre to run home and listen to the news of what was happening on the radio.

Transiting Venus (ruler of our twelfth house) was also conjuncting Mercury, at the same time ruling the conjunction of Saturn and Uranus in the twelfth house. Transiting Mercury was conjunct our Venus in the seventh house, making our hidden enemy our open enemy. Saturn and Uranus, rulers of the Axis of Awareness in the US Yod, describe the shock of sudden events that shattered our illusion of dependable structures. Change was coming despite our hiding our heads in the sand and avoiding involvement. There is also during this period a nodal reversal when external events are more likely to bring change in our lives. An additional influence is the transit of Mars through Aries, which will set off the unaspected duet that often is indicative of conflict happening when we try to avoid it.

In a matter of days, men were voluntarily enlisting by the thousands into the Army, Navy, and Air Force as well as the Coast Guard.[6] Jupiter in the first house describes the wave of patriotism that brought that feeling of "togetherness" in the face of a common enemy which lasted throughout the war. It was a taste of that motto, "From Many, One." (I realize it was not perfect at the time, but everyone cooperating in the war effort made it seem that way.) America's broad industrial base expanded to face the challenge, finally bringing the Great Depression to an end.

TIME LINE OF WORLD WAR II[7]

- December 8, 1941: US declares war on Japan, and 2 days later on Germany.
- January 1942: Over 100,000 Japanese Americans forced into remote internment camps, losing their homes and assets, a shameful event based on prejudiced national fear of their potential cooperation with the enemy.
- May 1942: The first mass extinction of Jews at Auschwitz begins. The US public was not aware of the depth of the horror going on under the Nazis.
- July 1942: Gas rationing begins.
- November 1942: General Eisenhower lands with British soldiers in Morocco and Algeria to fight the Axis powers.
- April 1943: Roosevelt freezes wages, salaries, and prices.
- May 1943: Roosevelt forbids racial discrimination in any companies taking government contracts.
- June 1943: Race riots break out in major cities, the Detroit riot on June 20 being the worst. Twenty-five African Americans and 9 whites lose their lives.[8]
- November 1943: United Nations Relief and Rehabilitation Ad-

ministration established by 44 nations to help war victims.
- June 6, 1944: D-Day marks the greatest military invasion in history.

- June 1944: Germans use the first rockets against Britain.
- November 1944: President Roosevelt reelected to a 4th term.
- January 1945: Japanese Americans released from internment.
- February 1945: Roosevelt, Churchill, and Stalin – the Big Three meet in Yalta.
- March 1945: US troops enter Germany.
- April 12, 1945: Roosevelt dies in Warm Springs, Georgia, and Harry S. Truman becomes president.
- May 1945: Germany surrenders and V-E -Day is celebrated.
- June 1945: The charter for the United Nations is signed by fifty
- nations.
- August 1945: First atomic bomb dropped on Hiroshima, Japan, followed by the second bomb on Nagasaki two days later.
- August 14, 1945: Japan surrenders, and V-J Day is celebrated worldwide.
- 1948: Truman signs an Executive Order desegregating the army, a bold step forward.

In 1939, the Einstein-Szilard letter had informed the president of research indicating that uranium fission chain reactions could release tremendous power. If such power could be harnessed, "the construction of 'extremely powerful bombs' was conceivable." The physicists expressed concern that Germany was doing the same research. Roosevelt set up a study committee which ultimately led to the Manhattan Project, led by Robert Oppenheimer.[9]

The letter changed the course of history.

In the following chart, you see the Sun (the president) receives a communication (third house) about the future of atomic energy development (Pluto conjunct the Sun and opposite Pluto in the US chart). The status of the project (tenth house) must be kept totally secret (Uranus in the twelfth house). Transiting Mars in Capricorn is setting off the unaspected duet of Sun/Mars square of the US chart. However, Saturn conjunct the South Node on the US Mars suggests serious karmic con-

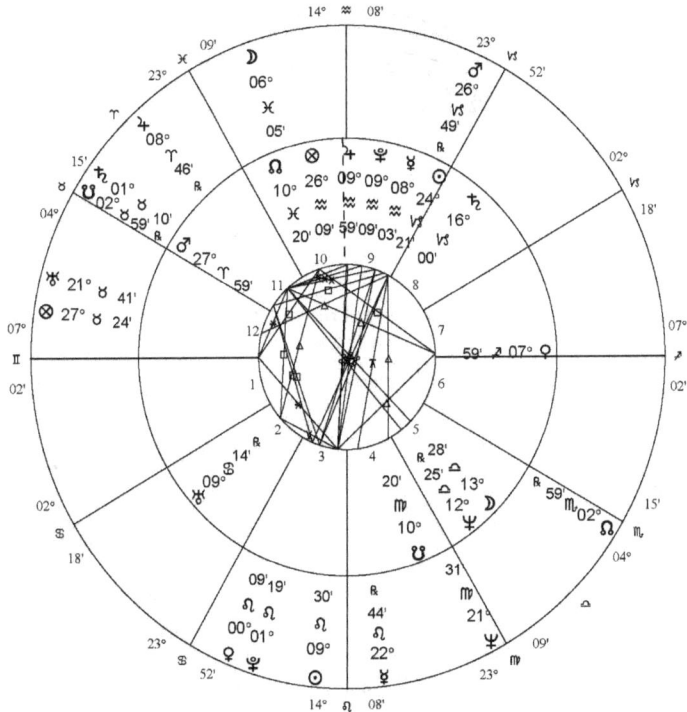

Figure 15-2
Inner wheel: US Chart / Treaty of Paris
Outer wheel: Einstein-Szilard Letter 8/2/1939, 12:00 PM;
Washington, DC

sequences of this project. The midheaven of the letter's chart (5° Leo) is straddled by Pluto and the Sun in Leo at 1° and 9° opposing the US chart's upper leg of the Yod in the fourth house (endings).

Work on the atom bomb proceeded during the war, and it was secretly detonated at Alamogordo, New Mexico, on July 16, 1945.[10] Truman had very recently assumed the Presidency following the death of President Roosevelt. It became his terrible task to decide whether to use the bomb on Japan or face a long and bloody invasion of that country. That choice has long been debated.[11]

The first bomb, dropped on Hiroshima, killed about 70,000 citizens at once.[12] Japan still refused to surrender. The second bomb, dropped on Nagasaki, resulted in the immediate deaths or mortal wounding of 45,000 people.[13] Japan surrendered shortly afterward.

Americans celebrated the end of World War II (Jupiter in the first house, the people, ruling the fourth house, endings). The happiness was

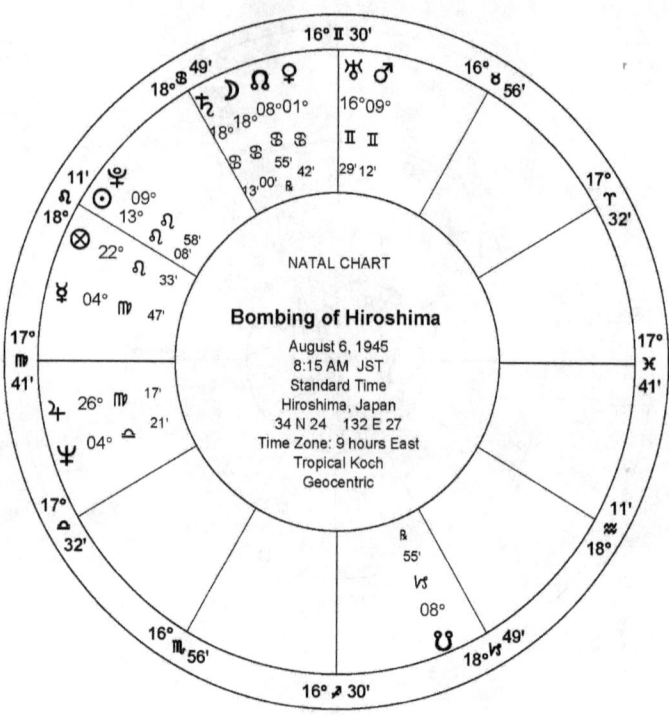

Figure 15-3
Hiroshima Atom Bomb Natal Chart
August 6, 1945, 8:15 AM; Hiroshima, Japan

later muted by recognition of the pain and suffering the US action had caused Japanese civilians. The regret continued for some time (Neptune in the first house, also with Chiron at the midpoint between the two). The conjunction of the Moon (people) with Saturn (death) is transiting in opposition to the US Saturn bringing awareness of our responsibility of what we have done. The Uranus at 16 Gemini sits exactly on the Midheaven of the chart with Mars on our Ascendant. The Sabian symbol for this degree explains that what has been "discovered" (atomic energy), revealed to the public, and now requires a global discussion.

In the following chart, you'll notice the event Mars conjunct the US ascendant trining our Pluto (atomic energy) and opposing US Venus (open enemy). The nodes are conjunct the Axis of Awareness of the Yod bringing it to world attention and our responsibility for it. There's a Pluto opposition between the event and US chart, as well as the Sun, ruler of US fourth house conjunct the IC, indicating the end of the war as it

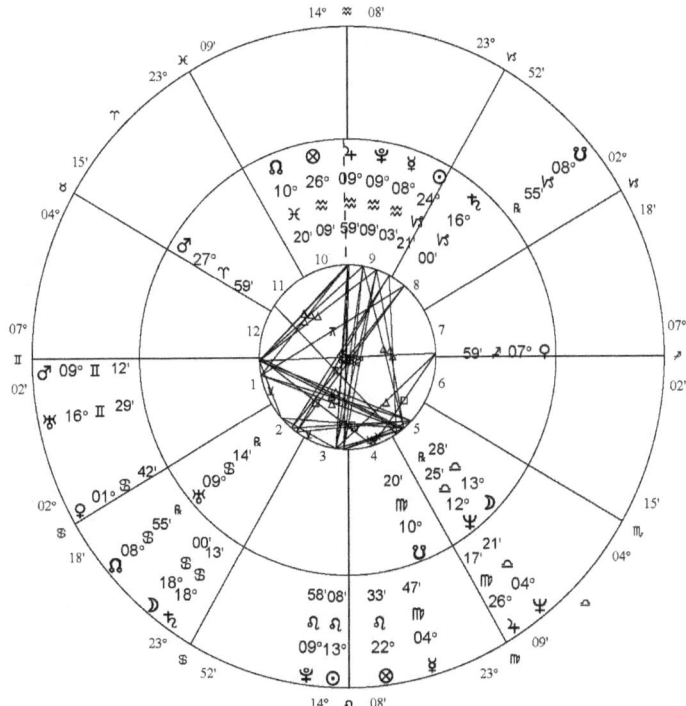

Figure 15-4
US chart/ Hiroshima Atom Bomb

trines US Venus in the seventh house, surrender of our enemy a few days later. The Moon conjunct Saturn in the event chart opposite the Saturn in the US eighth house indicates the thousands of lives lost as the result of two such powerful weapons. People who survived the blast continued to die because of radiation poisoning.

In 1946, President Truman created the Atomic Energy Commission to further study nuclear technology and promote its peacetime development. The commission also removed control from military hands and transferred it to civilians.[14] In 1949, the Soviet Union tested its first atomic bomb, propelling US development of the hydrogen bomb. The race to produce bigger and better bombs commenced.[15]

The Atomic Era had begun. Complete destruction of the Earth was now a possibility.

THE AFTERMATH

After World War II ended, America lost its isolationist stand, taking the world stage as a superpower. It helped war-torn countries recover and took a leading role to contain the growing threat of Russian communism in what became known as the "Cold War."[16] Military men returned home to an economic boom, taking advantage of the G.I. Bill to attend college, buy homes, and start new businesses, thus swelling the middle class.[17] Financial prosperity allowed the growth of the baby boomer generation. America would never be the same again.

The power of the executive branch of government grew as the president assumed the position of "leader of the free world." By 1948, the Marshall Plan was funded to aid 16 countries,[18] and in 1949, the North Atlantic Treaty Organization (NATO) was formed for mutual defense against the rising threat of Soviet Union aggression. The United Nations was dedicated in New York City.[19] After two World Wars, people wanted enduring peace and invested their hopes in the United Nations.

Women became more independent, many preferring to continue working in the postwar period. Most returned home to raise families in the new suburbs, tracts of affordable, single-family homes that blossomed around major cities. Major demographic changes included relocation of many African Americans to the North, which had begun during the war because of increased work opportunities. New technology reduced air travel expenses, computer technology evolved.[20]

The postwar period also saw the emergence of "a distinct youth subculture that would become even more influential in the future in shaping popular culture in America."[21] Teenagers with money to spend on clothes, radios, records, and big band concerts became the new consumer group. They jitterbugged to swing music and swooned to the music of Frank Sinatra. Magazines following their exploits bloomed.[22]

In 1947, Truman announced a new policy to limit communist expansion. The "Truman Doctrine" became a guiding element for NATO participants pledging mutual support throughout the Cold War and beyond. As previously noted, Russia's explosion of their own nuclear bomb in 1949 precipitated an arms race and persistent anxiety among Americans.[23]

The final chart shows the ties between Harry Truman and the US. President Truman stands in sharp distinction from the popular and eloquent FDR. He was a plainspoken man with only a high school education, but greatly admired by the public for his acceptance of responsibility for his own actions. Truman grew up on a farm, served in WW I, and then entered politics. As Senator, he saved millions in taxpayer funds by reducing fraud and improving efficiencies in defense work. Such successes won him the nomination as Vice President.²⁴

Truman's Saturn conjunct the US Ascendant and trine the Aquarius stellia links that sense of responsibility to the country. His sudden ascent to the presidency when FDR died was a shock. Asking Mrs. Roosevelt if he could help her with anything, he must have felt a chill when she replied, "Is there anything we can do for you? You're the one in trouble now."²⁵

Many, I suppose, questioned whether he was up to the job of filling

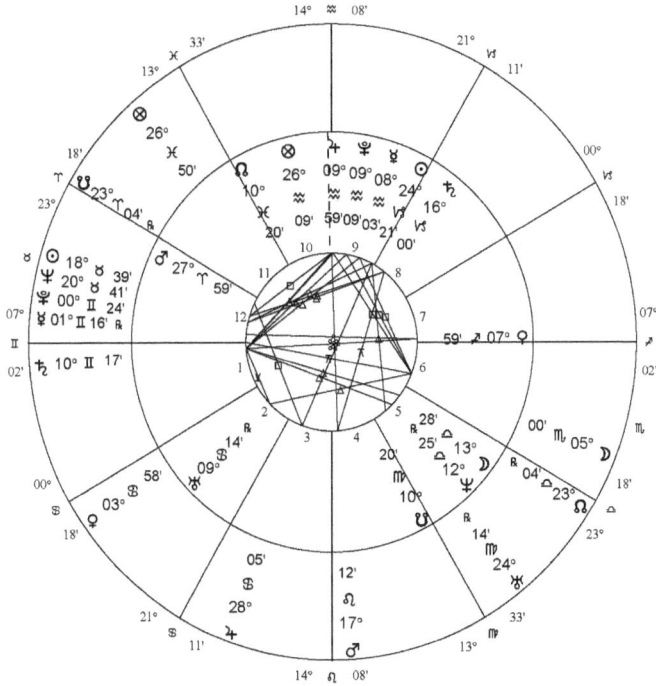

Figure 15-5
US chart /Harry S. Truman natal, 5/8/1884, 4:00 PM;
Lamar, MO

FDR's shoes in the middle of a war. He learned about the Manhattan Project only a week after his inauguration. The decision to use nuclear weapons was one of the most difficult ever faced by a president, but Truman took it in stride: "As president of the United States, I had the fateful responsibility of deciding whether or not to use the atom bomb for the first time. It was the hardest decision I ever had to make. But the president cannot duck hard problems- he cannot pass the buck."[26]

What's not shown here is the fact that his progressed chart for this date shows his Moon at 24 degrees of Capricorn conjunct the US Sun and his progressed Chiron was conjunct the US Ascendant. I don't think he understood the devastation he was releasing, no one really did, but he acted with the energy of his exalted Jupiter, thinking it better for humanity to end the war rather than prolonging it. Only history is allowed to judge, but his decision ushered in a whole new era.

CHAPTER FIFTEEN NOTES

1. Uschan, Michael V.: *The 1940s, a Cultural History of the United States Through the Decades*; Lucent Books, Inc. San Diego, CA, 1999. p. 116
2. Ibid. pp. 15-18
3. Ibid. p. 18
4. https://en.wikipedia.org/wiki/United_States_declaration_of_war_on_Germany_(1941) Accessed 7/4/2023
5. Uschan, Michael V.: *The 1940s, a Cultural History of the United States Through the Decades*; p. 19
6. Ibid. p. 20
7. Ibid. pp. 116-119, 77
8. https://detroithistorical.org/learn/encyclopedia-of-detroit/race-riot-1943 Accessed 3/06/2023
9. Manhattan Project: Einstein's Letter, 1939 (osti.gov) Accessed 3/08/2023
10. Manhattan Project: The Trinity Test, July 16, 1945 (osti.gov) Accessed 7/2/2023
11. Manhattan Project: Potsdam and the Final Decision to Use the Bomb, July 1945 (osti.gov) Accessed 7/2/2023
12. Manhattan Project: The Atomic Bombing of Hiroshima, August 6, 1945 (osti.gov) Accessed 7/2/2023
13. Langley, Andrew: *Hiroshima and Nagasaki*; Compass Point Books, Minneapolis, Minnesota, 2006. p. 67
14. https://en.wikipedia.org/wiki/United_States_Atomic_Energy_Commission Accessed 7/4/2023
15. Uschan, Michael V.: *The 1940s, a Cultural History of the United States Through the Decades*; p. 107
16. Ibid. p. 71
17. Ibid. pp. 97-98
18. Ibid. p. 104
19. Ibid. p. 121
20. Ibid. Chapter 5
21. Ibid. p. 88

22. Ibid. Chapter 6
23. Ibid. Chapter 7
24. Ibid. p. 103
25. American History: Roosevelt's Death Makes Truman President (voanews.com) *Accessed 3/8/2023*
26. Uschan, Michael V.: *The 1940s, a Cultural History of the United States Through the Decades*; p. 103

Chapter Sixteen

The Fifties and the Cold War

"Love and Marriage"
Sammy Kahn & Jimmy Van Heusen

The fifties were a pivotal period in US development. Two themes in this era require exploration: the economic and "baby" booms with related advancements in civil rights, and the Red Scare with its associated threat of atomic war.

On the positive side, the middle class expanded as war veterans used the GI Bill to attend college, start businesses, buy homes in the suburbs, and start raising families. Economic prosperity grew, allowing a man to support his family while women returned to their roles as housewives.[1] People flocked from the movies to television, where family shows like "Father Knows Best," "Ozzie and Harriet," "Leave it to Beaver," and especially "I Love Lucy" dominated, reflecting the changes in society.[2] More civil rights were extended to African Americans. With the United Nations at work, there was hope of a lasting peace.

On the negative side, although the United States had demobilized most of its armed forces, the Soviet Union had not. In fact, it had already gobbled up Estonia, Latvia, and Lithuania and set up communist puppet states in Eastern Europe. The Marshall Plan under President Truman was helping European countries recover from the war's devastation. Although this created much of the economic boom, poor relations between the free world and Communist countries increased. The development of the hydrogen bomb on both sides and the "space race" put a damper on the good things that were happening. The fear of an atomic war hung like a cloud over everything.[3]

TIME LINE[4]

- 1950: Korean War begins; Senator McCarthy begins anti-communist crusade.
- 1951: Truman fires General MacArthur; the Rosenbergs sentenced to death.
- 1952: First hydrogen bomb exploded by US; Eisenhower elected President.
- 1953: Korean War Armistice; Soviet Union explodes hydrogen bomb.
- 1954: Supreme Court ends segregation in US schools; Senator McCarthy's conflict with US Army ends his career; Hemingway wins the Nobel Prize for literature; Salk discovers polio vaccine.
- 1955: Rosa Parks arrested and bus boycott begins in Alabama.
- 1956: Eisenhower wins second term; Elvis Presley becomes a sensation.
- 1957: Russian Sputnik first satellite in space; Eisenhower sends troops to Little Rock to end segregation.
- 1958: Space race begins with the US Explorer; commercial jet planes introduced.
- 1959: Fidel Castro seizes Cuba; Hawaii and Alaska become states.

The first US-Communist confrontation began on June 25, 1950 when North Korean forces invaded the Republic of South Korea.[5] The United Nations, authorized to act against any country breaking the peace, responded. Along with the US, fifteen nations sent troops to South Korea while forty-one nations sent supplies. General Douglas MacArthur was designated the commander of all UN forces. By October, they had successfully liberated South Korea and chased their enemies across the 38th parallel.[6]

General MacArthur was not content with this, and his forces pushed on into North Korea. They were soon met by thousands of Chinese soldiers who repulsed them. Because MacArthur persisted in his pursuit of victory, President Truman officially fired him. The president feared starting another war, this time with China. Though his decision was criticized, he had made it clear that the commander-in-chief controlled

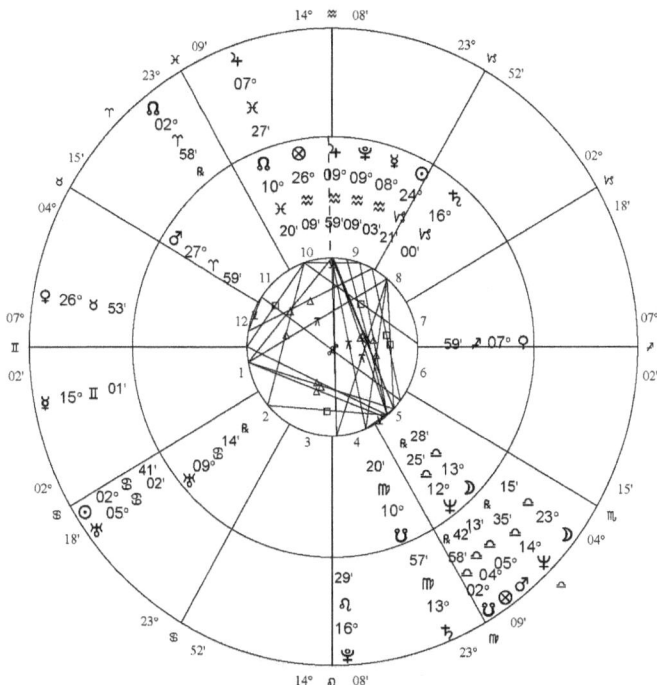

Figure 16-1
Treaty of Paris/Korean War Invasion, June 25, 1950; Korea 38th parallel

the military and was the one who made policy, not his generals.[7]

The peace treaty was finally signed on July 27, 1953. Despite the losses, the US strengthened its military, created the Southeast Asia Treaty Organization, and demonstrated "that through the collective action of the UN an aggressor could be prevented from conquering another country and without the use of dreaded atomic weapons."[8]

The important point to make in looking at this chart is the fact that the US was experiencing a Uranus return which continued to bring many changes, first squaring the Neptune and Moon conjunction in the fifth house, eventually opposing the Saturn and Sun in Capricorn and, finally, the stellium in Aquarius setting off the US Yod. It then entered Leo.

A major step forward for civil rights occurred on May 17, 1954, when Chief Justice Warren announced the Supreme Court's unanimous decision in Brown v. Board of Education. Racial segregation in public schools was ended, but many areas of the country resisted the decree.

Additionally, the ruling failed to specify how schools should be integrated. A year later, Brown v. Board of Education II directed "district courts and all school boards to proceed with segregation 'with all deliberate speed.'"9

The ruling was tested on September 4, 1957, when nine Black students approached Little Rock High School. An angry mob of segregationists met them, supported by the state National Guard that Governor Faubus had called out to protect citizens and property. In response, President Eisenhower signed Executive Order 10730 on September 23. The order commanded that "all persons engaged in such obstruction of justice do cease and desist therefrom, and to disperse forthwith." Eisen-

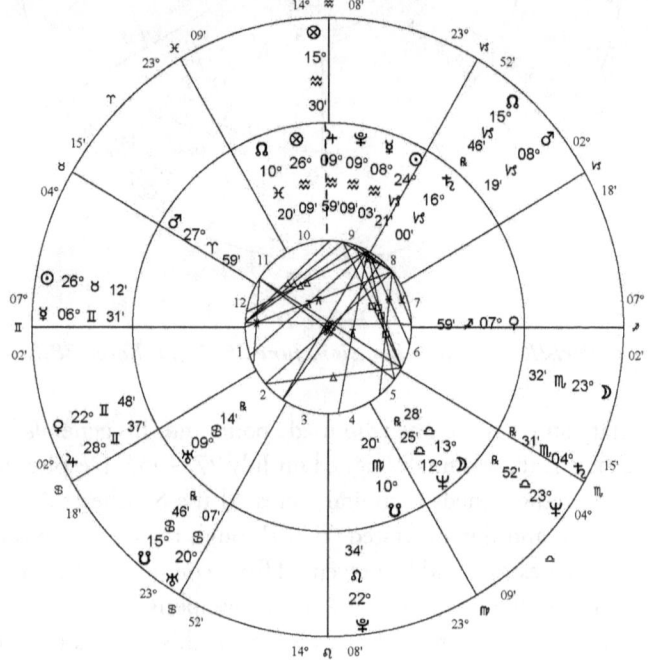

Figure 16-2
US chart/ Brown vs Board of Education, May 17, 1954, 12:00 PM Washington, DC

hower placed the National Guard under federal control and sent US paratroopers to assist in restoring order.10

The chart of Brown vs Board of Education clearly shows the prominence of the Uranus/Saturn Axis of Awareness of the US chart's Yod, the move for change versus the reaction of conservative forces against

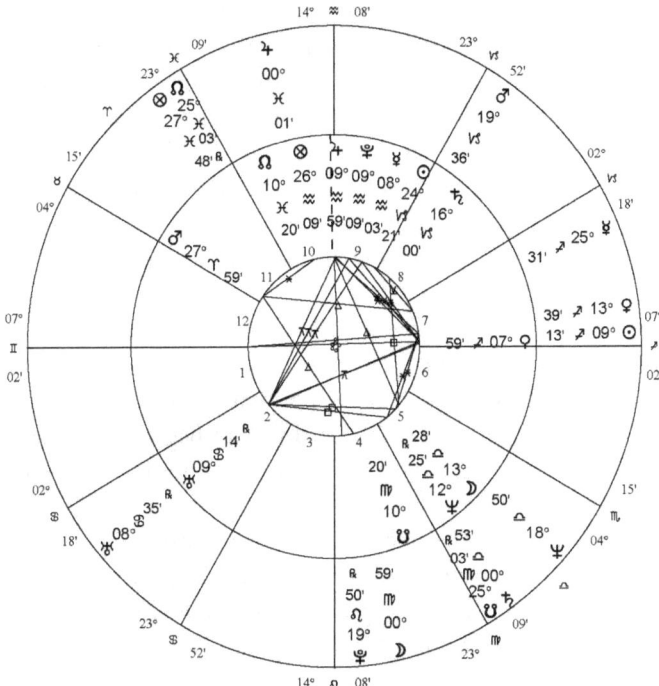

Figure 16-3
US chart/Rosa Parks arrest, December 1, 1950; 6:45 PM, Detroit, MI

change. The unresolved issue of slavery is still at play in the collective unconscious of the people. The Sun (fourth house, communities) and Mercury (the nation as a whole) are in the twelfth house, but the Venus that rules it has come to the first house of conscious awareness which triggers the Grand Trine of Air, reminding us of the concept of "From Many, One." The Grand Square of Neptune squaring the US Sun and Jupiter along with the opposition to natal Mars defines the confusion of this period related to this issue along with the delay in moving forward toward our ideal and the hostility against change.

We can see here the beginning of the Civil Rights Movement which was catalyzed by the actions of a single Black woman. Rosa Parks was small but greatly impacted our culture. Examine the chart above, detailing her revolt that stimulated the fight for not only the rights of Black Americans but also for women and the gay and lesbian communities.

Here you can see that the transiting Uranus in Cancer has made a return and has set the issue of the rights of others into vibration of the

Yod. On Thursday, December 1, 1955, Rosa Parks refused to relinquish her seat on the bus to a white man. Her action broke Montgomery law and she was arrested. She had been returning from a long day of work and had had enough of discriminatory treatment. She later stated that, no, she acted not because she was physically tired but because she "was tired of giving in." Her arrest sparked the Montgomery Bus Boycott led by Martin Luther King Jr. A US Supreme Court ruling rendered the Montgomery and Alabama laws unconstitutional, and the boycott ended on December 20, 1956.[11]

While civil rights were slowly progressing, the fear of communism was running rampant. The Cold War that began with President Truman's doctrine would last for the next 50 years. The fear was intensified by Wisconsin Senator Joseph McCarthy, who began a reign of terror, accusing individuals and organizations of communist ties without offering proof.[12]

The "Red Scare" commenced with McCarthy's campaign in 1950. His goal was to find communist agents in the State Department. On February 9, 1950, he made his first speech to the Ohio County Republican Women's Club in Wheeling, West Virginia, which started the snowball.[13]

The key phrase in the Senator's speech that day was: "I have here in my hand a list of 205 that were known being members of the Communist Party and who, nevertheless, are still working and shaping the policy in the State Department."[14]

Newspapers took up the call, informing citizens that the US government was riddled with communist spies. Seizing the opportunity, McCarthy set out to prove his statement.[15] His accusations stimulated further headlines, increasing public belief and arousing politicians' fears.[16]

The Senate investigated the State Department while other groups examined federal employees. The 1951-1952 House Un-American Activities (HUAC) questioned Hollywood writers, directors, and actors, who could only protect themselves by naming others as suspects. Labor unions, various "communist-front" organizations, college professors, teachers, and even churches were harrassed.[17] Finding that homosexuality might pose a risk in security judgments, McCarthy pursued this avenue as well.[18] He found suspects where he could and the HUAC investigated them.

In 1953, McCarthy was put in charge of the Government Operation Committee, giving him the funds he needed to pursue his agenda. His

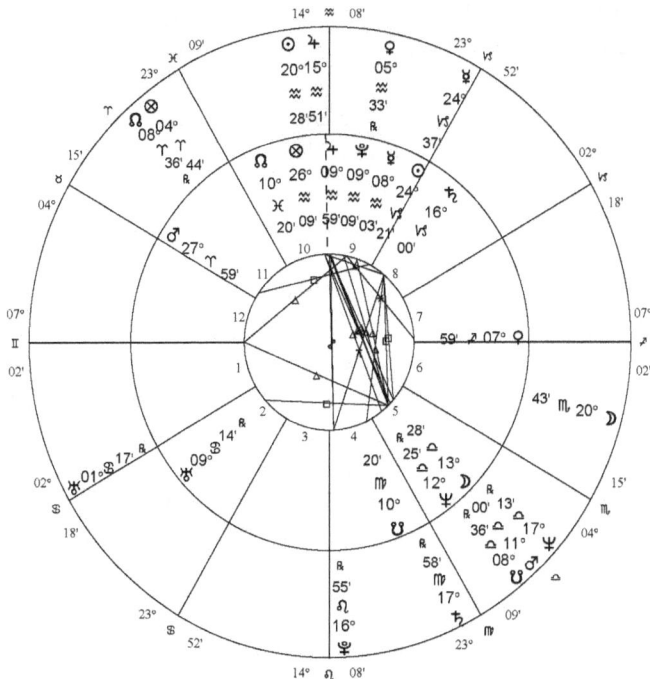

Figure 16-4
US chart/McCarthy speech, February 9, 1950; Wheeling, WV

next attack was on the Army Signal Corps. This would finally lead to his downfall. The Army-McCarthy Hearings began on March 16, 1954. They were broadcast on TV and over 20 million Americans watched McCarthy in action. It was not a pretty sight.[19]

People began to turn against him. Even his own state, Wisconsin, tried to recall him. The Senate voted to censure McCarthy on December 2, 1954, effectively ending his career. McCarthy died on May 2, 1957. Although the communist threat had lessened after the death of Stalin,[20] the McCarthy era was "one of the frightening and controversial periods in American history."[21]

Note in the chart that the Uranus at one degree Cancer is conjunct the event chart's ascendant, beginning a new four-year period of turmoil, fear, corruption of truth, intimidation and divisiveness in which people's names and lives were stained by the suspicion of "guilt by association." Here we also have transiting Saturn trining the US Saturn, a critical period of examining what we believe in. Transiting Pluto is, at the same time, inconjunct natal Saturn while transiting Neptune is square it.

The aspects of American life that need examination in this period relate to the move toward repression represented by McCarthy vs the move toward more freedom represented by the Civil Rights Movement spurred on by Rosa Parks' arrest. Neptune contributed to the anxiety and fear about these events. Eventually, the corrupt power sought and used by McCarthy ended, while the civil rights issue won more freedoms for Black Americans.

Another notable event initiated the Space Race in 1957. The launch of the first satellite by the Soviets shocked Americans and incited fear that they would next launch nuclear warheads at the US.[22] People demanded action, and Congress established the National Aeronautics and Space Administration (NASA) on July 29, 1958. This civilian agency would coordinate America's space activities.[23] The first successful US satellite, Explorer, was launched on January 31, 1958.[24] With relief, Americans looked forward to a competition that would eventually put a human on the Moon.

In some respects, the '50s were a time of conformity. People lived in tracts of similar houses, drove station wagons to accommodate children, sat around the TV in the evening, and enjoyed Sunday barbecues in the backyard. Disneyland opened and families made treks there to enjoy its many wonders.

Forty million births expanded the population and lifespan increased during the decade. Auto production soared, allowing more travel along newly constructed highways and freeways. A new vaccine discovered by Dr Jonas Salk considerably reduced cases of dreaded polio.[25] The stock market continued its upward trend. Americans enjoyed the prosperity of the time. It was a respite between World War II devastation and the conflicts of the decade to come.

CHAPTER SIXTEEN NOTES

1. Lindop, Edmund: *America in the 1950's*; Twenty-First Century Books, Brookfield, Conn., 2002. p. 65
2. Ibid. pp. 77-79
3. Ibid. pp. 5-6
4. Ibid. pp. 115-117
5. Ibid. p. 10
6. Ibid. pp. 12-13
7. Ibid. pp. 14-16
8. Ibid. p.. 18
9. https://www.history.com/topics/black-history/brown-v-board-of-education-of-topeka Accessed 4/14/2023
10. https://www.archives.gov/milestone-documents/executive-order-10730 Accessed 7/6/2023
11. www.history.com/topics/black-history/rosa-parks Accessed 1/23/2023
12. Zeinert, Karen: *McCarthy and the Fear of Communism in American History*; Enslow Publishers, Inc., Springfield, N.J., 1998. p. 69
13. www.ohiocountylibrary.org/wheeling-history/5655 Accessed 4/15/2023
14. Ibid.
15. Zeinert, Karen: *McCarthy and the Fear of Communism in American History*; Enslow Publishers, Inc., Springfield, N.J., 1998. p. 11
16. Ibid. p. 69
17. Ibid. Chapter 5
18. Cunningham, Jesse E., & Egandorf, Laura K., Eds.: *The McCarthy Hearings*; Greenhaven Press, Farmington Mills, MI, 2003. p. 90
19. Zeinert, Karen: *McCarthy and the Fear of Communism in American History*; Chapter 6
20. Ibid. Chapter 7

21. Ibid. p. 11
22. Lindop, Edmund: *America in the 1950's; Twenty-First Century Books*, Brookfield, Conn., 2002., p. 59
23. https://www.history.com/this-day-in-history/nasa-created *Accessed 4/16/2023*
24. Lindop, Edmund: *America in the 1950's; Twenty-First Century Books*, p. 59.
25. Ibid. Chapter 6

Chapter Seventeen

The Tumultuous Sixties

"The Times They Are A-Changin'"
Bob Dylan

The sixties were a time of great social and cultural changes. The baby boomers were coming of age, rebelling against the conformity and consumerism of the 1950s "Silent Generation." A new counterculture impacted the United States,[1] bringing with it movements for civil rights, women's rights, Chicano rights, and gay rights.[2] The Vietnam War escalated along with widespread protests. President Johnson's War on Poverty and other programs sought to improve economic equality.[3] The era was also notable for the unprecedented number of assassinations that occurred, including that of President John F. Kennedy.

Student activists impatient with slow reform "took over college campuses, organized massive antiwar demonstrations and occupied parks and other public places." Apolitical young people "dropped out" and joined the "flower generation" of hippies who grew their hair long and practiced free love.[4] Their peace and love message is reflected in the rock n' roll and protest songs of the era.

It was difficult to choose among the numerous events that happened in the sixties, so I will note important ones in the timeline, and focus on the charts reflecting issues of the Yod as touched on in the first chapter.

TIME LINE[5]

- 1960: Voting Rights Act passed; birth control pills made available; African American students engage in sit-in at lunch counter in North Carolina.

- 1961: John F. Kennedy sworn in as president; Soviets send first human into space to orbit the Earth; US defeat in Cuban invasion Bay of Pigs; Berlin Wall erected.

- 1962: Cuban Missile Crisis; John Glenn Jr first American to orbit Earth; *Silent Spring* by Rachel Carson stirs the environmental movement.

- 1963: President Kennedy assassinated in Texas; Supreme Court declares prayers in school unconstitutional; March on Washington with Martin Luther King Jr.

- 1964: Beatles come to US; Johnson signs Civil Rights Act, War on Poverty bill, and Voting Rights Act; Congress approves presidential action in Vietnam.

- 1965: US begins bombing in North Vietnam; Malcolm X is murdered; Medicare starts; immigration quotas of ethnic origin are abolished.

- 1966: Author Betty Friedan becomes first president of National Organization of Women; Cesar Chavez wins 1st migrant worker labor contract. (See Chapter 10)

- 1967: Thurgood Marshall first African American appointed to the Supreme Court.

- 1968: Martin Luther King assassinated; Robert Kennedy assassinated; peace protesters beaten by police at Democratic Convention in Chicago; Johnson announces he will not run for President; Shirley Chisholm, first Black woman elected to Congress.[6]

- 1969: Neil Armstrong first man on moon; Richard Nixon inaugurated as president; National Vietnam Moratorium launches antiwar protests, culminating in largest demonstration in US history with more than 250,000 protesters at Washington, DC; Woodstock Musical Festival draws 500,000 counterculture youth to a campout on a farm in New York; gay rights movement gains momentum following Stonewall Riots.[7]

Betty Friedan's book, *The Feminine Mystique*, was published in 1963, reinvigorating the crusade for women's rights. Friedan asked women to challenge the limits of their traditional social roles,[8] and was instrumental in the formation of the National Organization for Women (NOW),[9] the strongest group promoting women's rights since the convention at Seneca Falls and the suffrage fight (see Chapter 7). Its work is still ongoing.

NOW was founded on June 30, 1966, during the Third National Conference of Commissions on the Status of Women in Washington DC. Delegates at the meeting requested a resolution demanding that EEOC end sexual discrimination in employment but were informed they had no such authority. They decided to take action.[10]

That night many delegates met at Betty Friedan's hotel and by the end of the convention had set up a new organization to ensure a "movement toward true equality for all women in America." Betty Friedan became the first NOW president.[11] They also embraced movements against the war and civil rights for all who wanted to be equal and free.

A critical factor affecting women's status during this time was the recent availability of birth control. Contraceptives allowed women to control their childbearing, freed them of old Victorian mores, and ended the baby boom.[12] The controversy over a woman's choice began here and

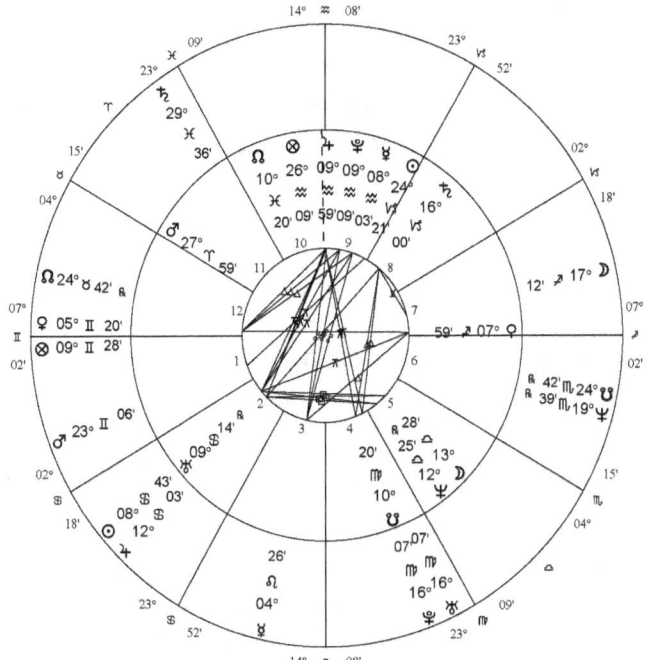

Figure 17-1
US chart/ Outer wheel: Founding of NOW, June 30 1966, 8:00 PM; Washington, DC

The Tumultuous Sixties

continues today.

Examine the above chart for the founding of NOW. I used 8 PM as the meeting time. The exact conjunction of Pluto (sex) and Uranus (liberation) in the fourth house of the people describes the revolutionary changes taking place in the country at the time, trining Saturn for lasting change. The second conjunction to note is the Sun (male) and Jupiter (ruler of US seventh house of women's affairs), being present in the second house with US Uranus bringing about a radical change in values of the people. Venus (females) conjuncts the Ascendant and brings equality of women to the forefront.

The next chart to be examined is that of Lyndon Johnson's State of the Union speech given on January 8, 1964, outlining his administration's agenda of "The War on Poverty." The speech addressed two of the issues related to the Yod: civil rights and the income gap.

Following are quotes from the speech pertaining to our journey:[13]

"Let us carry forward the plans and programs of John Fitzgerald Kennedy – not because of our sorrow or sympathy, but because they are right."

"In his memory today, I especially ask all members of my own political faith, in this election year, to put your country ahead of your party, and to always debate principles; never debate personalities."

"This administration today, here and now, declares unconditional war on poverty in America. I urge this Congress and all Americans to join with me in that effort."

Legislation soon followed that included the Civil Rights Act, the War on Poverty Act, and the Economic Opportunity Act (EOA). The EOA supported Head Start and civil rights, as well as Vista, a domestic Peace Corps of volunteers to work in poor communities.[14] Medicare and Medicaid were initiated to aid the elderly,[15] as indicated by the Moon/Neptune conjunction in Scorpio in the sixth house of health services.

Notice that the Axis of Awareness is set off by the passage of the North Node over this configuration, conjuncting Uranus. President Johnson's agenda for a "Great Society" is limited by the increasing costs of the Vietnam War. (Mars conjunct Sun in Capricorn with US Saturn conjunct the Sun all in the eighth house.) Jupiter in Aries opposing the natal Moon/Neptune conjunction complicates the picture by creating

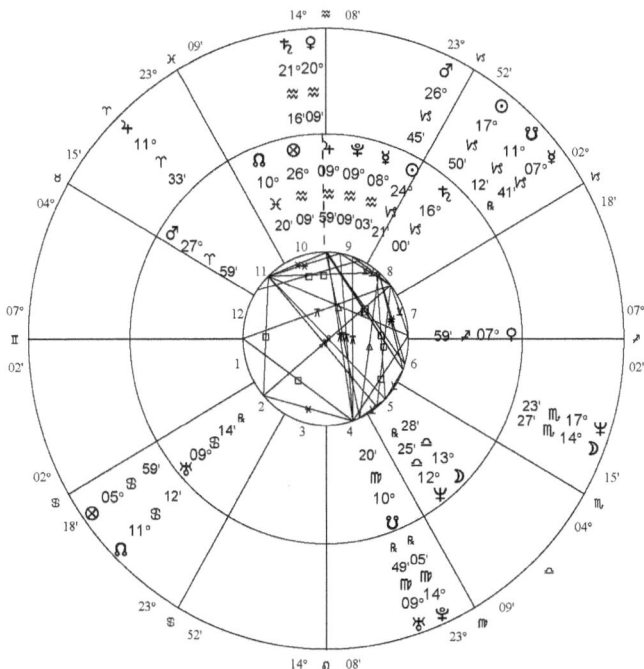

Figure 17-2
US chart/Lyndon B. Johnson State of the Union Speech, January 8, 1964, 9:15 PM; Washington, DC

a Grand Square, indicating the expansion of militant protesters against the war escaping into drugs.

Johnson later told his biographer, Doris Kearns Goodwin: "I knew from the start that I was bound to be crucified either way I moved. If I left the woman I really loved- the Great Society- in order to get involved with that bitch of a war on the other side of the world, then I would lose everything at home. All my programs. All my hopes to feed the hungry and shelter the homeless. All my dreams..."[16]

The problem of Vietnam had started with President Truman and continued through four more presidential terms. After the French-Indochina War ended in 1954, Vietnam was divided into communist and non-communist countries. An election to unify the two was scheduled. Fearful of losing the presidency to Ho Chi Minh, a war hero and the communist leader of North Vietnam, Ngo Dinh Diem, the South Vietnam leader, cancelled it. In an effort to contain communism as the Truman

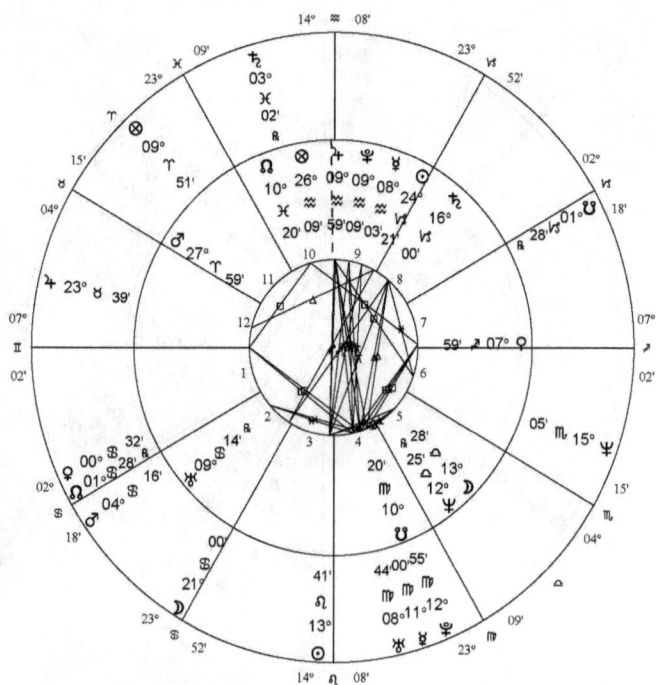

Figure 17-3
US chart/Outer wheel: US Enters Vietnam War August 5, 1964, 11:30 PM, Washington, DC

Doctrine advocated, America supported Diem despite his corruption. Presidents Eisenhower and Kennedy continued this support, sending "advisors" and aid, the goal being to prevent "the domino effect" that could lead to communist control of Indochina.[17]

President Johnson, inheriting this situation, finally made the war legal. He requested and received a congressional resolution allowing him to order military strikes in Vietnam.[18] A militant antiwar movement ensued, with young men burning their draft cards and returning veterans speaking out against the war.[19]

This "legal war" in Vietnam began with President Johnson's announcement to the American public on August 5, 1964, as noted in the chart. North Vietnam had reportedly attacked American ships in the Gulf of Tonkin and Johnson planned to retaliate. The Gulf of Tonkin Resolution was passed on August 7th and empowered the president to increase America's participation in Vietnam.[20]

The resolution resulted in an increase in antiwar sentiment. People had already been questioning the conflict's legality and now viewed the government with suspicion. Television brought all the news of Vietnam into American homes,[21] and finally the horror of the My Lai massacre of more than 500 Vietnamese civilians by US soldiers created a turning point in public support.[22] Mars in Cancer is transiting the US Uranus but at the same time, the Moon (public) is opposing the president (US Sun). The stellium in Virgo of Uranus, Mercury and Pluto indicate the transformation of public sentiment, culminating in the largest single anti-war demonstration in US history occurring on November 15, 1969. Johnson declared he would not seek reelection.[23]

It would take another election and another decade to end the war.

A noteworthy event involving the civil rights issue, detailed in the next chart, was the march from Selma, Alabama to the state's capi-

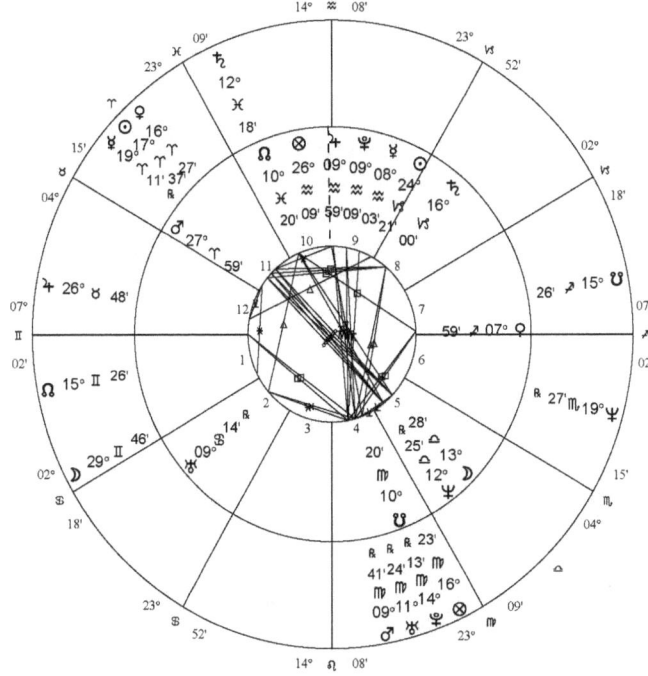

Figure 17-4
US chart/Outer wheel: Selma March 7, 1964, 10:00 AM; Selma, AL

tal Montgomery. The initial march on Sunday, March 7, 1964, later dubbed "Bloody Sunday," was led by John Lewis, head of the Student Nonviolent Coordinating Committee.[24]

The Tumultuous Sixties

The march started on Sunday morning (I used a 10:00 AM time for the chart) after participants were reminded of the non-violent tactics they were to use. They reached the Edmund Pettus Bridge where they confronted dozens of state troopers, deputized men on horseback, and other law enforcement officials. The marchers were brutally beaten with bullwhips and billy clubs, attacked with tear gas, overrun by horses, and spat on. Lewis and over 50 people required hospitalization.[25]

Televised, the brutality of the event shocked Americans and resulted in demonstrations across the country in support of the marchers.

Here you see the stellium in Aries in the eleventh house (groups) squaring US Saturn (repression) and inconjunct the Virgo stellium in the 4th House with Mars opposite US Pluto (power struggles with police and military). Another Yod is formed with Neptune in Scorpio ruled

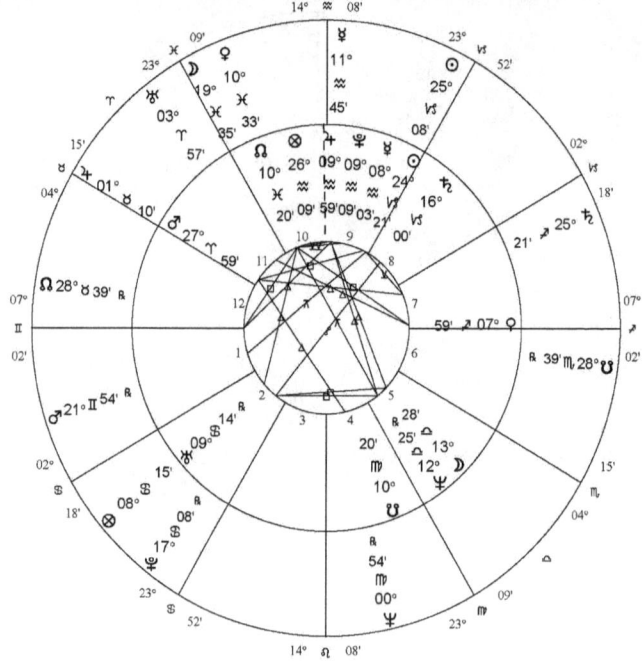

Figure 17-5
US chart/Martin Luther King natal January 15, 1929; 12:00 PM; Atlanta, GA

by Pluto in sextile with the Virgo stellium in a second inconjunction to the Aries stellium. The reaction point falls on the US Moon (the people) in the fifth house (television performers).

One cannot leave the '60s without examining the chart of the greatest civil rights leader of that time, Martin Luther King Jr. He was present for the bus boycott in Montgomery and was there for the March to Selma. His famous "I have a dream" speech was made at the March on Washington. He was cut down in his prime by assassination. King's birthday, one day after this nation's, is recognized as a holiday in his honor.[26]

King's Pluto is in the US second house of values opposite of US Saturn in the eighth, helping to revolutionize the values of the status quo. His Mercury in Aquarius conjunct the US Midheaven also conjuncts the Aquarius stellium in the US Yod, setting off America's restlessness and our search for meaning and identity as it also trines our Ascendant. His Neptune in the US fourth house, trine Jupiter in the US eleventh house, demonstrates his dream for a better America with his Venus in Pisces conjunct our North Node pointing the way. His Saturn in Sagittarius

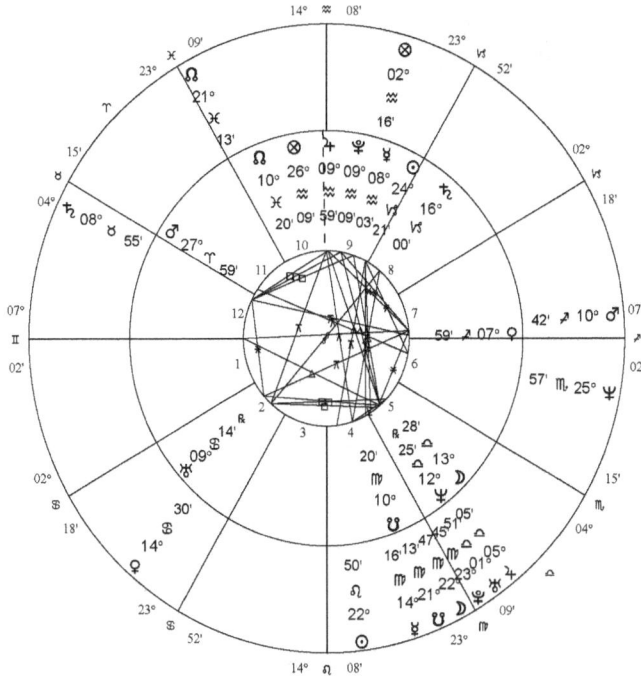

Figure 17-6
US chart/Outer wheel: Woodstock Music Festival August 15, 1969, 5:00 PM, Bethel NY

in the seventh house trines the US Mars, restraining violence with the non-violent methods he used in protests.

King was a greatly admired leader by both the high and the low. He reminded us of the need to throw out our "white man's burden" baggage and embrace the principles that our Founding Fathers endorsed: "All men are created equal" and "Justice for all."

The last chart ends the sixties on a positive note. The Woodstock Music Festival is a legend. It started on August 15, 1969 on a farm in upstate New York and lasted three days. Half a million people attended performances of thirty-two musicians which included both local and global talents, and enjoyed "a lot of sex, drugs, rock 'n' roll and rain."[27]

Max Yasgur, the farmer who owned the land, addressed the crowd on the third day: "...You've proven something to the world...the important thing that you've proven to the world is that half a million kids, and I call you kids because I have children who are older than you are, a half a million young people can get together and have three days of fun and music and have nothing but fun and music and God bless you for it."[28]

Woodstock was a symbol of this decade of the '60s. I'll let you examine the ties to the US chart for yourself.

CHAPTER SEVENTEEN NOTES

1. Holland, Gini: *The 1960s: a Cultural History of the United States Through the Decades*; Lucent Books, Inc. San Diego CA, 1999. pp. 7-8
2. Ibid. p. 77
3. Ibid. p. 9
4. https://www.history.com/topics/1960s/1960s-history *Accessed: 4/20/2023*
5. Holland, Gini: *The 1960s: a Cultural History of the United States Through the Decades*; pp. 126-129
6. Ibid. p. 91
7. https://en.wikipedia.org/wiki/Stonewall_riots *Accessed: 7/10/2023*
8. Holland, Gini: *The 1960s: a Cultural History of the United States Through the Decades*; p. 90
9. https://obamawhitehouse.archives.gov/blog/2015/06/30/day-history-national-organization-women-was-founded *Accessed: 4/19/2023*
10. https://now.org/about/history/founding-2/ *Accessed 4/19/2023*
11. https://obamawhitehouse.archives.gov/blog/2015/06/30/day-history-national-organization-women-was-founded *Accessed: 4/19/2023*
12. Holland, Gini: *The 1960s: a Cultural History of the United States Through the Decades*; p. 89
13. Lyndon Johnson's State of the Union Address, 1964 -Ballotpedia *Accessed: 7/10/2023*
14. Holland, Gini: *The 1960s: a Cultural History of the United States Through the Decades*; pp.31-33
15. Ibid. p. 35
16. Goodwin, Doris Kearns: *Lyndon Johnson and the American Dream*; St Martin's Press, New York, NY, 1991. p. 251
17. Holland, Gini: *The 1960s: a Cultural History of the United States Through the Decades*; pp, 41-43
18. Ibid. p. 43

19. Ibid. pp. 48-50
20. https://www.history.com/topics/vietnam-war/gulf-of-tonkin-resolution-1 *Accessed: 4/22/2023*
21. Holland, Gini: *The 1960s: a Cultural History of the United States Through the Decades*; pp.43-45
22. https://www.history.com/topics/vietnam-war/my-lai-massacre-1 *Accessed: 7/10/2023*
23. Holland, Gini: *The 1960s: a Cultural History of the United States Through the Decades*; p.129
24. https://www.britannica.com/event/Selma-March *Accessed: 4/19/2023*
25. Ibid.
26. https://en.wikipedia.org/wiki/Martin_Luther_King_Jr. *Accessed: 7/10/2023*
27. https://www.history.com/topics/1960s/woodstock *Accessed: 4/20/2023*
28. Ibid.

Chapter Eighteen
The Backlash 1970s

"Imagine all the people, sharing all the world"
John Lennon

Near the beginning of the new decade, President Richard Nixon ushered in the "New Right" political movement, decrying the breakdown in traditional social values[1] with his November 3, 1969 speech from the Oval Office. He appealed to the "Silent Majority," a group he had described in a previous speech as "the forgotten Americans, the non-shouters, the non-demonstrators."[2] His first move was to abolish as much of Johnson's agenda as he could, hoping to get rid of the welfare state and discourage "spoiled hippies and whining protesters."[3]

The Vietnam War persisted into the seventies but with increasing loss of public support. Not wanting the US to look weak, Nixon did not end the war. Instead, he tried to make it more publicly acceptable by limiting the number of soldiers drafted and forcing the South Vietnamese to carry the burden of military action. Despite this, the invasion into Cambodia stimulated further antiwar protests, culminating in the killing of four students at Kent State University on May 4, 1970.[4]

Environmental issues continued to be prominent in the '70s. The first Earth Day was celebrated in April 1970. Congress passed several environmental laws, including the National Environmental Policy, the Clean Water, and the Endangered Species Acts. The energy crisis stemming from the OPEC oil embargo served to draw further public attention to conservation issues.[5]

TIME LINE of 1970s[6]

1. 1970: NOW holds Women's Strike for Equality march in New York City; Environmental Protection Agency (EPA) created; first Earth Day celebrated in the United States.
2. 1971: Pentagon Papers published in New York Times; Nixon creates the secret Plumbers unit.
3. 1972: Nixon makes historic trip to China; Congress passes Equal Rights Amendment (ERA) and Title IX in support of women's rights; Plumbers unit breaks into the Democratic National Committee headquarters in Watergate; Senate approves the S.A.L.T. Agreement with the Soviet Union, limiting antiballistic weapons.[7]
4. 1973: US exits Vietnam; Congressional committee established to investigate Watergate break-in; Roe v. Wade legalizes a woman's right to abortion.
5. 1974: Nixon resigns after impeachment papers are approved by Congress; Gerald Ford becomes President; Ford pardons Nixon.
6. 1975: North Vietnam wins the war and takes over South Vietnam[8]; the US and Soviet Union cooperate in space test.
7. 1976: Carter wins the presidential election.
8. 1977: Carter unconditionally pardons draft deserters; tax codes revised for the first time in 30 years, requiring higher payments by the wealthy.
9. 1978: Equal Rights Amendment ratification period extended by Congress; American Indian Movement organizes peaceful march from San Francisco to Washington, D.C., in protest to forced removal of Native Americans from their homelands.
10. 1979: President Carter negotiates with Israeli prime minister Begin and Egyptian president Sadat, followed by the signing of the Israel-Egypt Peace Treaty in Washington; Three Mile Island radiation leak alerts public to nuclear power risks; Iranians seize US embassy in Tehran, capturing sixty-six American hostages.

Several movements sought improved civil rights but worked independently rather than collectively. Antiwar protests continued, the push for gay liberation expanded, Native Americans fought for equality, and women renewed their struggle for equal rights. Success was mixed.[9]

The Women's Strike for Equality March in August 1970 at the time was the largest women's rights protest since the suffrage movement. Organized by NOW on the 50th anniversary of the 19th Amendment's passage, it brought 50,000 feminists to New York City where they "paraded down… Fifth Avenue with linked arms."[10] Another near victory emerged in March 1972 with Senate approval of the Equal Rights Amendment (ERA). The ERA had originally been proposed in 1923 but had never gotten through Congress before. It was quickly ratified by 30 states but did not achieve the requisite 38-state confirmation in the allotted time frame, leaving the hope of gender equality still a distant dream.[11]

True victory arrived January 22, 1973 when the Supreme Court granted women the right to an abortion in deciding the case of Roe v. Wade.[12] (See Chapter Seven). However, today the issue remains unresolved, recent activities bringing it to the forefront once again in this transition period.

The Stonewall Riots occurred in June 1969 when gay activists confronted police outside a gay bar in Greenwich Village. The riots lasted several days and catalyzed an international gay rights movement, homosexual and transgender people recognizing the value in fighting for a common cause.[13] In 1973, the American Psychiatric Association removed homosexuality from its list of psychological disorders, one early victory for the movement.[14]

The American Indian Movement (AIM) staged a protest at Wounded Knee, South Dakota in February 1973. This location was infamous for the massacre of almost 300 Lakota tribe members by the US Army in 1890.[15] Native protesters seized the town, which was cordoned off by FBI agents, US marshals, and other law enforcement. The siege lasted 71 days. Although the protesters' demands were not met, wide public support developed. Wounded Knee became a symbol for continued Native American activism.[16] AIM arranged many protests throughout the decade, and the "Red Power" movement resulted in some increased funding for Native American social needs such as housing, education, and healthcare.[17]

The most prominent '70s event was the Watergate break-in by Nixon's "plumbers" in 1972.[18] Two young reporters for *The Washington Post*, Carl Bernstein and Bob Woodward, initiated an investigation that uncovered Nixon administration crimes,[19] and eventually led to Congressional impeachment proceedings and Nixon's resignation. By then, Vice President Spiro Agnew had resigned to avoid a trial for tax evasion, and unelected Gerald Ford had been chosen as his replacement.[20]

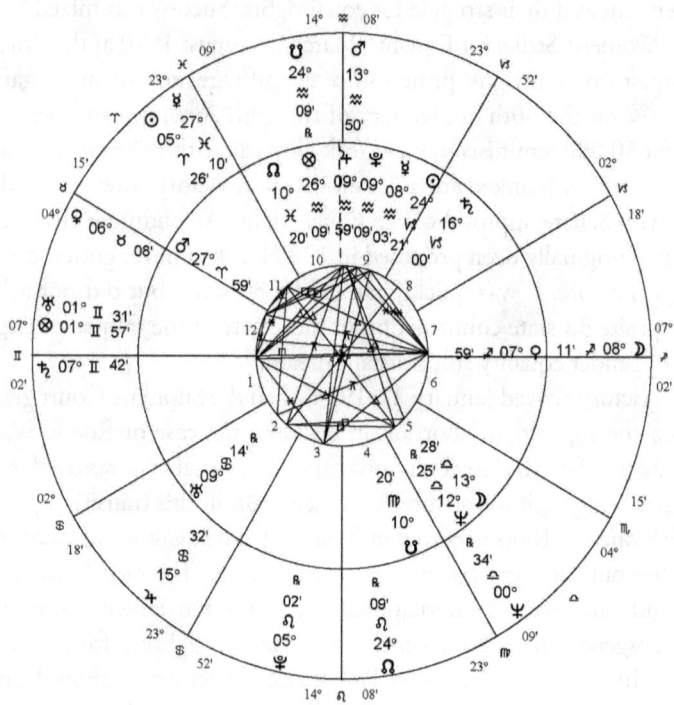

Figure 18-1
Inner wheel: US chart/Bob Woodward natal March 6, 1943, 6:35 PM; Geneva, IL

Note the chart for Bob Woodward, the investigative reporter in Washington who was instrumental in exposing the Nixon administration's misdeeds. His work earned *The Washington Post* the 1973 Pulitzer Price for public service.[21] In the US chart's third house (newspapers), his Pluto (investigations) sits in trine to his Moon in the US seventh house conjunct the US Venus, ruler of the twelfth house, bringing out the "hidden" enemies behind Watergate. Many of Nixon's private circle were imprisoned, including his attorney general, John Mitchell. Woodward's Saturn sits on the US Ascendant bringing his reporting to the public, emphasized by his Natal Mars conjunct the US Pluto (hidden crimes) as well as the Midheaven (the administration).

The Senate Watergate Committee and House Judicial Committee thereafter began investigations of the Nixon administration. Nixon's poll numbers dropped dramatically. Impeachment was inevitable, and no support existed for him in Congress. Republican leaders confronted him. "For the good of the Republican Party, and the nation, Nixon must resign."[22]

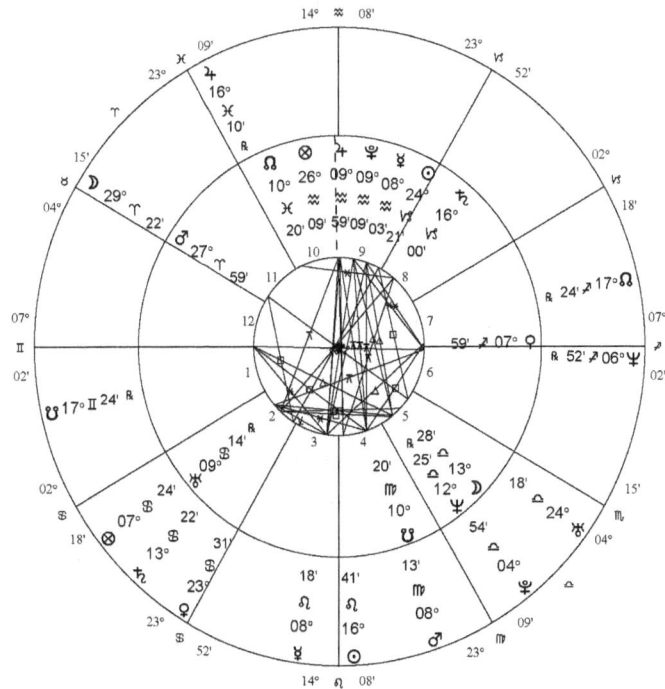

Figure 18-2
US chart/Nixon resigns August 9, 1974, 12:00 PM; Washington, DC

In this chart, you can see that transiting Uranus is squaring the US Sun and, coincidentally, is conjunct the Ascendant of the event chart. The event Moon and US Mars conjunction opposes Uranus, creating a powerful Cardinal T-Square demonstrating the hostility of the public as well as that of Nixon's colleagues. The event chart also has Saturn opposing Saturn in the US chart, indicating the doubt and despair of the president. This was the first time in US history a president had resigned. He left at noon, the same time Vice President Ford took the oath as the new president.

Gerald Ford was unique in not having been elected to either the presidency or vice presidency. Early in his term, he pardoned Richard Nixon and named Nelson Rockefeller, a party liberal, to the vice presidency, irritating fellow Republicans. His attempts to lower inflation resulted in a severe recession and rising unemployment. Conflicts with the Democratic-controlled Congress led to legislative gridlock.[23]

Although the Paris Peace Accords had ended the war in Vietnam on

January 27, 1973, and American troops had left, the fighting continued. Foreign assistance was cut off by Congress in 1974. The North Vietnamese invaded South Vietnam, threatening Saigon. President Ford evacuated remaining American personnel in the weeks preceding the fall of Saigon on April 30, 1975.[24]

In 1976, Jimmy Carter became the next president. Carter had ambitious plans for reform but Congress resisted them. The lack of legislative successes undermined his administration and popularity.[25] The outstanding achievement of his term in office was the peace treaty he brokered between Egypt and Israel. He won the Nobel Peace Prize in 2002 for this as well as for his work in social welfare and human rights.[26]

The 1970s saw a transition to a more conservative public. Some groups made progress toward the goal of "From Many, One." Local, national, and global recognition of environmental issues occurred for the first time.[27] Carter's failure to free the American hostages taken in the Iran revolution led to his defeat in the 1980 election,[28] ushering in the Reagan Era.

CHAPTER EIGHTEEN NOTES

1. https://history.com/topics/1970s/1970s-1 *Accessed 4/24/2023*
2. https://historynewsnetwork.org/article/184301 *Accessed 4/24/2023*
3. https://history.com/topics/1970s/1970s-1 *Accessed 4/24/2023*
4. Ibid.
5. Ibid.
6. Richards, Marlee: *America in the 1970s*; Twenty-First Century Books, Minneapolis, MN, 2010. pp. 132-133
7. https://www.britannica.com/event/Anti-Ballistic-Missile-Treaty *Accessed 7/20/2023*
8. Richards, Marlee: *America in the 1970s*; p. 28
9. https://history.com/topics/1970s/1970s-1 *Accessed 4/24/2023*
10. https://time.com/4008060/women-strike-equality-1970/ *Accessed 4/30/2023*
11. https://www.history.com/this-day-in-history/equal-rights-amendment-passed-by-congress *Accessed 4/29/2023*
12. Richards, Marlee: *America in the 1970s*; p. 66
13. https://www.britannica.com/event/Stonewall-riots *Accessed 4/29/2023*
14. https://www.infoplease.com/history/pride-month/the-american-gay-rights-movement-a-timeline *Accessed 4/30/2023*
15. Richards, Marlee: *America in the 1970s*; pp. 72-73
16. Wounded Knee Occupation - Wikipedia *Accessed 7/20/2023*
17. Richards, Marlee: *America in the 1970s*; p. 73
18. Fremon, David K.: *The Watergate Scandal in American History*; Enslow Publishers, Inc., Springfield, NJ, 1998. pp. 39-42
19. Ibid. pp. 46-47, 115
20. Ibid. p. 73
21. https://www.britannica.com/biography/Bob-Woodward *Accessed 5/3/2023*
22. Fremon, David K.: *The Watergate Scandal in American History*; p. 111
23. https://www.britannica.com/biography/Gerald-Ford *Accessed*

5/2/2023
24. https://www.thoughtco.com/vietnam-war-end-of-the-conflict-2361333   *Accessed 5/3/2023*
25. https://www.britannica.com/biography/Jimmy-Carter *Accessed 5/3/2023*
26. https://www.nobelprize.org/prizes/peace/2002/carter/facts *Accessed 5/3/2023*
27. Richards, Marlee: *America in the 1970s*; p. 129
28. https://history.com/topics/1970s/1970s-1 *Accessed 4/24/2023*

Chapter Nineteen

The Avaricious Eighties

*"Working 9 to 5; What a way to make a livin';
Barely gettin' by; It's all takin' and no givin'"*
Dolly Parton

This decade saw the widening gap in American incomes advance (See Chapter Ten). If you look over the previous chapters, a pattern begins to emerge involving Saturn and Uranus, the Axis of Awareness of the US chart's Yod, as America seeks its identity. The '80s were a turning point. Many of the tensions and conflicts of previous generations met head on. The '50s consumer-generation style of living was heatedly confronted by a liberal generation of the '60s, who in turn were dominated by an emerging new conservative right movement in the '70s.[1]

Traumatized by such conflicts, the public looked for a solution, and thought they had found it in the 1980 Republican presidential candidate, Ronald Reagan. He "was the perfect projection of the nation's hopes and aspirations, suffering clearly after the defeat in Vietnam, the disgrace of Watergate, and the disintegration of the economy in the 1970s. The man acted like a president, and in the 1980s, acting was enough."[2]

Ultimately, however, the nation became more economically, socially, and politically divided during this decade. Reagan's policies gave large tax breaks to the rich, decreased government regulation of industries, and encouraged lax antitrust enforcement. American jobs were compromised as businesses pursued cheap foreign labor. Companies merged unchecked into multinational corporations, inhibiting economic competition.³ Under Reagan and the next Republican president, George H. W. Bush, the public saw the federal debt increase to the largest in history.⁴

Other results of Reagan's policies included declining wages, an increased need for women to work to support their families, reduced education scores because of cuts to education, expanding handgun sales, increasing inner city violence and police brutality, child abuse scandals, a 25 per cent increase in the homeless, and new depths of poverty.⁵

As one economist stated, "America had thrown itself a party and billed

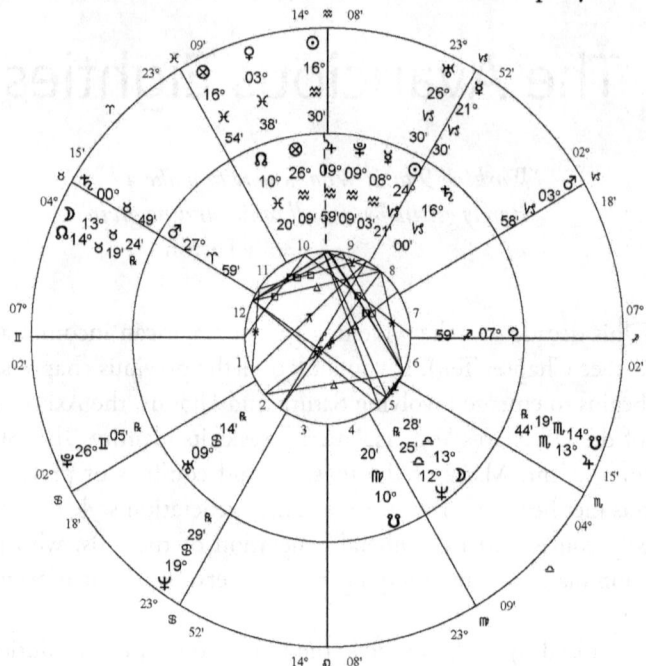

Figure 19-1
US chart/Ronald Reagan natal February 6, 1911 3:43 AM;
Tampico, IL

the tab to the future."⁶

Note the chart above. Although Reagan's Aquarius Sun sits on the US Midheaven, closer inspection shows that Reagan's Capricorn side is much stronger, with Uranus, Mercury, and Mars all in Capricorn in the US eighth house (international finance, multinational and transactional corporations). The Uranus in the eighth shows a change in the economy which Reagan's "supply-side" economics clearly caused in America. The

Mars in Capricorn in the eighth is also trine Saturn, its ruler in the eleventh house, showing the long-lasting effect of his policies, which were not obvious at first, with the North Node conjunct the Moon in Taurus in the twelfth house opposing Jupiter in Scorpio conjunct the South Node in the sixth house (military affairs). The Neptune in the US second house shows the gradual leak of money from the people.

Labor issues fared poorly under Reagan. Most notable was his reaction to the Professional Air-Traffic Controllers Association. The union had gone on strike August 3, 1981, requesting higher wages and a reduced workweek, emphasizing the heavy pressure their jobs entailed. Reagan declared the strike illegal, stating any controller not returning to work in 48 hours would be fired. On August 5, he began to fire almost 12,000 controllers and announced a lifetime ban that would preclude their ever being hired again.[7]

Labor Day parades the next month were filled with thousands of terminated air traffic controllers as well as disgruntled workers from other unions protesting Reagan's labor policies. Although the president had promised his programs would create millions of jobs, he did not attend New York's first Labor Day parade in 13 years. AFL-CIO's leader Kirkland ridiculed that promised employment, noting that 1.25 million jobs had already been eliminated. "His actions speak a lot louder than his words," he declared.[8]

Issues regarding separation of church and state grew dominant in the 1980s as the evangelical movement's participation in American politics increased. The initial impetus was not the abortion question. Rather, it was a court decision disallowing the tax-exempt status of private, often Christian, schools because of their segregationist policies. Paul Weyrich, a religious conservative activist and co-founder of the Heritage Foundation, decided he could marshal a formidable bloc to support conservative candidates like Ronald Reagan based on Christian concerns.[9]

However, because supporting racial segregation was not palatable, Weyrich looked elsewhere for a rallying issue. Since abortions had increased following Roe vs Wade, he focused on this concern. Six years after Roe vs Wade was passed, the abortion issue became the evangelical call to arms.[10]

Shortly after Reagan's election, the National Association of Evangelicals and National Radio Broadcasters met in Washington, D.C. at the Washington Sheraton Hotel, their goal to bring a "moral rebirth" to America.[11] They blamed secular humanism for the rise in atheism and

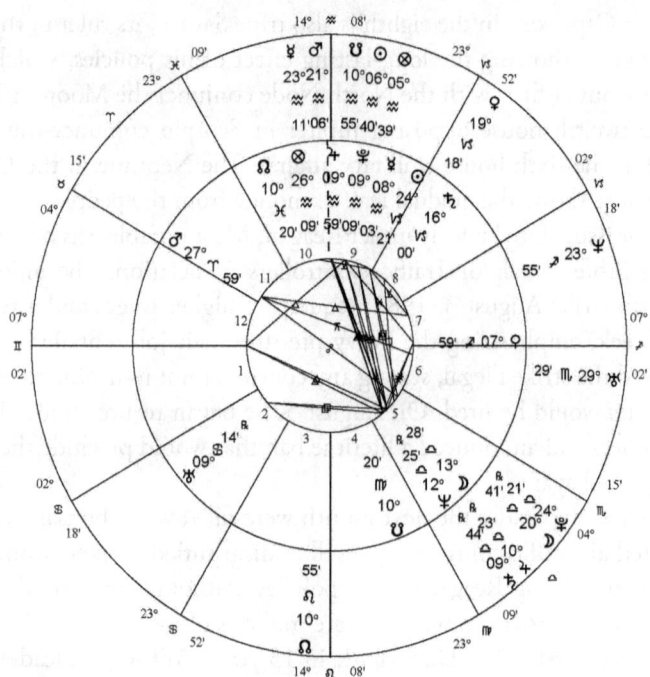

Figure 19-2
US chart/Evangelical march on Washington January 26, 1981;
Washington, DC

increasing social acceptance of pornography, homosexuality, and abortion. During five days of speeches, they proclaimed that the Constitution did not restrict church-related political activity, and that this belief resulted from a "brainwashing" of the public.[12] Reagan himself was "unabashed in his expressions of support for causes of the New Christian Right."[13]

In this event chart, there is a conjunction of Jupiter (religion) and Saturn (conservativism) marking the birth of the "religious right" movement that will affect future presidents. This conjunction also melds with the US conjunction of Moon and Neptune which reminds us of "brainwashing," public's idealism of the president (trine the Sun), and the "moral majority" that dominated this decade and continued into the next. Both conjunctions fall in the fifth house of the US chart (affairs related to children). Uranus in the sixth house is the desire to change medical policies to prevent more abortions.

The move to the right resulted in avoidance of discussion and treatment of the deadly AIDS (Auto Immune Deficiency Syndrome) virus which appeared in the summer of 1981. Almost 600 people had died from it before it got front-page space in the New York Times in 1983. Reagan had cut National Institutes of Health and CDC funding, frustrating public health experts. As AIDS was little understood and seemed mostly confined to the gay community, the media and government largely ignored it.[14]

President Reagan publicly mentioned AIDS the first time on September 17, 1985. The death from AIDS on October 2 of Reagan's close friend, actor Rock Hudson, shocked the public into awareness. That day, Congress funded AIDS research with almost 190 million dollars.[15] On May 26, 1988, Surgeon General Everett Koop mailed out 107 million copies of Understanding AIDS, a pamphlet that was the first co-

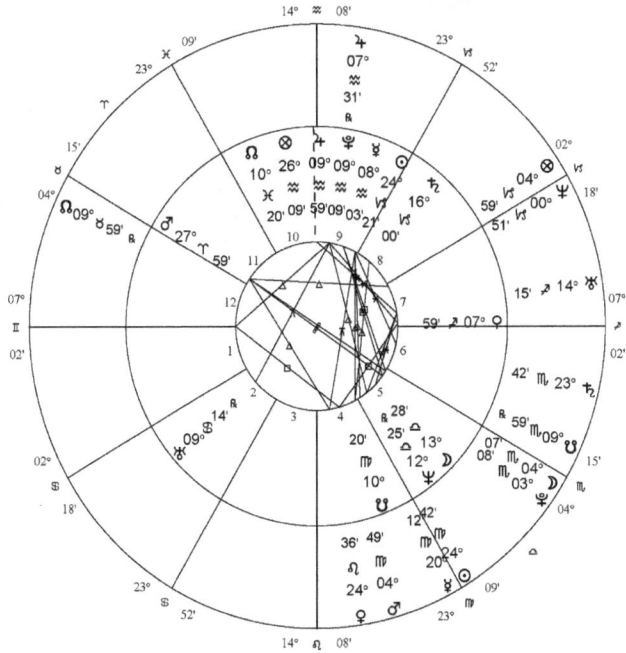

Figure 18-2
US chart/Reagan announces AIDS crisis September 17, 1985, 12:00 PM;
Washington, DC

ordinated education strategy for the public. Federal funds were authorized for AIDS prevention, testing, and research in HOPE, Reagan's first comprehensive AIDS bill.[16] By then, 47,000 people were infected with HIV.[17]

In this chart the Aquarius stellium is being set off by transiting Jupiter while squaring the Moon conjunction with Pluto in the fifth house of the US chart. AIDS is a sexually transmitted disease that became an epidemic in the United States during the 1980s. Because it started in the gay community, they became early targets of discrimination. (Uranus in the seventh house of the US chart). Later, the disease was found to be spread by addicted people injecting drugs. These people also became targets of discrimination. (Neptune also in the seventh house). Saturn in Scorpio is transiting the sixth house of health conditions, indicating the fatal nature of this mysterious disease. Once Reagan made it publicly his "first priority," Congress moved swiftly to authorize funds to fight it.

Racism contributed to the growing public division and urban whites' fear of Black and Brown crime. A representative event was a trial of po-

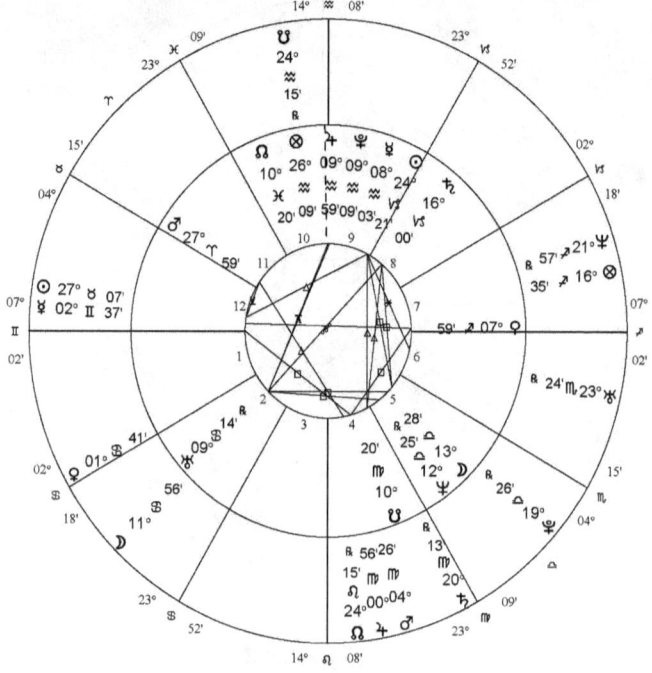

Figure 18-2
US chart/Miami Riots May 17, 1980, 6:00 PM; Miami, FL

lice officers that led to the Miami riots in May 1980. Arthur McDuffie was a Black lance corporal in the US Marine Corps and an insurance salesman. Police officers beat him to death after a traffic stop. Their trial on charges of manslaughter and evidence tampering ended on May 17, 1980 with acquittal.[18]

Protests began in Miami streets that afternoon, turning into riots by 6 p.m. and spreading into other neighborhoods. Burglaries, fires, and looting ensued. The governor called up the National Guard. Riots continued and more troops were sent. A curfew from 8 p.m. to 6 a.m. was imposed, and gun and liquor sales temporarily banned, reducing the violence by the third day. Eighteen people were killed, 370 people hurt and 787 arrested. Destruction of property was more than 100 million dollars.[19]

In the preceding chart you see the Moon in Cancer (the people) con-

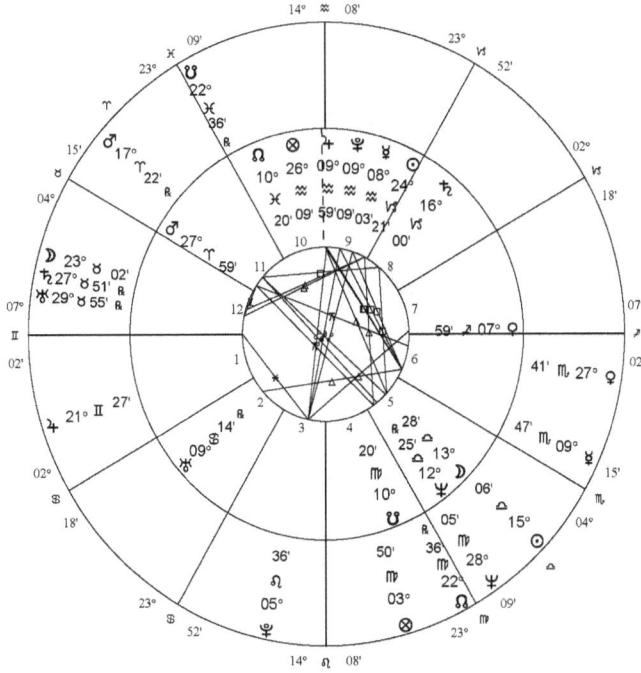

Figure 18-2
US chart/Jesse Jackson natal October 8, 1941, 2:15 PM; Greenville, SC

junct US Uranus (protest) opposing the authority of the government (Saturn) which expanded over the area, Jupiter conjunct Mars in the fourth house. The National Guard (Pluto, ruler of US sixth house) creates a T-square with the Moon in the event chart and the US Saturn. This event illustrates the racism issue still at work in the country but moving backward, not forward.

A positive note for Black advancement was the emergence of Reverend Jesse Jackson as a public figure. He was "the first African American to launch a full-scale campaign for a major-party presidential nomination," running in both 1984 and 1988. His "Rainbow Coalition" of various minorities left behind by Reagan's "vision of America"[20] consisted of the poor, Blacks, Hispanics, unions, liberal whites, and others who supported his populist ideas.[21] His second campaign in 1988 was better financed, and he was second in total delegates in the Democratic primaries.[22] His influence as an activist gave hope to young Black males who saw him as a model, and he continued to have a strong voice in the Democratic Party.

Jackson's Taurus Moon and Virgo Neptune form a Grand Earth Trine to the US Sun, enabling him to build a strong base which brought him close to the nomination for president. His Pluto in Leo falls in the US third house (communication), opposing the US Mercury (the people) which puts the emphasis on his eloquent speeches designed to influence public opinion in favor of his goals. In addition, his Ascendant is conjunct the US Sun. He increased hope in the Black community that one day they would see a president of color.

Women's rights showed little advancement in this decade. The Equal Rights Amendment was defeated, a blow after ten years of fighting.[23] Although many women had to work to support the family, they were still expected to take care of domestic tasks alone.[24] Positive events, however, included the appointment of the first woman, Sandra Day O'Connor, to the Supreme Court by Reagan in 1981. Sally Ride became America's first female astronaut in 1983,[25] and in the 1984 election, Congresswoman Geraldine Ferraro, a Democrat, became the first woman to run for vice president.[26]

TIME LINE[27]

1. 1980: Mount St. Helens in Washington State explodes; Ronald Reagan becomes 40th US president.
2. 1981: Iran hostages are released; Reagan is injured in an attempted assassination.
3. 1982: Highest unemployment rate since 1940, a reported 10.4 percent.
4. 1983: Invasion of Grenada by US troops where Cuban military

advisors were running the country.

5. 1984: Reagan is elected for second term; Vietnam veterans poisoned by Agent Orange win suit against chemical companies.
6. 1985: Reagan meets Russian leader, Mikhail Gorbachev in Geneva.
7. 1986: A new national holiday is named for Martin Luther King; the public discovers America has sent Iran ammunition and other materials.
8. 1987: Senate and House committees hold hearings on the Iran-contra hearings issue; Dow Jones Industrial Average drops 508 points; Russians agree with Reagan to dismantle missiles.
9. 1988: Reagan visits Moscow and attacks Soviet human rights record; George H. W. Bush is elected president.
10. 1989: Oliver North convicted in Iran-contra scandal; Congress bails out the savings and loan industry debacle at the cost of $166 billion over 10 years and $400 billion over thirty years; US troops invade Panama and overthrow Manuel Noriega.

The 1980s saw the development of opposing forces. Liberals believed that an active government could make a positive difference in people's lives, whereas conservatives thought that "making people more self-sufficient would lower crime rates, cause welfare to dry up, give people a sense of purpose, and reinvigorate the entire country."[28]

The struggle between these views continues.

CHAPTER NINETEEN NOTES

1. Bondi, Victor, Ed.: *American Decades 1980-1989*, A Manly, Inc. Book by Gale Research, Inc., Detroit, MI, 1996. p. viii.
2. Ibid.
3. Ibid. p. ix-xi
4. Ibid. p. viii
5. Ibid. p. x-xi
6. Friedman, Benjamin: *The Day of Reckoning: The Consequences of American Economic Policy Under Reagan and After*, Random House, New York, 1988. p. 4 Random House, New York, 1985. p. ix.
7. https://www.history.com/this-day-in-history/reagan-fires-11359-air-traffic-controllers Accessed 5/5/2023
8. https://www.newspapers.com/article/the-salina-journal-reagan-fires-12000-/124118687/ Accessed 5/5/2023
9. https://www.politico.com/magazine/story/2014/05/religious-right-real-origins-107133/ Accessed 7/17/2023
10. Ibid.
11. Evangelical Christians Meet to Develop Strategy for 1980s - The Washington Post Accessed 5/7/2023
12. https://www.nytimes.com/1981/01/27/us/evangelicals-debate-their-role-in-battling-secularism.html Accessed 5/7/2023
13. Reasons Why Liberalism Declined in the Late 1970s - Synonym Accessed 5/7/2023
14. https://www.history.com/news/aids-epidemic-ronald-reagan Accessed 5/4/2023
15. Ibid.
16. https://www.history.com/topics/1980s/hiv-aids-crisis-timeline Accessed 5/5/2023
17. https://www.history.com/news/aids-epidemic-ronald-reagan Accessed 5/4/2023
18. https://en.wikipedia.org/wiki/1980_Miami_riots# Accessed 5/5/2023
19. Ibid.
20. Bondi, Victor, Ed.: *American Decades 1980-1989*; p. 289
21. Ibid. p. 556

22. Ibid. p. 557
23. Wright, David: *America in the 20th Century, 1980-1989*; Marshall Cavendish Corp., New York, 1995. p. 1290
24. Ibid. p. 1287
25. Ibid. p 1290
26. Ibid. p. 1176
27. Ibid. p. 1290-1291
28. Ibid. p. 1282

Chapter Twenty

The "Good Decade" – the 1990s

"Get in the Groove and Let the Good Times Roll"
Sam Cooke

The 1990s were "good" because of the longest recorded economic expansion in US history, beginning in 1991. The stock market surged, job creation reached a new peak, productivity rose, and inflation remained low. The prior decade had ended with a brief recession due to the savings and loan crisis, a gas price spike, and other factors. The country wanted a change. After twelve years of Republican governance, Bill Clinton was elected president in 1992.[1] Under his leadership, the country went from a huge deficit to a record surplus of $236 billion.[2] Consumerism increased with the expanded use of credit cards. Increased internet use and the World Wide Web boosted globalization. The end of the Cold War established the United States as the largest world superpower, and eased fears of a potential third world war.[3]

IMPORTANT FACTS ABOUT THE NINETIES[4]

1. Despite healthcare business expansion, many Americans had no health insurance. Clinton's attempts to pass healthcare legislation failed.
2. The homeless population increased as did alcohol and drug abuse.
3. Gun violence remained a serious issue. Guns were the leading US cause of death, and homicide the 3rd leading cause of death

in children ages 5-15. Eighty per cent of homicides resulted from domestic arguments. However, any attempt at gun legislation was followed by increased gun sales.

4. American education was inadequate in providing young adults necessary job skills.
5. Social changes were profound. The number of nuclear families declined. More women entered the work force, and fewer families were sustainable on a single income. Divorces and single-parent households grew in number. Although the birth rate dropped, teenage pregnancy increased. Poverty resulted in more crime and gang membership.
6. The religious right increased their opposition to abortion and sex education, while advocating the teaching of creationism in schools.
7. Iraq invaded Kuwait in August 1990. The US spearheaded a UN coalition of 39 countries to oust Iraq in the Gulf War beginning in January 1991. It took only a few weeks.[5]
8. Apartheid ended in South Africa in June 1991 and relations to the US were normalized.
9. The Soviet Union dissolved in December 1991.
10. North American Free Trade Agreement went into effect in 1993, promoting free trade between Canada, the United States and Mexico.
11. Two bombings occurred, one an Islamic terrorist bombing in New York City in 1993; another, a domestic terrorist bombing in Oklahoma City in 1995.[6]
12. Clinton and Gore were reelected in 1996.[7]
13. Bill Clinton was acquitted of all impeachment charges in 1999.[8]

What did Bill Clinton bring to the country? Examine the following chart.

Clinton was one of the most popular presidents – even during impeachment his approval ratings stayed in the 60s, peaking at 73 percent immediately after the House filed impeachment articles.[9] Look at his stellium in Libra conjuncting the US planets in Libra. With his Venus conjunct Neptune in the fifth house of the US chart, his empathy for

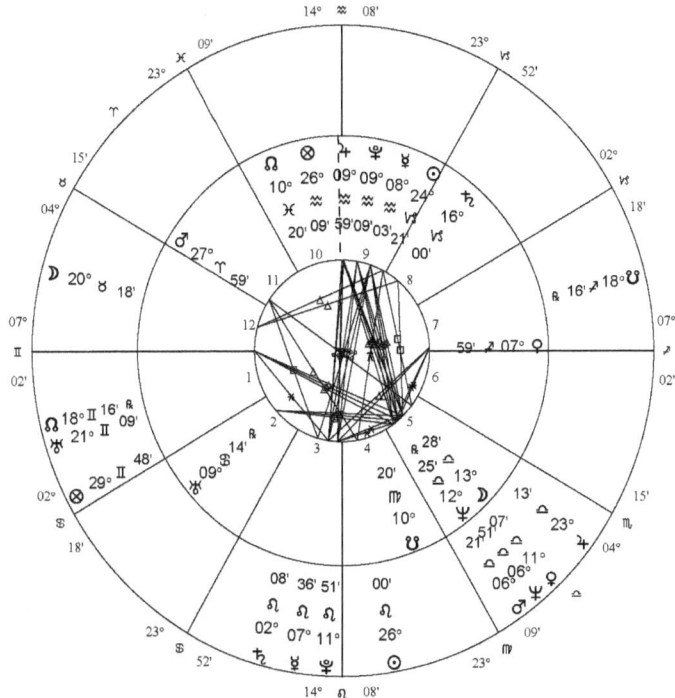

Figure 20-1
US chart/Bill Clinton natal August 19, 1946, 8:51 AM; Hope, AR

people was sincere and people knew it. The Mars conjunct Neptune gave him a lot of charisma.

Clinton had hoped to repair the rift among political parties, urging Congress in his second inaugural speech to concentrate on America's mission rather than extreme partisan issues.[10] His Leo stellium opposite the US Aquarian planets reflects a balance Americans desired between the individual and the group. In addition, his Uranus sextile to his Sun forms a Yod with the US Sun, thus enabling his ability to make changes acceptable within traditional conservative viewpoints.

Despite scandals and investigations plaguing his second term, "Clinton's presidency is also remembered as one of the most successful of the 20th century – not only for its enormous domestic accomplishments and significant foreign-policy achievements, but also for creating a stronger nation at the beginning of a new century."[11]

Both George H. W. Bush and Clinton had an impact on social issues. Civil rights took a step forward with the signing of the Americans with Disabilities Act in 1990 by the elder Bush. The law banned discrimination against people with physical or mental disabilities, including alcoholics, drug abusers, and people with AIDS.[12] Under Clinton, the Violence Against Women Act was passed in 1994 for the purpose of reducing domestic violence and sexual assault.[13] However, Clinton's attempt to end discrimination against homosexuals in the military was unsuccessful. Strong Congressional and armed services opposition led only to a feeble compromise of "don't ask, don't tell, don't pursue" policy.[14]

Even in a "good" decade bad things happen. The charts included in this chapter are related to the issues involved with the Yod in the US chart.

In 1991, motorist Rodney King was severely beaten by four LAPD officers. The event was videotaped, but the officers were still acquitted of assault. Rising tensions between African Americans and police exploded, and by 5:30 p.m. on April 29, 1992, protests turned violent. Buildings were firebombed, windows smashed, and stores looted. Governor Pete Wilson called out the National Guard, but President Bush had to send federal troops by the third day. Curfew was finally lifted May 4th by Mayor Bradley.[15]

Rebuilding eventually began with the help of corporate investments, federal grants, and tax proposals. An investigation of the LAPD response resulted in the resignation of Chief Daryl Gates. It wasn't until 1993 that two of the involved officers were sentenced to thirty months for violating King's civil rights. However, serious reforms did not occur until the late 1990s after widespread corruption within the LAPD was revealed.[16]

The event brought racism to the forefront and was transformative in the sense that officers were held accountable and some reform took place. But what a price - 2000 injuries, 63 deaths, 3000 buildings destroyed, one billion dollars in damages[17]- and only a small progression.

Examine the chart of the riots which follows and consider its impact on the country.

The most powerful conjunction of Pluto/Moon in Scorpio describes the confrontation between the police (sixth House) and people (workers) which is intense and violent, especially since it brings up repressed anger issues on both sides. Add to that the Mars in Cancer in the second House (the people's values) opposing the US Saturn in Capricorn (authority) enhanced by the event chart's Uranus conjunct US Saturn (disruption of the status quo) and Neptune (confusion). The media is

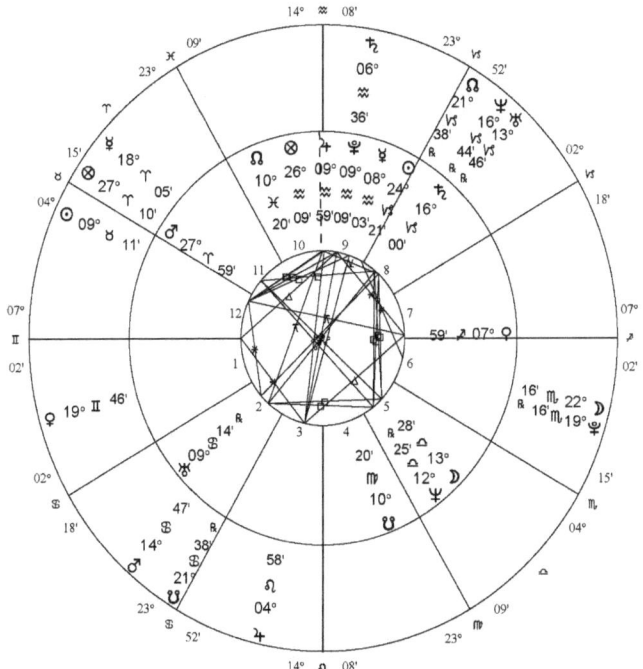

Figure 20-2
US chart/Rodney King riots April 29, 1991, 5:30 PM, Los Angeles, CA

also involved (Mercury in US chart) opposed to event chart Jupiter in the third House which was the instigator (the video of King's beating).

The first World Trade Center bombing in 1993 alerted the American public to the danger of global terrorism and foreshadowed the much larger attack on 9/11. Radical Islamist terrorists parked a van loaded with explosive material and cyanide under the North Tower. The resulting explosion killed six people and injured more than 1000. The perpetrators eventually were caught and imprisoned for life. The plot leader's uncle later became the principal architect for the 2001 attack.[18]

The Oklahoma City bombing is the deadliest domestic terrorist event thus far in American history. Examine the following chart for this event.

Friends since military service, Timothy McVeigh and Terry Nichols were anti-government militants who planned and carried out the Oklahoma City bombing. They had been radicalized by the Ruby Ridge shoot-out in Idaho and the Waco siege in Texas against the Branch Davidian religious sect. They selected the Alfred P. Murrah Federal Building in Oklahoma City, Oklahoma for revenge bombing of federal agencies

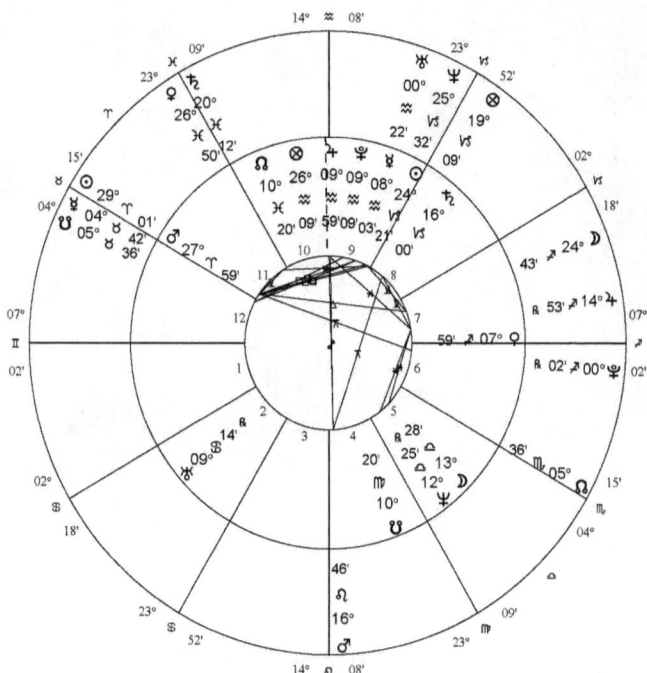

Figure 20-3
US chart/Oklahoma City bombing April 19, 1995, 9:10 AM;
Oklahoma City, OK

such as the ATF and DEA housed within it. Placing a diesel fuel-fertilizer bomb they had built in a rented truck, they parked next to the building and fled.[19] The explosion was timed for April 19, 1995, the second anniversary of Waco and the 220th anniversary of the American Revolution Battles of Lexington and Concord. It killed 168 people including children, left hundreds injured and nearby buildings damaged or destroyed.[20]

In the chart, find the attack (Mars in Leo) in the fourth House of the US Chart (federal buildings) inconjunct Saturn in the eighth House (death). It is also trine to Jupiter in the seventh House (open enemies) and opposed to the tenth House (government).

The event chart also has a Gemini Ascendant with the individual in the twelfth house (terrorists, plots) square US Mercury conjunct the Uranus (bomb) of the event chart. In addition, the Sun of the event chart sets off the unaspected duo of Mars square the US Sun chart, repeating the theme of citizen hostility toward the government.

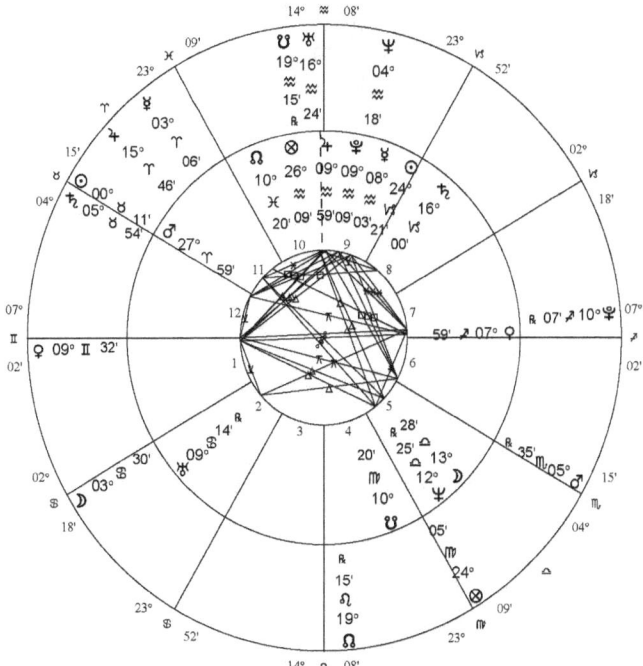

Figure 20-4
US chart/Columbine school shooting April 20, 1999, 11:19 AM;
Littleton, CO

Gun violence continued to be an issue. The 1999 Columbine shooting was, at the time, "the worst high school shooting in U.S. history and prompted a national debate on gun control and school safety." After they placed bombs in the cafeteria that failed to explode, the two teen perpetrators entered the school and began shooting. They killed a teacher and 12 students, wounded 20 others, then killed themselves. More severe school shootings were to follow in later years.[21]

The Moon in Cancer, which rules the third house of schools in the US chart, also rules the ascendant of the event chart and falls in its twelfth house of terrorists and secret plots. It also is in range of the US Uranus setting off the Yod. The event chart Mars (anger) is opposing Saturn (restriction) which illustrates this has been brewing for some time, taking students (Mercury) as victims (Neptune) to satisfy these two disturbed teens' need for revenge. The gun control issue has continued to make its face known over time and is part of the US Yod under the ruler Pluto (death, crime, murder, and suicide).

The "Good Decade"- The 90s

The (mostly) "good times" of the '90s rolled away and the period of the 2000s followed, but now with more terrorists, wars, recessions, and President George W. Bush.

CHAPTER TWENTY NOTES

1. https://en.wikipedia.org/wiki/1990s_United_States_boom *Accessed 5/11/2023*
2. http://www.cbo.gov/sites/default/files/cbofiles/attachments/43904-Historical%20Budget%20Data-corrected.pdf *Accessed 6/21/2023*
3. https://en.wikipedia.org/wiki/1990s *Accessed 5/11/2023*
4. Holland, Gini: *America in the 20th Century – 1990s*; Marshall Cavendish Corp., N.Y., 1995
5. https://en.wikipedia.org/wiki/Gulf_War *Accessed 6/21/2023*
6. Anderson, Dale: *America in the 20th Century – 1990-1999*; Marshall Cavendish Corp.,N. Y., 2003. p. 1375
7. Ibid. p. 1420
8. Ibid. p. 1425
9. https://news.gallup.com/poll/4111/clinton-receives-record-high-job-approval-rating-after-impeachment-vot.aspx *Accessed 6/21/2023*
10. https://www.pbs.org/wgbh/americanexperience/features/clinton-legacy/ *Accessed 5/11/2023*
11. Ibid.
12. Holland, Gini: *America in the 20th Century – 1990s*; p. 1434
13. https://en.wikipedia.org/wiki/Violence_Against_Women_Act *Accessed 6/21/2023*
14. Holland, Gini: *America in the 20th Century – 1990s*; p.1321
15. https://www.history.com/topics/1990s/the-los-angeles-riots/ *Accessed 5/10/2023*
16. Ibid.
17. Ibid.
18. https://history.com/news/world-trade-center-bombing-1993-facts *Accessed 5/20/2023*
19. https://www.history.com/topics/1990s/oklahoma-city-bombing *Accessed 5/14/2023*
20. https://en.wikipedia.org/wiki/Oklahoma_City_Bombing *Accessed 5/23/2023*
21. https://www.history.com/topics/1990s/columbine-high-school-

shootings_ Accessed 5/23/2023

Chapter Twenty-One

The New Millennium

"A Few Words in the Defense of Our Country"
Randy Newman

The year 2000 started out with a joke called the Y2K "bug." Computers utilized a two-digit format for the year before 2000. If "00" was interpreted as 1900 instead of 2000, worldwide digital catastrophe might occur. Anticipating a computer apocalypse, frightened Americans hoarded guns, water, and food. But programmers had worked on the issue for years. Came the dawn of the New Year and nothing happened. It was a big hoax, cried Americans, as they heaved a sigh of relief.[1]

What happened at the end of the year wasn't so funny. The 2000 election was close, and results in Florida, the state determining the final electoral vote, needed a recount. "Hanging chads" seemed to have blurred the results. The US Supreme Court stopped the Florida count, giving the election to George W. Bush, despite Albert Gore having won the popular vote. This was the fourth time in the history of America that the popular vote loser became president.[2]

What did George Bush's inauguration bring to the United States? Examine the chart below.

Although the Sun here is in Aquarius, both rulers, Saturn and Uranus, are in Capricorn. Bush was considered a very conservative Republican with strong ties to the Evangelical movement (Neptune in Capricorn between both Saturn and Venus). Natally, Bush has a Gemini Sun which falls in the US chart's first house, giving him a strong identification with the United States but not as a "man of the people." He called himself a "doer, a decider, a provoker, a charger,"[3] not an academic or a self-reflec-

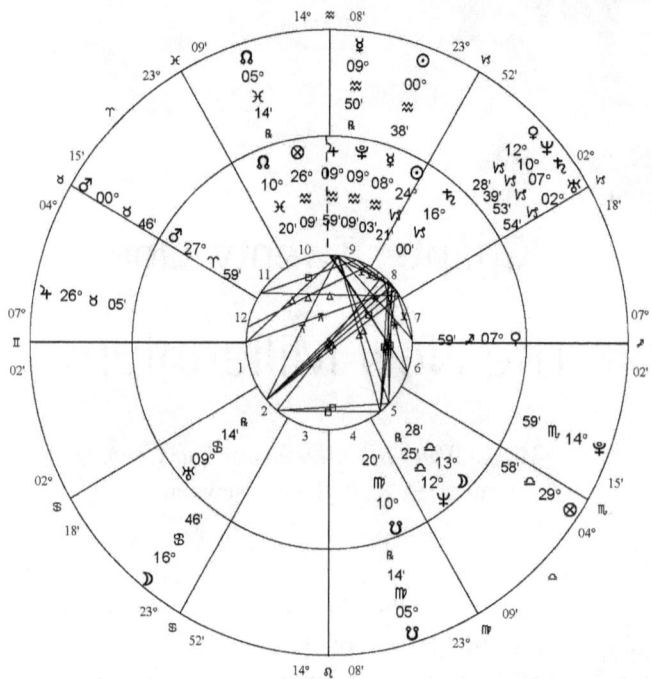

Figure 21-1
US chart/George Bush inauguration January 20, 1989; 12:00 PM, Washington, DC

tor. He wanted to know the point of something, not the details. He also didn't like surprises. He was an optimist, believing "I've never run a race where I thought I wouldn't win."[4]

Although he didn't like surprises, Bush's presidency was shaped by several of them during his two terms: the 9/11 terrorist attack on the New York Trade Center; the start of an unending war in Afghanistan; the devastation of Hurricane Katrina in Florida; a war in Iraq that didn't end as soon as he thought it would; and lastly, a deadly recession, the worst since the Great Depression.

There went the big government surplus!

In the chart you can see the evidence by the heavy Capricorn stellium in the eighth house (international finance) draining the second house finances, opposing Cancer Moon which is also opposite the US Saturn. Broad tax cuts plus fighting two wars led to annual budget deficits starting in 2002.

Bush considered himself a "compassionate conservative" who promoted a "responsibility era" in response to the "boomer" generation which he equated with self-indulgence.[5] The 9/11 attack surprised him, but he quickly charged into action and invaded Afghanistan, where the Taliban government was harboring Osama Bin Ladin, leader of the terrorist group Al Qaeda, responsible for the attack. He declared a global "war on terrorism" by establishing the Department of Homeland Security. America supported him and his popularity grew.[6]

Worldwide sympathy poured into America, supporting the US attack against Afghanistan. But George Bush did not stop there- his next goal was Iraq. His father had chased Saddam Hussein out of Kuwait in 1991 during the first Gulf War. Iraqi intelligence later attempted to assassinate him. The younger Bush resented this action. Although he publicly supported his father's decision not to make war with Iraq, he told a friend, "Dad made a mistake not going into Iraq when he had an approval rating in the nineties."[7]

Notice that Mars is conjunct the US Mars which triggers the unaspected duet of Sun and Mars. Mercury is conjunct the US Pluto which allows him to use manipulation to carry out his goals regarding the country. The attack on 9/11 set off a string of events that finally led to the invasion of Iraq, the first time the United States took preemptive action against another country.

The president saw connections between Afghanistan and Iraq. Hussein, he was sure, supported terrorists like Al Qaeda. Hussein also refused to have inspectors monitor his country for atomic bomb production. Bush had support from his inner circle, including Vice President Cheney, and the fever began to grow. Bush failed to get a UN mandate, but Congress passed a resolution giving him the right to use force against Iraq. It was believed that the Iraqi people would welcome the troops and freedom from a brutal regime.[8] President Bush informed the nation of the invasion on March 19, 2003 as Baghdad skies were filled with a barrage of missiles. "My fellow citizens, at this hour, American and coalition forces are in the early stages of military operations to disarm Iraq, to free its people and to defend the world from grave danger."[9]

Examine the chart of this announcement, which started a war lasting eight years. Although the US defeated Hussein in six weeks, it was not prepared for the insurgent backlash, Iraqis angered by US occupation, and later civil war between two Muslim sects. The war finally ended under President Obama on December 15, 2011.[10] The opposition of Saturn to Pluto had been going on since the 9/11 attack across the 1st/7th

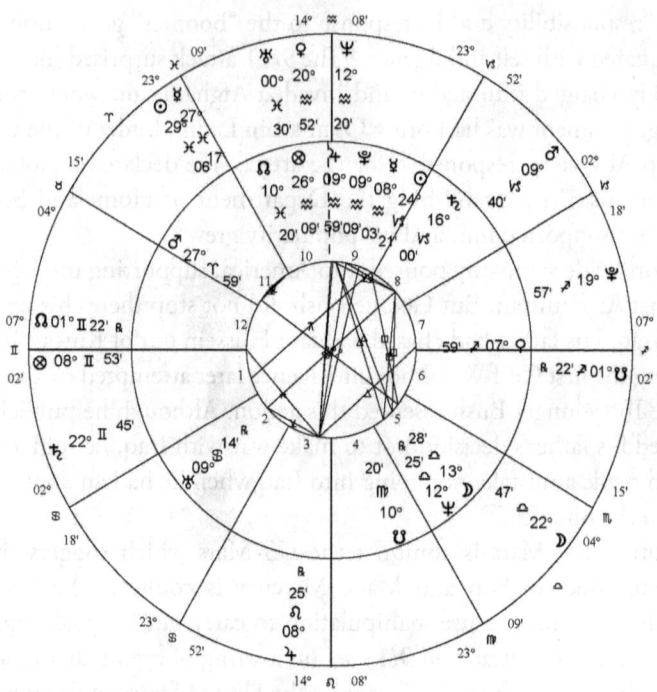

Figure 21-2
US chart/Iraq war announcement March 19, 2003, 10:05 PM, Washington, DC

House Axis, connecting these two events.

The enemy strikes us (Pluto in the seventh) and we retaliate (Saturn in the first). The Moon (the people) supports this action, opposing US Mars while trining Saturn. Another strong opposition between Mars and the US Uranus sets off the planets of the Yod. The natal Mercury and Pluto are opposed by Jupiter in Leo in the third house and show the subterfuge being used on both sides in an obsessional way, as Neptune hovers over the Pluto/Mercury conjunction. This configuration taken together demonstrates Bush's total belief in what he is announcing, regardless of the opposition of any other point of view, including those of the UN, France, Spain, and Russia.

Another significant point is the transiting North Node over the US Ascendant, beginning a new cycle and bringing karmic issues from the past. Many Muslims likened the invasion/occupation to the Crusades, with Christians intruding on their land to alter their way of life and beliefs. The growing insurgence in Iraq seemed to reflect that view.[11] A major transition often coincides with this movement of the North Node through the first house, but takes time to play out.

A presidential election occurred during the Iraq War, with Senator John Kerry, a Democrat, running against Bush. The war dragged on with no end in sight and continuing American casualties. No evidence for WMDs had been found. Such issues dominated the highly contested campaign. Debate also focused on the US role in the international com-

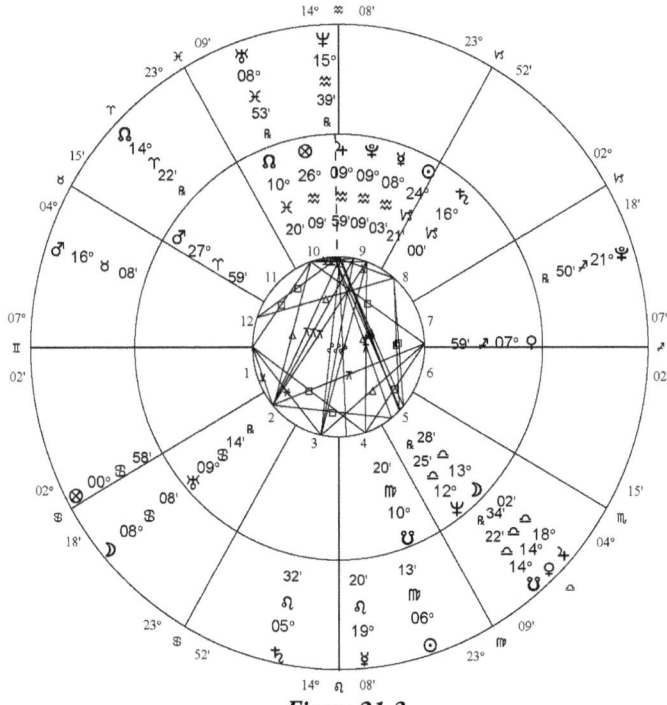

Figure 21-3
US chart/George Bush inauguration January 20, 1989; 12:00 PM; Washington, DC

munity, religion, abortion, gay rights, and civil rights- recurring issues related to the US Yod. Bush won the election by a short margin, 50.7 percent of the vote.[12]

Another surprise hit President Bush during his long vacation after the war. One of the worst natural disasters in US history, Hurricane Katrina, hit the Gulf Coast on the morning of August 29, 2005. Bush had isolated himself from the country, but his aides finally alerted him to the catastrophe. He left for the White House on August 31, but refused to

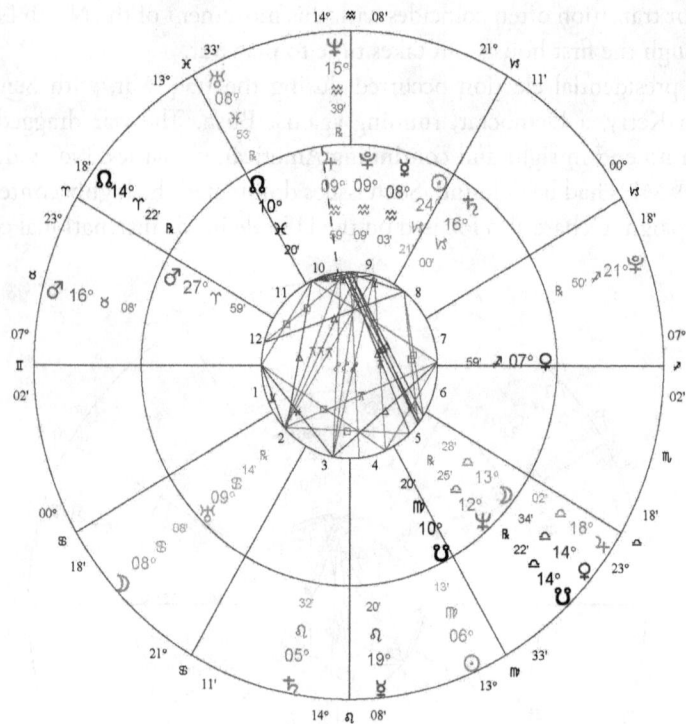

Figure 21-4
*US chart/Hurricane Katrina, August 29, 2005, 6:10 AM,
Baton Rouge, LA*

visit the site, saying he didn't want to disrupt the rescue efforts. Bush's slow reaction plus the weak governmental response to the crisis undermined his reputation as a decisive leader and crisis manager. Although he made several visits to the area and spent billions of federal dollars for recovery, his popularity dropped. It was clear he and FEMA had done an inept job of responding, and the public blamed him.[13]

The chart shows the event Moon (the people) conjunct the US Uranus (crisis in loss of money, assets, and homes) plus the transiting Uranus (hurricane) square to the Ascendant (the nation) plus opposite the Sun in the fourth house. Saturn in the third house shows the delay in communication (opposite Mercury) and the resistance of the public to what Bush had to say. In addition, the Saturn (levees) is opposite Pluto (destruction) which was revealed by the Army Corps' investigation that "the levees failed due to flawed and outdated engineering practices used to build them."[14]

Katrina widened public awareness of the particularly severe effect on the poor and the black population of New Orleans, who were stranded in the city with no way out. Water covered New Orleans for weeks, resulting in 1392 deaths and billions of dollars in damage.[15] This awakened a new conversation about an old issue, poverty and race and the need for solutions. But the conversation died out within the year.[16]

TIME LINE 2000-2009[17]

1. 2000: George W. Bush certified president by Supreme Court after presidential election results inconclusive.

2. 2001: 9/11 terrorist attack on the Twin Towers in NYC and elsewhere with more than 3000 killed; United States invades Afghanistan; Patriot Act passed to enhance law enforcement counterterrorism abilities and resources; legislation passed to cut taxes significantly; educational reform bill (No Child Left Behind) passed.

3. 2002: Bush signs legislation creating the Department of Homeland Security.

4. 2003: Republicans take control of Senate in 2002 elections; invasion of Iraq by US, UK, Australia, and Poland begins; Saddam Hussein is captured.

5. 2004: Massachusetts becomes the first state to legalize same-sex marriage; Ronald Reagan dies; Facebook is launched; Bush elected for second term.

6. 2005: Hurricane Katrina devastates Louisiana, Mississippi, and Alabama.

7. 2006: Democrats take control of both houses of Congress.

8. 2007: Nancy Pelosi becomes first woman Speaker of the House; Bush orders huge troop surge to Iraq; Virginia Tech Massacre – 32 students and professors shot – spurs gun control debates; first IPhone comes out; recession officially begins in December.

9. 2008: Hurricane Ike kills 100 people in Texas; oil prices hit a record high; global financial crisis begins as stock market crashes; Bush signs legislation to buy failing bank assets.

10. 2009: First Black American, Barack Obama, is elected president; Tea Party becomes established and marches on the Capitol to

United States Bear Market of 2007-2009[22]

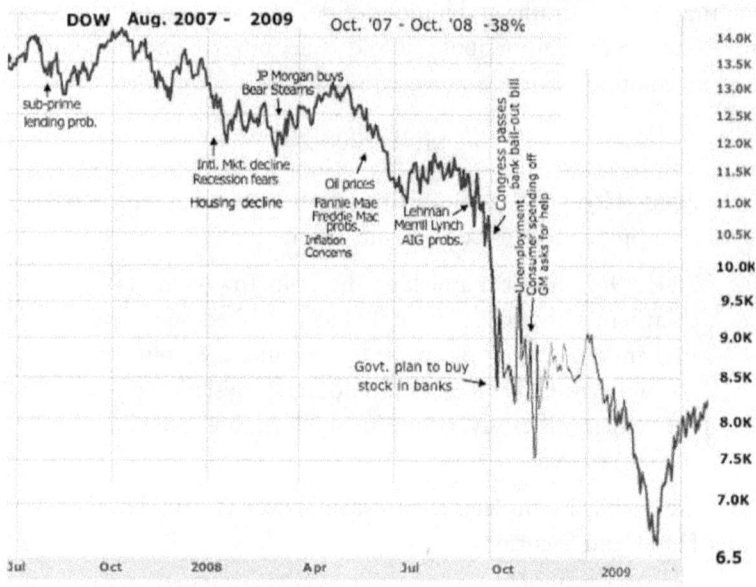

Figure 21-5: Graph of the United States Bear Market of 2007 — 2009

demonstrate against health care reform.

The last surprise for President Bush was the fourth quarter 2007 onset of the Great Recession beginning with a housing bubble burst. The Glass-Steagall Act of 1933, which prevented commercial banks from using depositors' money for investment activities, was partially repealed in 1999, eliminating those restrictions. Banks then pursued more risky activities that included subprime lending,[18] which "enabled banks to issue mortgage loans at lower interest rates to millions of customers who normally would not have qualified for them."[19]

Home prices fell as interest rates began to climb, resulting in mortgage loans costing more than the houses themselves. Banks increased foreclosures. Millions of people lost their homes, jobs, and savings. The financial crisis spread globally. It is estimated that households sustained a 26 percent loss in net worth during the crisis. By the end of the recession, the richest had recovered their losses, but many in the other classes did not and would remain poorer than previous generations. Awareness

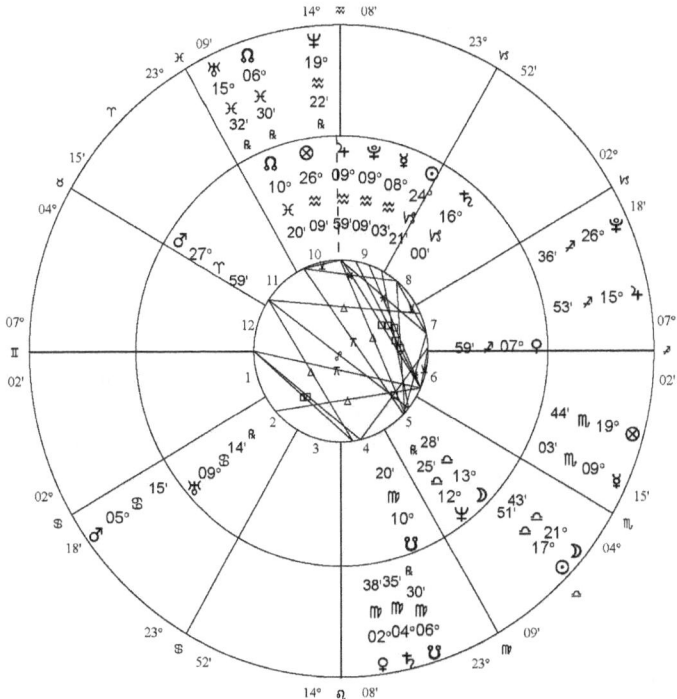

Figure 21-6
US chart/Stock Market crash of 2007

of economic inequality in America drew a lot of public resentment.[20] The median net worth of families in the top 20 percent increased by 13 percent between 2007 and 2016, whereas it dropped by at least 20 percent in the lower 80 percent.[21] The next chart denotes the beginning of the bear market of 2007 to 2009, known now as the Great Recession. The stock market reached an intra-day peak on October 11, 2007, and started its rapid decline thereafter. A record-breaking drop occurred September 29, 2008, then a market low March 6, 2009. The value lost between the peak and low dates was 54 percent. The market rebounded thereafter.[23] It is important to note the continuing wealth gap that increased divisiveness in the following decades.

The first thing to notice is Saturn's exact conjunction to the South Node in the fourth house of the US Chart (the land and the common people), plus it is also conjunct Venus on the other side. Note a strong opposition to the government (tenth house), as well as a double dose of Saturn as it rules the US eighth house of finances as well as international finances. Mars is transiting Uranus in the second house of the economy, setting off the issues of the Yod, in this case the wealth gap. The government chooses to bail out the big banks and corporations over helping the lower classes with unemployment increases.

Rick Santelli, a CBNC commentator speaking from the Chicago Mercantile Exchange, blamed Obama and the US government for interfering in the housing market. He proposed a Chicago Tea Party protest, which became a rallying cry around the country. The Tea Party movement, a conservative force against newly elected President Obama and the government, was born.[24] Members included "birthers" (who believed Obama was born outside the United States, was also a socialist and a secret Muslim), disaffected Republicans, and the paramilitary. The Tea Party was loosely organized but did have unofficial spokespersons such as Sarah Palin and Glenn Beck. Their influence continued to affect politics into the next decade,[25] and will be discussed further in Chapter Twenty-Two.

This decade was a mixed bag. It started out with a laugh, but disasters followed. By the end of this time, America was broke, poor, confused, and divided. Changes were coming that no one could see as Pluto began to move into Capricorn to deepen the division.

CHAPTER TWENTY-ONE NOTES

1. https://time.com/5752129/y2k-bug-history/ *Accessed: 5/24/2023*
2. https://www.historycentral.com/elections/2000.html *Accessed: 5/24/2023*
3. Draper, Robert: *Dead Certain – The Presidency of George W. Bush*; Simon & Schuster, Inc., New York, NY, 2007. p. 7
4. Ibid. p. x
5. Ibid. p. 6
6. https://www.history.com/topics/us-presidents/george-w-bush *Accessed: 5/24/2023*
7. Draper, Robert: *Dead Certain – The Presidency of George W. Bush*; pp. 172-173
8. Ibid. Chapter 8
9. https://english.elpais.com/international/2023-03-20/operation-iraqi-freedom-20-years-since-the-war-that-undermined-us-credibility.html *Accessed: 6/4/2023*
10. https://en.wikipedia.org/wiki/IraqWar *Accessed 6/18/2023*
11. Iraq War Raises Suspicion of New 'Crusade' - ABC News (go.com) *Accessed 6/18/2023*
12. 2004 United States presidential election - Wikipedia *Accessed 6/18/2023*
13. Hurricane Katrina Was the Beginning of the End for George W. Bush (usnews.com) *Accessed: 6/5/2023*
14. https://www.history.com/news/hurricane-katrina-levee-failures *Accessed: 6/5/2023*
15. https://en.wikipedia.org/wiki/Hurricane_Katrina *Accessed 6/18/2023*
16. What Katrina Taught Us About Race : NPR *Accessed 6/5/2023*
17. Timeline of United States history (1990–2009) - Wikipedia *Accessed: 6/6/2023*
18. https://www.investopedia.com/articles/03/071603.asp *Accessed 6/18/2023*
19. https://www.britannica.com/topic/great-recession *Accessed: 6/7/2023*
20. https://www.britannica.com/money/topic/financial-crisis-

of-2007-2008 *Accessed: 6/7/2023*
21. 6 facts about economic inequality in the U.S. | Pew Research Center *Accessed: 6/18/2023*
22. 2008-09 Recession (donsnotes.com) *Accessed: 6/16/2023*
23. United States bear market of 2007–2009 - Wikipedia *Accessed: 6/7/2023*
24. https://washingtonmonthly.com/2021/02/19/the-tea-party-began-12-years-ago-whats-changed-and-what-hasnt/ *Accessed: 6/6/2023*
25. https://www.britannica.com/topic/Tea-Party-Movement *Accessed: 6/6/2023*

Chapter Twenty-Two

The Turning Point Decade - The Obama Years

"A Change is Gonna Come"
Sam Cooke

Although the decade opened with a deepening recession and anxiety, Barack Obama's election brought hope that the American dream could be reclaimed. The ascent of a Black man to the presidency had seemed improbable, but now this achievement seemed to promise that America was entering a new realm of possibilities. Examine the chart of his inauguration and the response his presidency elicited in America.

The first thing to notice is that Pluto has entered Capricorn for the first time and will continue until November 20, 2024, when it makes its final entry into Aquarius to stay for some time. For the next fifteen years, Pluto will slowly move through Capricorn like an unstoppable bulldozer, tearing at our roots, turning up major issues we tried to keep covered, and revealing corruption we don't want to acknowledge. The purpose of Pluto's visit through Capricorn is to force us to look at all our traditions and structures, both political and cultural, that have been rotting away underneath. Pluto's journey, like a thorough spring cleaning, brings dust and turmoil, leaving us confused, anxious, and angry. But its ultimate purpose is to clear the way so that something better can be established. We have seen previous paradigm shifts caused by Pluto in times past (see Prologue) when the major authorities and cultures have been transformed.

Another important transit to the US chart which adds power to Plu-

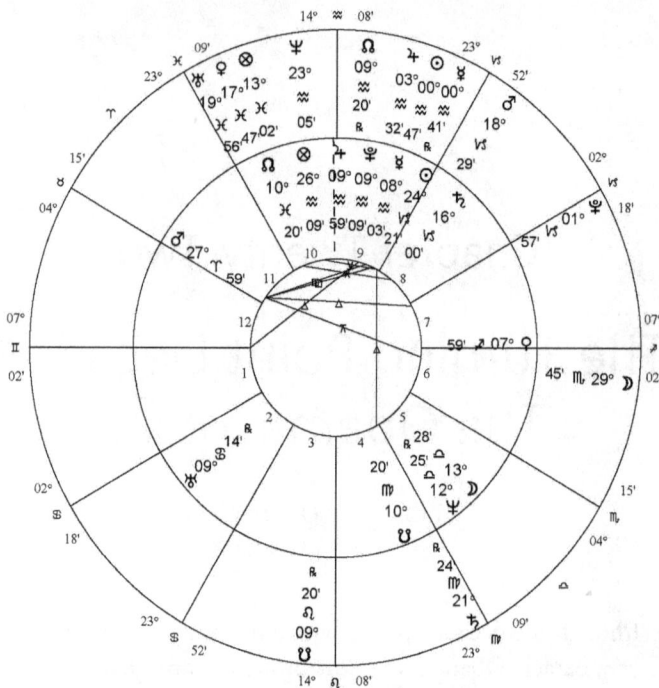

Figure 22-1: *Inner wheel: US chart/ Treaty of Paris*
Outer wheel: Barack Obama inauguration, January 20, 2009, 12:00 PM;
Washington, DC

to's transit into Capricorn is the North Node (in Aquarius) conjunct the US Pluto in the upper leg of the Yod, which suggests large scale changes in society that do not have to be violent. The shift comes from the individual (Leo) to the group (Aquarius). From the "me" to the "we." Division may give way to cooperation for the betterment of all.

The oppositions of transiting Saturn and Uranus across the 4th/10th House axis echo the Axis of Awareness of the US Chart, which will increase the divisiveness between the status quo and the forces for change as it did before our Revolution. Even today talk of revolution or Civil War echoes of state secession have returned. Things will become clearer as we go through this decade and into the next. It's important to remember that long time cycles, like Pluto's, repeat some of the themes of the past but never in the same way. Evolution performs like a spiral formation, but the motion, hopefully, is upward to higher levels.

TIME LINE OF EVENTS UNDER OBAMA[1]

1. 2009: First bill signed promotes fair pay regardless of sex, race, or age; Hillary Clinton appointed Sec. of State; Obama wins the Nobel Peace Prize; Recovery Act passed.
2. 2010: Dodd-Frank Wall Street Reform Act; Affordable Health Care Act passed.
3. 2011: Obama signs nuclear arms reduction treaty with Russia; Obama signs legislation to repeal "Don't ask, don't tell"act;[2] Occupy Wall Street demonstration.[3]
4. 2012: Obama announces support for same-sex marriage; Obama elected for 2nd term; Sandy Hook Massacre.
5. 2013: Obama announces proposals for gun control; he addresses the Trayvon Martin shooting.
6. 2014: Obama announces US to restore full relations with Cuba.
7. 2015: Obama participates in UN Climate Change Conference in Paris; Supreme Court legalizes gay marriage;[4] treaty with Iran and other powers including US, relieves sanctions against Iran for ending their nuclear program and admitting inspectors.[5]
8. 2016: Obama announces Merrick Garland as his Supreme Court nominee, but Senate refuses to hold hearings for him in order to wait for the next president;[6] Obama endorses Hillary Clinton for president; Trump is elected and GOP narrowly retains majorities in both houses.

The next chart to examine is that of the Tea Party, a conservative movement that developed in response to perceived government overreach. Resentment about government bailout loans to banks initiated during the George W. Bush administration and extended by Obama exploded with passage of Obama's expensive economic stimulus package.[7]

Rick Santelli, a CNBC reporter, set off the firestorm with a "rant" you can view on YouTube.[8] Referring to "losers" who lost their homes because of banks' shaky loans, he declared, "The government is rewarding bad behavior!"[9] He questioned why taxpayer money was being used to bail out these losers and suggested that American capitalists come to a Chicago Tea Party.[10] The tirade was widely televised and conservatives were quick to use it as a cry to rally others. "We need to take our country back" became the theme for people while marching in protest.[11]

The movement spread. Its diverse membership included evangelical

Christians, anti-abortionists, Libertarians[12] and people concerned with immigration, welfare programs for the poor, and entitled young people that Tea Partiers considered "undeserving freeloaders."[13] Major billionaires who didn't like government regulations were eager to support candidates with connections to the Tea Party. In many ways, the grassroots activism of initial members- generally older white conservative citizens- was eventually commandeered by large ultra-free-market organizations and conservative media.[14]

Proposal of the Affordable Care Act (ACA) further enraged the Tea Party against Obama. A new rallying cry, about the ACA's alleged "death panels," brought Tea Party supporters into town halls shouting down any Democratic lawmakers considering ACA passage.[15] Racial divisions accelerated after it passed, many whites believing it benefited Blacks more than it did whites. How much of the division relates to white backlash against an African American president is unclear.[16]

Tea Party influence was demonstrated in the 2010 midterm election.

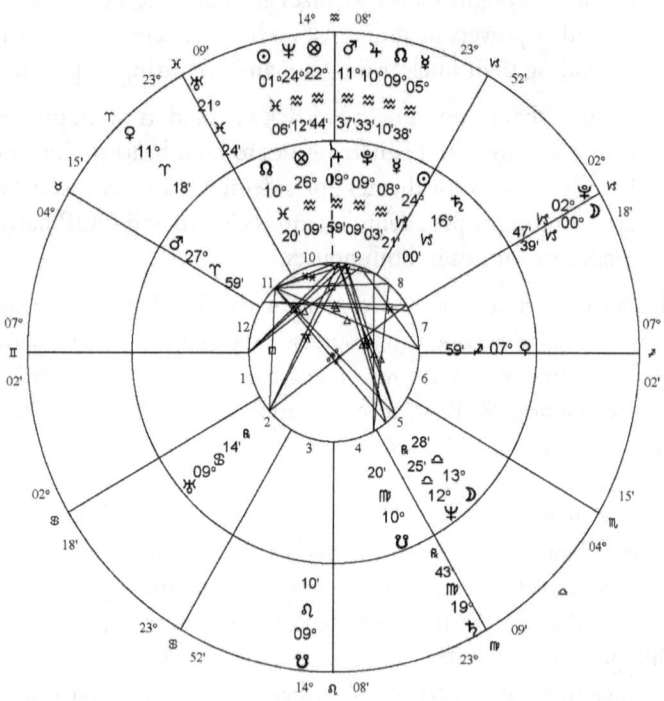

Figure 22-2: Inner wheel: US chart/ Treaty of Paris
Outer wheel: Tea Party begins February 19, 2009; 8:45 AM; Chicago, IL

204   An Astrological Journey of the United States

Republicans took over the House of Representatives, gained six Senate seats, and won numerous state legislatures and governorships.[17] In addition, an ideological shift to the right occurred among Republicans that continued throughout Obama's term, with 77 percent of the newcomers further right than previous Congressional members.[18]

In the above chart, Saturn in the fourth house shows this is a grassroots movement in opposition to the government. The Sun in Pisces conjunct its ruler Neptune in the tenth house shows Obama is the target. The Moon/Pluto conjunction in Capricorn brings to the surface emotions reflecting the deepest part of the American psyche, the conflict between a central controlling government and individual/state rights. During the previous cycle in the 1700s, citizen colonists resisted the imposition of a federal government and president that they feared would become tyrannical. The battle between state and federal rights has continued throughout US history and is complicated by issues of immigration, racism, civil rights, economic status, and social support.

The Tea Party represents the surfacing of these deep unresolved conflicts, triggered by the election of a Black man to the presidency. The co-opting of the movement by other groups focused on free market, religious, radical conservative and other issues has further confused the people as to what a government should or should not do. The public (Moon) has embraced Pluto in Capricorn (despots), which will try to crush any efforts toward change (opposite US Uranus) under the banner call of "freedom" and "patriotism." Pluto also points out paramilitary groups such as the Oath Keepers, active in the Tea Party, along with extremists such as members of the John Birch Society.[19]

The next chart highlights the increasing wealth gap between the 99 percent and the top one percent during the Great Recession. Occupy Wall Street, a protest against economic inequality, targeted the financial sector. Barricaded from other areas in New York City by the police, the protestors occupied Zuccotti Park for 58 days with the slogan "We are the 99 percent." The American protest inspired an Occupy movement throughout the world.[20]

The Virgo Mercury (young people and workers) occupies the fourth house of the land opposing the tenth house of the establishment. Because it is conjunct the US South Node, it brings up the issue from the past of a "landed gentry" that Americans insisted did not belong here. Venus opposing Uranus describes the shortness of the protest as well as nature of the protesters- young people seeking justice from financial

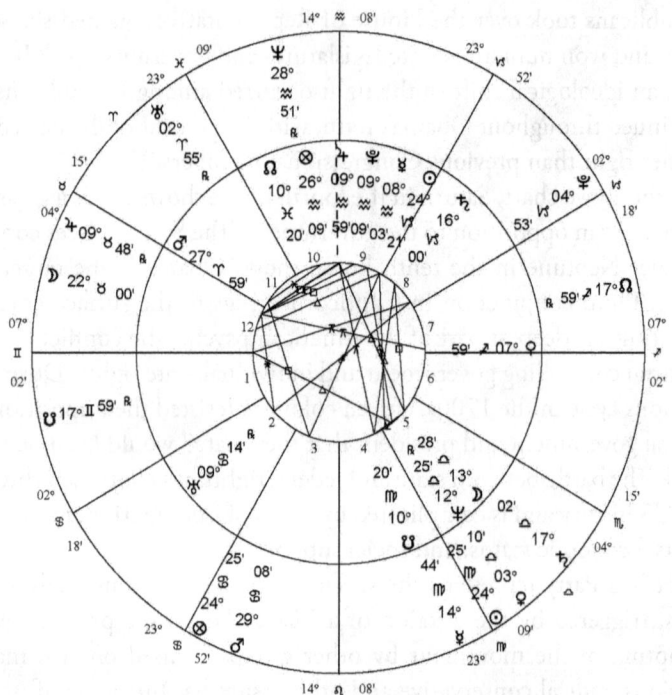

Figure 22-3: Inner wheel: US chart/ Treaty of Paris
Outer wheel: Occupy Wall St September 17, 2011, 12:00 PM; New York, NY

groups because of lack of jobs (square Pluto in Capricorn in the eighth house). Mars in Cancer in the third house (communications) shows the hostile attitude of these groups concerning their financial problems and the need for a living minimum wage. Although the groups disbanded, this attitude persisted, inspiring activism in later elections for a fifteen dollar minimum wage.

Gun control issues were brought to the forefront on December 14, 2012 in Newton, Connecticut. A mass shooting, one of the worst school massacres in American history, took place at Sandy Hook Elementary School. After killing his mother at home, Adam Lanza, the perpetrator, used an AR-15 and 30-round ammunition magazines in the assault, taking his own life afterward. Twenty children and six adults were murdered. Another debate about 2nd Amendment rights was sparked, resulting in a congressional bill to ban such weapons. Despite public support, the bill was defeated in the Senate. The Sandy Hook families sued the gun maker, Remington, and after 8 years they were awarded 73

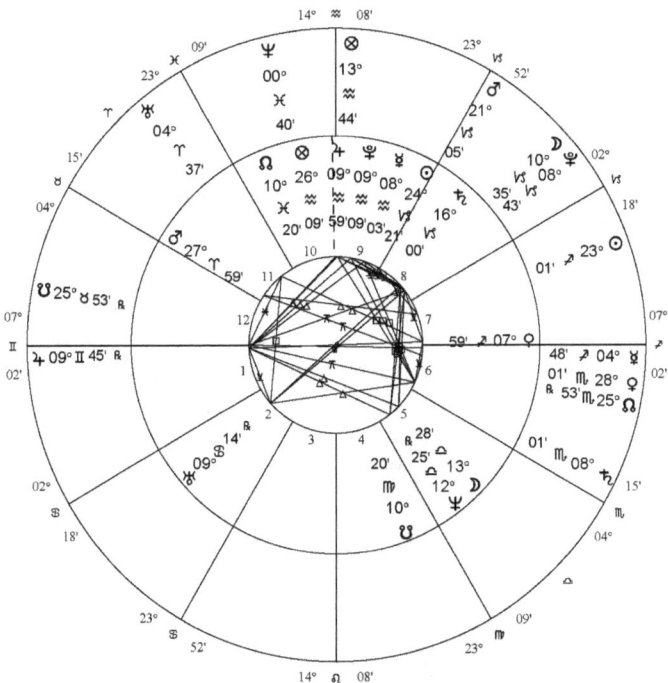

*Figure 22-4: Inner wheel: US chart/ Treaty of Paris
Outer wheel: Sandy Hook massacre, December 14, 2012, 9:30 AM;
Newtown, CT*

million dollars.[21]

In the chart a conjunction of the Moon and Pluto opposes US Uranus, setting off the Yod. The attack was surprising and deadly. The event Mars is conjunct the US Sun, ruler of US fourth house (communities). Jupiter conjunct the US Ascendant (the people) and trine US Pluto (massacres) is brought to conscious awareness so there is public support for change. The pressure for change in gun laws will increase over the next decade along with the increase in mass shootings.

The racism issue was brought to public awareness this decade with the multiple shootings of young Black males. The killing of Trayvon Martin on February 26, 2012 in Sanford, Florida is representative, and notable for the origination of the slogan "Black Lives Matter" and protests across America continuing into the next decade.[22]

Teenaged Trayvon was walking home from his nearby convenience store when he was confronted by a neighborhood watch volunteer. George Zimmerman was patrolling the local community and fatally shot him. Zimmerman was charged with second-degree murder and went to trial. His defense was based on Florida's "stand your ground" law. He also claimed that he was shooting in self-defense during a physical altercation.[23]

Zimmerman was found not guilty in 2013. The acquittal enraged Alicia Garza, an activist who on July 13, 2013 posted the phrase "Black Lives Matter" on social media. The slogan became popular and led to the organization of grassroots protest movements across the country. Although initially Americans did not approve of the movement, public support increased as shootings continued in the ensuing years.[24]

The time on this chart comes from a resource that states: "An officer

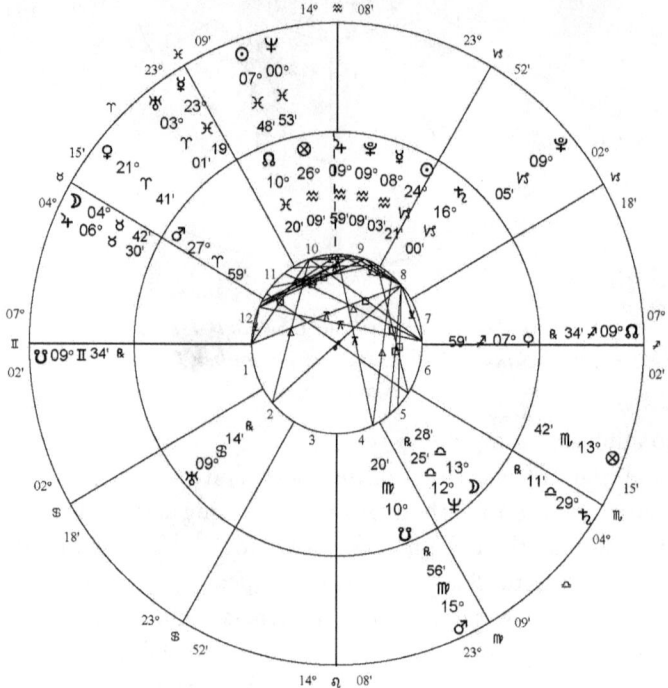

Figure 22-5: Inner wheel: US chart/ Treaty of Paris
Outer wheel: Trayvon Martin shooting, February 26, 2012, 7:00 PM;
Sanford, FL

arrived on the scene at 7:17 p.m. He found Martin dead and Zimmerman on the ground..."[25]

In the chart, Pluto is beginning a long transit opposing US Uranus, releasing powerful emotional forces from the US collective unconscious

(Moon conjunct Jupiter in the twelfth house) related to the Axis of Awareness (change versus the status quo) and the issues of the Yod which need recognition and healing. At the same time, the event chart's Uranus is moving into a square to transiting Pluto to transform all worn-out structures into something new. It may take some time because Pluto moves so slowly, but eventually it will transit all the planets in Capricorn and Aquarius, including the Midheaven. Pluto demands change, whether we like it or not, so "Fasten your seatbelts; it's going to be a bumpy ride!" Who can surmise what is waiting on the other side?

Further racism-related deaths throughout the decade kept the issue in public awareness: Eric Garner in 2014, Michael Brown a month later, Tamir Rice three months after that, Freddie Gray in 2015, nine churchgoers in South Carolina in 2015, Sandra Bland's suicide in a jail cell following a traffic-stop arrest a month later. Black Lives Matter protests continued to grow.[26]

This chapter has covered the Obama presidency and some of the events during his two terms. The next chapter will cover the Trump years and events of his one term.

CHAPTER TWENTY-TWO NOTES

1. https://en.wikipedia.org/wiki/Timeline_of_the_Barack_Obama_Presidency Accessed 6/17/2023
2. https://www.britannica.com/event/Dont-Ask-Dont-Tell Accessed 8/18/2023
3. https://www.britannica.com/topic/Occupy-Wall-Street Accessed 6/17/2023
4. https://www.hrw.org/news/2015/06/26/us-supreme-court-upholds-same-sex-marriage Accessed 8/18/2023
5. https://www.cfr.org/backgrounder/what-iran-nuclear-deal Accessed 8/18/2023
6. https://en.wikipedia.org/wiki/Merrick_Garland_Supreme_Court_nomination Accessed 8/18/2023
7. Skocpol, Theda & Williamson, Vanessa: *The Tea Party and the Remaking of Republican Conservatism*; Oxford University Press, New York, New York, 2012. pp. 6-7
8. CNBC's Rick Santelli's Chicago Tea Party - YouTube Accessed 8/18/2023
9. Skocpol, Theda & Williamson, Vanessa: *The Tea Party and the Remaking of Republican Conservatism*; p. 7
10. https://washingtonmonthly.com/2021/02/19/The-Tea-Party-began-12-years-ago-whats-changed-and-what-hasnt/ Accessed 6/16/2023
11. Skocpol, Theda & Williamson, Vanessa: *The Tea Party and the Remaking of Republican Conservatism*; p. 7
12. Ibid. pp. 35-36
13. Ibid. pp. 68, 72
14. Ibid. pp. 83-89
15. How False Claims Of Obamacare 'Death Panels' Stuck With The President : NPR Accessed 6/16/2023
16. https://washingtonmonthly.com/2021/02/19/The-Tea-Party-began-12-years-ago-whats-changed-and-what-hasnt/ Accessed 6/16/2023
17. Skocpol, Theda & Williamson, Vanessa: *The Tea Party and the Remaking of Republican Conservatism*; p. 4
18. Ibid. p 170

19. Ibid. p. 33
20. https://www.britannica.com/topic/Occupy-Wall-Street *Accessed 6/17/2023*
21. https://www.britannica.com/event/Sandy-Hook-Elementary-School-shooting *Accessed 6/17/2023*
22. https://www.history.com/this-day-in-history/florida-teen-trayvon-martin-is-shot-and-killed *Accessed 6/17/2023*
23. Ibid.
24. Ibid.
25. https://www.biography.com/crime/trayvon-martin *Accessed 6/18/2023*
26. https://www.pewresearch.org/internet/2016/08/15/the-hashtag-blacklivesmatter-emerges-social-activism-on-twitter/ *Accessed 6/18/2023*

Chapter Twenty-Three

The Turning Point Decade – The Trump Years

"We're Not Gonna Take It"
Twisted Sister

Donald J. Trump won the 2016 election with electoral but not popular votes after a turbulent campaign against Hillary Clinton. The Great Recession had resolved under Obama and prosperity had increased as Trump assumed leadership. The populist new president projected himself as "the only one who can fix it" to voters angry at the establishment for troubles incurred during the preceding economic downturn. He was welcomed by Tea Party members, militia groups, evangelicals, and white supremacists as their new icon: a leader who spoke their language and sympathized with their lot. They saw him as one of them.

The Trump administration was a pivotal time. During this period, underlying unresolved conflicts represented by the Yod and present since the Revolution continued to become more apparent, resulting in increased polarization and violence. Progressive changes were met with regressive backlash, in a futile attempt to return to an imagined ideal time of stability, peace, happiness, and economic prosperity. Such issues as states' rights vs federal control, immigration, and civil rights of Blacks, women, LGBTQ groups, and other minorities became center stage.

Examine the inauguration chart for clues to Trump's presidency.

Many interesting points are to be made here. First, Neptune in the event chart is conjunct the US North Node in the tenth house of government administration. Is Trump here to move the country forward? In a way. Also note that the event chart shows that the Nodes are in reversal, which

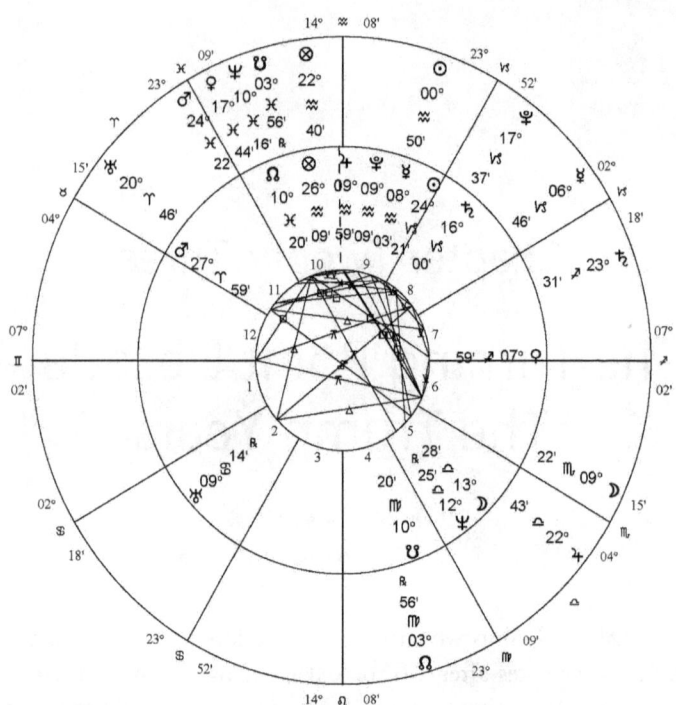

Figure 23-1
US chart/Trump inauguration, January 20, 2017, 12:00 PM, Washington, DC

indicates an opportunity to work out ancestral karma or past mistakes (especially in the 4th/10th axis). Our collective unconscious issues will be presented to us to deal with during the next nine-year cycle. Transiting Pluto will be conjunct the US Saturn which is the reaction point of the Axis of Awareness in the Yod. This indicates a stressful period in which our values as Americans will be tested and transformed. It may also signify a national death and rebirth.

The Scorpio Moon in the house of health is square the US Pluto in the ninth house suggesting the appearance of a foreign virus which will bring devastation and death in its wake. Jupiter in the event chart in the fifth house makes a T-Square with the opposition to the US Mars and square the US Sun. This shows that a lot of enthusiasm is brought to the office but not a lot of discipline.

Uranus in the event chart in Aries (conjunct US Mars) also suggests erratic governance since it rules all the Aquarian planets and the energy of transiting Pluto provides secrecy as well as control seeking. In addition, Uranus opposes Mercury in the US chart implying there will be changes in the way things are usually done. Saturn transiting the seventh house brings tensions in foreign relations. The last thing to note is the square in the event chart between Mars in Pisces square Saturn in Sagittarius in the seventh. This contributes tension to his presidency due to restrictions from others as Trump struggles to achieve his goals.

After an election, the new president usually tries to unify the country. Not so with Trump. He delivered a populist, dark description of America filled with crime, empty factories, illegal immigration, and drug lords. He promised that "From this moment on, it's going to be America first." He painted his administration as one which would transfer the power of Washington over to the people.[1] Ironically, the persons most benefiting from the preceding economic downturn were Trump and his cabinet composed of numerous billionaires, unlikely to compromise their own wealth for the supporters who voted them in.[2]

The Women's March on Washington took place on January 21, 2017,

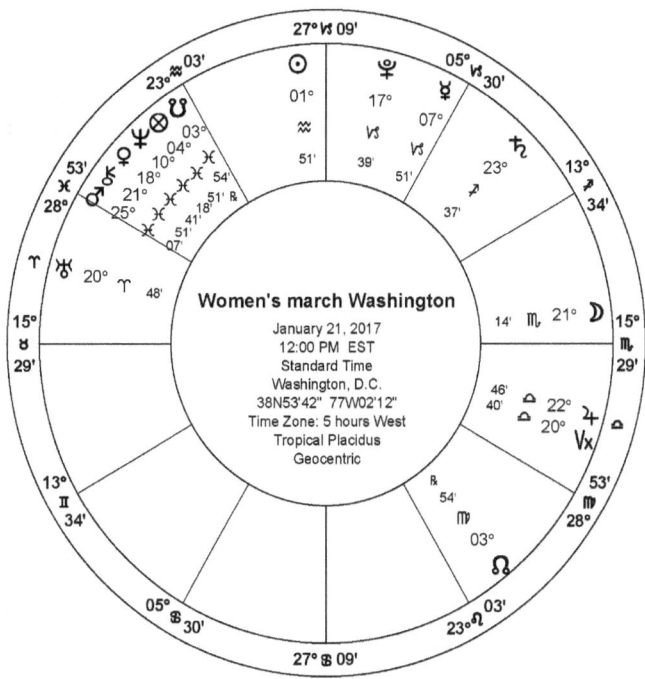

Figure 23-2
Women's March on Washington, January 21, 2017,
12:00 PM, Washington, DC

the day after Trump's inauguration. Prompted by his threat to women's rights, between 3 and 5 million participants attended marches across the country. Over 7 million people worldwide engaged in marches in 81 countries. The primary march in Washington DC drew around 500,000 people and had much news media coverage.[3]

A precise time was not available, so noon was used for the event chart. According to the organizers' website, the goal of the march was to "send a bold message to our new administration on their first day in office, and to the world that women's rights are human rights."[4] It was also promoted as an event supporting other human rights issues encompassing immigration, race, ethnicity, religion, and healthcare.[5]

The strong message (ruler of the 3rd House) comes from the Moon in Scorpio in the seventh house of women's affairs. The Moon is trine a conjunction of Venus and Mars to Chiron. This illuminates one of the US issues from the twelfth house of the collective unconscious that is a call to action and a shared expression of feelings for women's rights. The opposition of Jupiter expands the movement globally. The message is intended for the new administration, the Sun in the tenth house of government.

Immediately after his inauguration, Trump began reversing policies initiated by President Obama. On that very day, he announced his plan to repeal the Affordable Care Act and replace it with "something better."[6] On January 27, he signed an executive order that became known as the Muslim Ban, reducing the number of refugees allowed into the US and suspending immigration from several Muslim countries.[7] He appointed Neil Gorsuch to the Supreme Court on January 31, filling the seat that Senator Mitch McConnell had kept open during the Obama administration.[8]

Environmental protections took a hit starting in June as Trump announced withdrawal from the Paris Climate Agreement, an international accord to reduce greenhouse gases, and later that year reversed several climate change mitigation policies that Obama had initiated.[9] He aimed to defund Obama's Clean Power Act and to lift the ban of coal leases on federal lands.[10]

Trump's first big legislative achievement was the Tax Cuts and Jobs Act of 2017, which amended the IRS Code of 1986.[11] It included the largest corporate tax rate cut in history.[12] His appointment of another two conservative prolife justices to the Supreme Court, Brett Kavanaugh in 2018 and Amy Coney Barrett in 2020,[13] profoundly altered the political direction of the country. In May 2018, he withdrew from the Iran Nuclear Deal,[14] reversing carefully negotiated foreign policy.

Immigration became a major issue during Trump's administration. In addition to the Muslim Ban, Trump introduced 472 executive actions that reduced humanitarian protections, made it harder for immigrants to enter the country legally, initiated historic border restrictions, attempted to rescind the Deferred Action for Childhood Arrivals (DACA) program, and introduced sweeping changes in the agencies responsible for immigration enforcement.[15]

The most criticized action was the "Zero Tolerance" policy, which im-

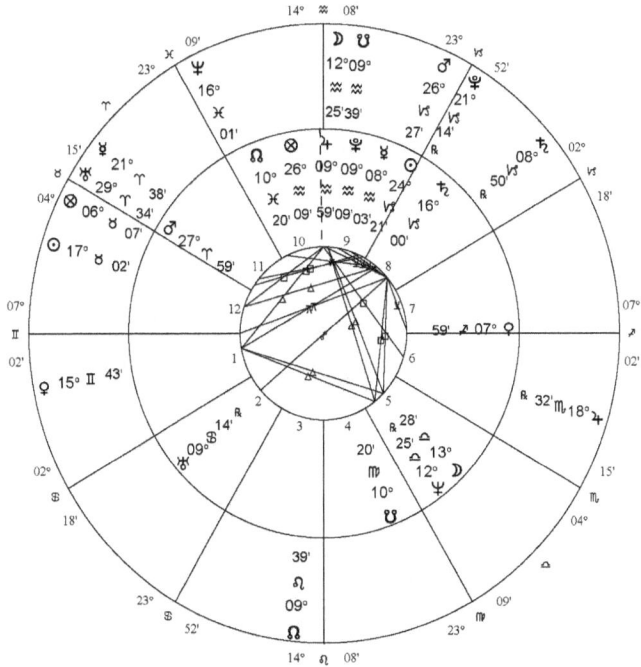

Figure 23-3
US chart/Zero Tolerance Policy May 7, 2018, 12:00 PM, Washington, DC

prisoned undocumented asylum seekers who crossed the border without permission. Children under the age of 18 accompanying them were separated and shipped to refugee camps and other institutions. Many of these children were less than 5 years of age.[16] Prior to the institution of this policy, families had generally been kept together in the United States while their immigration cases were adjudicated. The administration claimed that a policy of separation would act as a deterrent to future migrants.[17]

In the chart, Jupiter (the law) in the sixth house is being carried out by civil service workers who separate families (Sun in the twelfth house, ruler of the fourth house), incarcerating adults (twelfth house) as well as consigning children to shelters (Mercury square Pluto). The media soon brought it to public attention (Event Moon conjunct the US Midheaven), which caused an outrage across the country.

Numerous mass shootings occurred during Trump's presidency, augmenting concerns about gun control and domestic terrorism. In 2017, 348 people were killed, including 26 people in a Texas church. The deadliest attack that year included 59 killed and over 500 injured at a music festival in Las Vegas. In 2018, a total of 336 were killed, 417 in 2019, and 615 in 2020.[18]

Many mass shootings were motivated by hate crimes targeting people of differing religion, race, and sexual orientation. Domestic terrorist in-

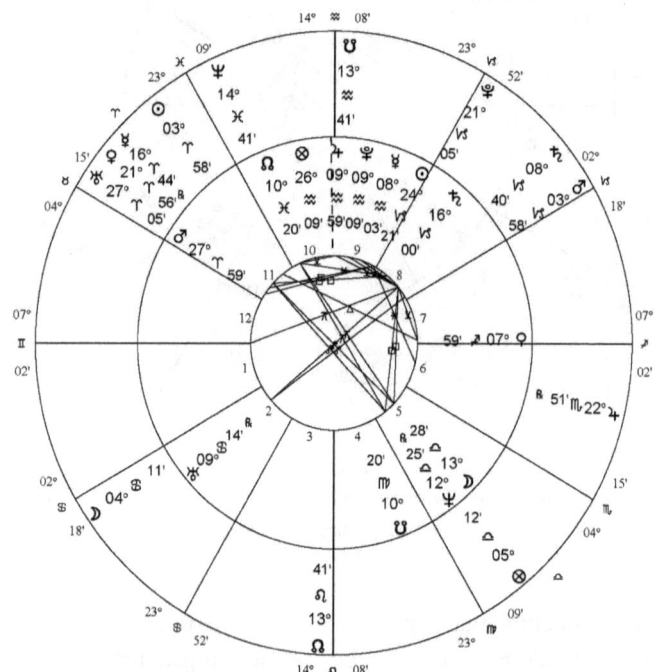

Figure 23-4
US chart/March For Our Lives, March 24, 2018, 12:00 PM, Washington, DC

cidents began increasing in the 2010s, often linked to far-right extremist and white supremacist groups. Such hate crimes involved eleven members of the Tree of Life synagogue murdered in Pittsburgh in 2018,[19] and 22 people killed in a Texas WalMart by a gunman reacting to a perceived "Hispanic invasion."[20]

The Parkland, Florida shooting at Marjory Stoneman Douglas High School that resulted in the death of 17 students and teachers in 2018 precipitated a youthful gun control advocacy movement called "Never Again." March for Our Lives, a protest organized by this group in Washington DC, took place on March 24, 2018, accompanied by "Hundreds of sister marches…across the country and around the world."[21]

In the above chart you find transiting Uranus exactly conjunct the US Mars setting off the unaspected duet to the Sun. The event Moon is conjuncting the US Yod's Uranus while opposing Mars and squaring the event Sun, creating a T-square. Again, the gun issue takes center stage as these young people express their anger toward a government that refuses to address the problem.

The killing of George Floyd while in police custody was a seminal event initiating national discussion about racism, police brutality, government overreaction, and civil rights. Floyd, an African American living in Minneapolis, Minnesota, was arrested on May 25, 2020 for allegedly passing a counterfeit bill. During a struggle, Floyd fell to the ground, still handcuffed, and police restrained him, one placing his knee between Floyd's head and neck for over 9 minutes, resulting in his death.[22]

A witness posted a video of the event on Facebook, provoking historic protests across the country almost immediately. Protestors in over 2000 towns and cities in all 50 states sounded the message that "Black Lives Matter." They were often met with riot-control tactics.[23]

The protest differed from previous demonstrations in its length, diversity of the marchers, and its spread throughout the world. People of various ethnicities, whites and Blacks, and families with children were all present. Solidarity with the message was displayed by one demonstrator's sign that read "I may never understand, but I will stand with you."[24]

In some cases, violence occurred. Protestors were met with tear gas, rubber bullets, arrests, and curfews. The Trump administration responded with a violent backlash. President Trump threatened a crackdown while bipartisan elected officials expressed concern that this would only further divide the country. Trump threatened protestors with "the most vicious dogs, and the most ominous weapons, I have ever seen."[25] Pro-

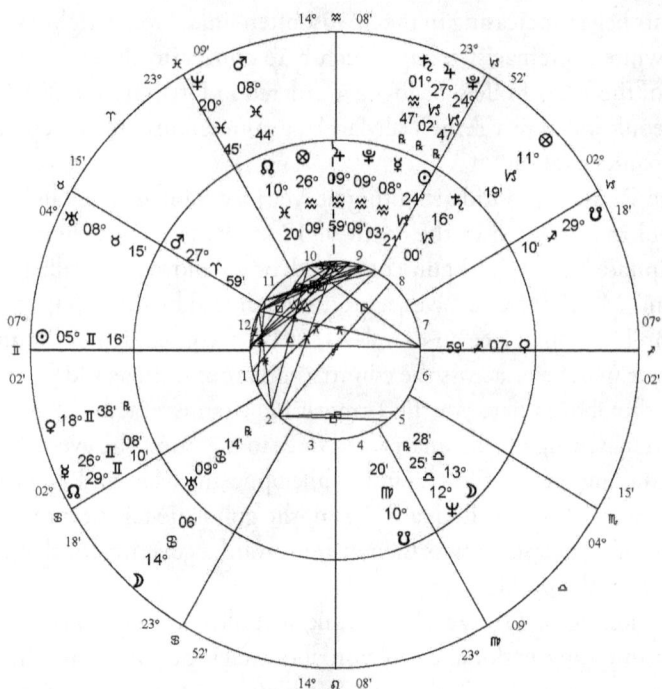

Figure 23-5
*US chart/Death of George Floyd, May 25, 2020, 8:27 PM,
Minneapolis, MN*

testors in Washington DC reached the White House gates on May 29, leading to a lockdown of the facility. The Secret Service rushed Trump and his family to an underground bunker, where they remained for an hour. He later claimed he was "only inspecting" the bunker.[26]

In the chart, Pluto conjuncting the US Sun demonstrates the power the president is using to control the situation. The Moon in Cancer in the second house illustrates the people's message being suppressed by the US Saturn in the eighth house. Meanwhile, the president is sheltered in the bunker – Sun in the twelfth house of the event chart. The Venus and Mercury in the first house show the upbeat mood of the protesters which was at first peaceful. The event chart Uranus is square the US Mercury, describing the message from the people has changed by becoming more inclusive and global.

The coronavirus (COVID-19) pandemic began in the US when the CDC reported the first case on January 20, 2020 (See Chapter Twelve). Instead of uniting the country in a common cause, the spread of disease

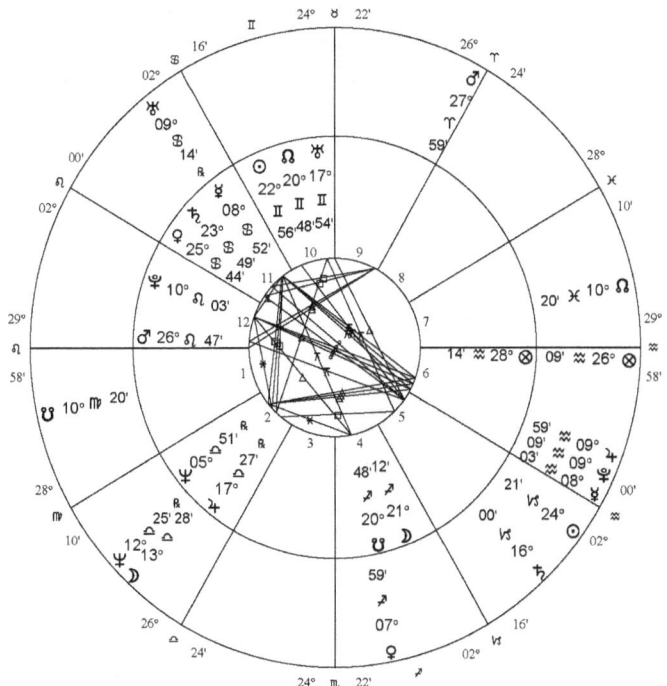

Figure 23-6
Inner wheel: Trump natal: June 14, 1946, 10:54 AM, Jamaica, NY
Outer wheel: US chart

strengthened the divide between states and federal government. Misinformation and conspiracy theories blossomed, offsetting CDC health information. Partisan gaps in attitudes and behaviors related to efforts to control the virus affected health policies and media coverage. Severe damage to health, safety, and the economy was the consequence.[27]

The last chart to examine is one of a comparison chart between the US chart and Trump's.

Notice the conjunction of Trump's Mercury (his Gemini ruler) to the US Uranus, setting off all the issues of the US Yod. At the same time, his Pluto in Leo opposes the Aquarius stellium on the upper leg of the Yod, emphasizing the individual over the group.

Opposition to Mercury from the twelfth house shows Trump's need to dominate the thinking of Americans (US chart ruler) as well as the institutions of the government and Congress. The Saturn opposition to Pluto indicates mistrust and conflict over administrative matters, even a threat to survival. The Saturn opposition to US Jupiter shows the tendency toward exaggeration, unrealistic expectations, and eventual lawsuits. The opposition of his Saturn to the US Sun suggests opposite views on administrative affairs and the "Who's in charge here?" struggle. His Jupiter in the second house (money) allows him to count on an unending stream of donations from the people.

How did Trump become such a populist icon for Americans? Most of his planets fall in the 4th quadrant, the configuration reflecting Trump as a symbol of the ongoing American populist movement.[28] His Neptune in the second house suggests that he is recognized for his achievements. Although he calls himself a self-made man, projecting himself as an American idol who became rich through his own efforts, this is a façade. But he never feels loved for himself, only for his status.[29]

Trump seems to be a revolutionary: he talks back to the elites, disparages them with nicknames; he is a bully, emulating the iconic figure of John Wayne, a tough, independent fighter, a macho figure that can't be overcome, a rebel without a real cause. He is a man who seems to have achieved the American Dream. He does not reveal his family background that was the real basis for his apparent success (the ruler of his fourth house is in the twelfth house). He talks like a man of the people, not an academic, and the public adores him for it.

Trump represents all the issues of the American collective unconscious, and he is not afraid to expose them. He therefore becomes the voice of the people. Even Republican leaders have fallen into the role of followers because they recognize the power he wields. Democracy for white property owners has always been acceptable in the US, but the addition of "others" into the democratic process such as Blacks, women, the poor, different ethnic groups, and immigrants that has occurred with the natural development of the country has never been adequately managed. Trump presents these "outsiders" as a threat to the populace.

So where does this leave us? Scholars of democracy have noted since the late 2010s an increase in "democratic backsliding" in the US, that is, a process in which a democratic government moves towards autocracy. Having peaked in 2015, the US democracy score fell quickly after 2016, earning the designation of a "flawed democracy."[30] The causes of democratic backsliding include the issues we've discussed here: increasing gaps in wealth and political power, white ethnic identity politics with erosion of voting rights, religious and white nationalism, racism, and increased acceptance of violence in pursuit of political outcomes.[31]

One scholar noted that democratic backsliding was more pronounced in states with Republican Party control and was associated with legislation restricting voting rights, abortion rights, and civil rights of gender and sexual minorities.[32]

During the Trump administration, the demise of democratic norms and institutions accelerated. Political violence was supported, the media was maligned, and belief in fair elections undercut. Like an autocratic leader preserving his racial group, Trump tacitly accepted white supremacy support and threatened immigration. Authoritarian populist views have been an undercurrent in American politics, but the Trump administration has exposed them.[33]

What we now see is the reality of that power and what Trump did and is still doing with it. Step by step, the issues of patriarchy, women's rights, civil rights, immigration, the income gap, states' rights versus federal rights, the separation of church and state, and, most importantly, democracy versus authoritarianism become prominent in the fight for "the soul of America."

In summary, this decade saw a strong turn in our democracy toward authoritarian agendas. The issues from the collective unconscious stemming from America's Yod are being brought to our awareness for solutions. This theme was part of the 2020 election and continues today. I leave you with a quote from Professor of History at Yale University Timothy Snyder's book *On Tyranny*: "The Founding Fathers tried to protect us from the threat they knew, the tyranny that overcame ancient democracy. Today, our political order faces new threats, not unlike the totalitarianism of the twentieth century. We are no wiser than the Europeans who saw democracy yield to fascism, Nazism, or communism. Our one advantage is that we might learn from their experience."[34]

CHAPTER TWENTY-THREE NOTES

1. Analysis: Trump's short, dark and defiant Inaugural address (usatoday.com) *Accessed 6/22/2023*
2. https://www.theguardian.com/world/2017/jan/20/donald-trump-inauguration-speech-analysis *Accessed 6/22/2023*
3. 2017 Women's March - Wikipedia *Accessed 6/22/2023*
4. Women's March On Washington Aims To Be More Than Protest : NPR *Accessed 9/20/2023*
5. 2017 Women's March - Wikipedia *Accessed 9/20/2023*
6. First 100 days of Donald Trump's presidency - Wikipedia *Accessed 9/20/2023*
7. Executive Order 13769 - Wikipedia *Accessed 9/20/23*
8. Presidency of Donald Trump - Wikipedia *Accessed 9/20/2023*
9. Ibid.
10. First 100 days of Donald Trump's presidency - Wikipedia *Accessed 9/20/2023*
11. History of the United States (2008–present) - Wikipedia *Accessed 9/20/2023*
12. US tax cuts: Are they the biggest in American history? - BBC News *Accessed 9/20/2023*
13. History of the United States (2008–present) - Wikipedia *Accessed 9/20/2023*
14. History of the United States (2008–present) - Wikipedia *Accessed 9/20/2023*
15. https://www.migrationpolicy.org/sites/default/files/publications/mpi-trump-at-4-report-final.pdf pp. 1-5 *Accessed 9/20/2023*
16. https://www.splcenter.org/news/2022/03/23/family-separation-timeline *Accessed 6/25/2023*
17. https://www.reuters.com/article/us-usa-immigration-children-idUSKBN16A2ES *Accessed 6/25/2023*
18. https://marketrealist.com/p/how-many-mass-shootings-happened-under-trump/ *Accessed 6/25/2023*
19. History of the United States (2008–present) - Wikipedia *Accessed 6/25/2023*
20. https://marketrealist.com/p/how-many-mass-shootings-happened-under-trump/ *Accessed 9/20/2023*
21. March for Our Lives: What you need to know | CNN *Accessed 6/25/2023*

22. George Floyd: What happened in the final moments of his life - BBC News *Accessed 6/23/2023*
23. https://www.history.com/this-day-in-history/george-floyd-killed-by-police-officer *Accessed 6/23/2023*
24. George Floyd: Huge protests against racism held across US - BBC News *Accessed 6/23/2023*
25. https://www.cnn.com/2020/05/31/politics/trump-george-floyd-protests/index.html *Accessed 6/24/2023*
26. https://en.wikipedia.org/wiki/George_Floyd_protests_in_Washington,_D.C. *Accessed 6/23/2023*
27. https://www.brookings.edu/articles/politics-is-wrecking-americas-pandemic-response/ *Accessed 6/25/2023*
28. Schlieffen, Alexander Graf von: *When Chimpanzees Dream Astrology*; Centre for Astrology Press, London, UK, 2004. p. 49
29. Ibid. p. 152
30. History of the United States (2008–present) - Wikipedia *Accessed 6/25/2023*
31. https://journals.sagepub.com oi/10.1177/00027162211069730 *Accessed 9/22/2023*
32. History of the United States (2008–present) - Wikipedia *Accessed 6/25/2023*
33. https://journals.sagepub.com/oi/10.1177/00027162211069730 *Accessed 9/22/2023*
34. Snyder, Timothy: *On Tyranny*; Tim Duggan Books, New York. 2017. p. 130

Chapter Twenty-Four

The 2020s — America Divided: The Crisis Point

"Tear It Down"
Twisted Sister

The first years of the 2020s have been a trying, chaotic, and anxiety-ridden time as we seek to deal with the unconscious issues plaguing us since the birth of the United States. I kept a personal journal for the entire year of 2020 because I knew it was a pivotal year and I wanted to keep an accurate record of events as they happened. All information was taken from the press, the internet, and TV news broadcasts with some personal observations on astrological transits. Some of this information will be included in the text of this chapter.

On January 21, 2020, the first US case of Covid-19 was reported in Seattle, Washington. Subsequently, the US began a slow slide into decline due to the pandemic and economic collapse resulting from shutdowns all over the country and severe jobs loss. Division in the country widened with the politicization of the pandemic. Misinformation filled the media along with conspiracy theories. People were confused and did not know whom they could trust. The public was advised to stay home, wear masks, and practice safe self-distancing. Theaters, restaurants, schools, and sports events were closed. People felt isolated and alone. Fear and distrust led to many citizens defying government health officials' recommendations. Polarization between groups supporting or denying the presumed scientific evidence grew. The ongoing presidential campaign only served to increase polarization.

Against this backdrop, the Black Lives Matter protests following

George Floyd's death increased. It peaked with a military backlash in Washington DC when the Trump administration sent troopers armed with batons, pepper spray, and firebombs to remove the protestors in Lafayette Park. Shortly afterward, President Trump held a photo-op, raising a Bible in front of a church. This action was criticized by the military. I noted in my journal that General Milley stated that the military should not be used by the president for his own personal reasons. Trump's intense reaction to peaceful protests seemed to indicate a potential slide to autocratic control.

Such events gave evidence to emergence of the unconscious issues so long repressed in our history. I noted in my journal that national reaction from the public polls showed 67 percent of Americans felt Trump mostly increased racial tensions. TV talking heads called this a "turning point in American history." The National Science Foundation Survey found Americans the unhappiest they've been in fifty years with less optimism about their kids having a better standard of living than themselves.

Biden's campaign message to the voters declared that he was "fighting for the soul of the country" to save our democracy from becoming authoritarian. Advisors were dubious about this strategy, but when Biden was elected, voters in exit polls affirmed that it had worked.

Election day was a nail-biter as votes were slowly counted. The voter turnout was the highest in 120 years. No winner was projected by day's end, but Trump declared himself winner anyway. When Biden was declared winner in Wisconsin the following day, Trump called for a recount. By Saturday, Biden had reached the required number of electoral votes. As European leaders were calling to congratulate Biden, Trump claimed voter fraud and filed lawsuits in various states. Republicans in Congress held with Trump, not stating the election was stolen but not conceding that Biden had won. During this time, Trump began firing senior defense officials and replacing them with loyalists, causing great alarm at the Pentagon.

The General Services Administration finally recognized Biden as the 2020 winner more than 2 weeks after the election. The transition of power was delayed as a result and was further slowed by the Trump administration's limited cooperation with Biden's team as Trump sought legal remedies for presumptive election fraud. Meanwhile, Trump and the Republican Senate rushed to confirm a series of conservative judges. When Trump was questioned about leaving the White House in January 2021, he said he certainly would, then added "There will be a lot of things between now and January 20th, a lot of things," as I noted in my journal.

Bad news continued as the inauguration approached. Coronavirus cases topped 10 million cases, and many states were overwhelmed with hospitalizations and lack of nursing staff. Deaths and new viral cases continued to increase. The new virus vaccines did not reach the states as planned due to unexplained shipment delays. Jobless claims, poverty and hunger were up.

In the Senate, Majority Leader McConnell finally congratulated Biden and Harris on their win on 12/15 following the official Electoral College vote, warning Republican Senators not to object to the election results certification on January 6th. A week later, Attorney General Barr resigned and was replaced by Jeffrey Rosen. Trump promised "wild protests" in Washington, D.C. on January 6, 2021, when Congress was to meet to finalize the Electoral College election results.

I had noted in my journal 8/30/2020 that "many people I talked to this last week feel the same as I do, the 'low-grade' depression Michelle Obama described. It's a feeling of being tired all the time, not able to focus on anything, not wanting to do anything, difficulty finding anything happy or to look forward to, tension related to the uncertainty of the time we are living in." It felt like being in a void, waiting for something to happen which would point us in a new direction. The negativity and hostility that surrounded us was exhausting. Even the temporary feeling of hope a new president might bring seemed out of reach, especially considering all the looming challenges he would face. Uncertainty took its toll every single day.

Then came the explosion on January 6– the attack on the Capitol that kept us glued to the TV all day, watching the chaos, and listening to commentators on the whole event.

The time used for the chart is when the marching protesters reached the barricades and confronted the Capitol police. Uranus from the twelfth house is squaring the Aquarius stellium in the ninth house, the law, the people, our values, the very structures of our Constitution and our government. The event Sun is conjunct the US Saturn, setting off the Axis of Awareness in the US Yod. The event Pluto is conjunct the US Sun, but the power of Pluto is being used for individual ego purposes, not for positive transformation. The event Mars in Aries is conjunct the US Mars, releasing the hostility of the unaspected duet. The event Libran Moon creates

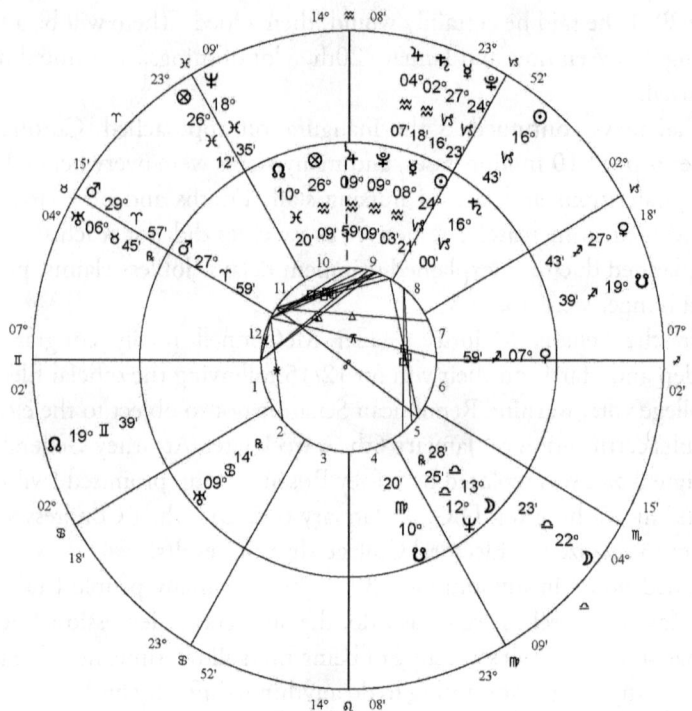

Figure 24-1
US chart/January 6 riots, January 6, 2021, 3:00 PM; Washington, DC

a T-square with the duet, goading the hostility of the protesters into violence that has become out of control, the opposition occurring across the 5th/11th Houses of Congress. The conjunction of the event chart Saturn and Jupiter illustrates the need to break from perceived restriction which is being triggered by the event Uranus in the twelfth house.

Examine the next chart for Biden's inauguration to see what he brings to the country. He called himself the "transition" president though not everyone knew what that meant. His real transition of power from Trump was delayed because Trump refused to recognize Biden's presidency and was the first president in 150 years to not attend the inauguration ceremony of the new president- a factor adding to the building of hostility against the new administration.

With Pluto conjunct the US Sun, it seems to indicate the truth of Biden's statement, this would be a different kind of presidency. However, the many indications of resistance, hostility, and rebellion suggest that it won't be a peaceful one. The Moon is setting off the unaspected

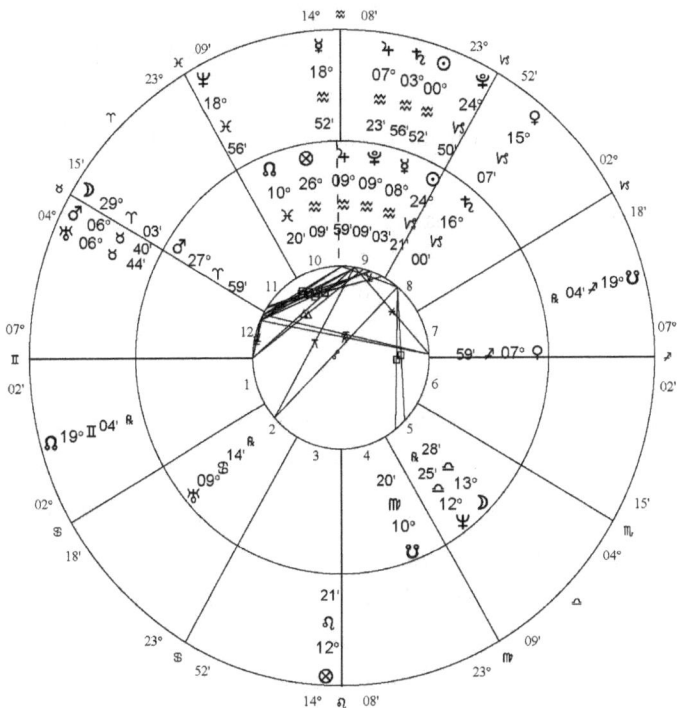

Figure 24-2
US chart/Biden inauguration January 20, 2021, 12:00 PM, Washington, DC

duet of Mars square the Sun, while event chart Mars conjunct Uranus in the twelfth house both suggest a hidden anger brewing that has already exploded on January 6th and will continue through the first two years of Biden's presidency.

During the next hundred days, President Biden signed many executive orders to rescind Trump's policies. The US reentered the Paris Agreement on climate change and the US withdrawal from WHO was canceled. Without Republican support, Congress was able to pass a pandemic relief program which included one-time payments to Americans, financial aid to states, and more. Eventually, a bipartisan bill of Infrastructure Investment and Jobs Act was passed. To end the 20-year war in Afghanistan, Biden ordered troop withdrawals from the country, though not without a lot of criticism. The Respect for Marriage Act allowed for same-sex marriages by repealing the former Defense of Marriage Act which did not. Biden's attempt to protect voting rights was blocked by filibusters in the Senate.¹

Despite strong opposition in his first 2 years, Biden had several accomplishments:²

- Bipartisan investment package provided $1.2 trillion for national infrastructure.
- American Rescue Plan provided 500 million Covid-19 vaccinations, cut child poverty in half, and lowered ACA healthcare premiums by $800 annually.
- Bipartisan Safer Communities Act addressed gun violence for the 1st time in 30 years.
- The longest war in American history- Afghanistan – was ended.
- Covid-19 relief deal provided $1400 to struggling citizens.
- Paris Agreement to fight climate change was rejoined.
- Inflation Reduction Act imposed a 15% corporate tax on large businesses, empowered Medicare to negotiate drug prices, and reduced government health spending.
- NATO support of Ukraine strengthened by including Sweden and Finland into the alliance.
- 6.6 million jobs created in one year, greater than any other president in history.
- Violence Against Women Act reauthorized through 2027.
- Historically low unemployment rates achieved.
- All federal executions that had been reinstated by the previous administration were stopped.

Midterm elections took place in 2022. While a "red wave" did not happen as expected, the Republicans did win the House by a small margin, guaranteeing division in Congress. Democrats increased their majority by one seat in the Senate. Because of division among House Republicans, it took 15 ballots to elect the Speaker, Kevin McCarthy.

Throughout Biden's administration, however, hostility and division have continued to grow. The hidden issues that have continually affected our country have again surfaced and demand attention. Authoritarianism vs democracy, federal vs states' rights, civil rights, gun violence, religious freedom vs theocracy, immigration, the rights of Blacks and other minorities, and women's rights are concerns that must be confronted.

Examine the recent events that have led us to the crisis point.
The Supreme Court has continued to chip away legal precedents and people's rights:

- Ruled in favor of Lorie Smith, who stipulated that the First Amendment's guarantee of free speech supported her refusal to create websites for same-sex couples. The ruling enabled businesses to circumvent state and local anti-discrimination laws based on "free speech."[3]
- Reduced the EPA's (Environmental Protection Agency) ability to regulate the carbon emissions of individual power plants by requiring congressional approval before implementing any restrictions.[4]
- Ruled that the First Amendment allowed school employees to engage in prayer on a public school's football field.[5]
- Ruled that New York's requirement of a license for carrying a concealed weapon was a violation of the Second Amendment.[6]
- Effectively ended race-conscious admission (affirmative action) programs at colleges and universities, reversing decades of precedents.[7]
- Overturned Roe vs Wade.[8]

In addition, the Supreme Court has come under corruption accusations, with Congress calling for an ethics panel to be created to assure this branch of our government adheres to rules of ethics just like the other two branches.[9] The public's opinion of the Court has gone down considerably.[10]

Let us review one of these rulings in more detail. The next chart examines Roe vs Wade, using the time when the upcoming reversal was leaked to the press.

The reason I used this chart was because transiting Uranus was coming to a conjunction with the US Chiron in the twelfth house of the United States. To me, this signaled the "awakening" to the unconscious issues we've been ignoring, such as women's rights, that we have taken for granted so long (50 years) and how easily rights can be taken away by the stroke of a pen. It also forced public awareness on the Supreme Court, and how religion was shaping its decisions. The right of abortion was now in states' hands, and they moved rapidly to pass legislation to restrict access, some states worse than others. Chiron in the US chart is at 15 Taurus 11

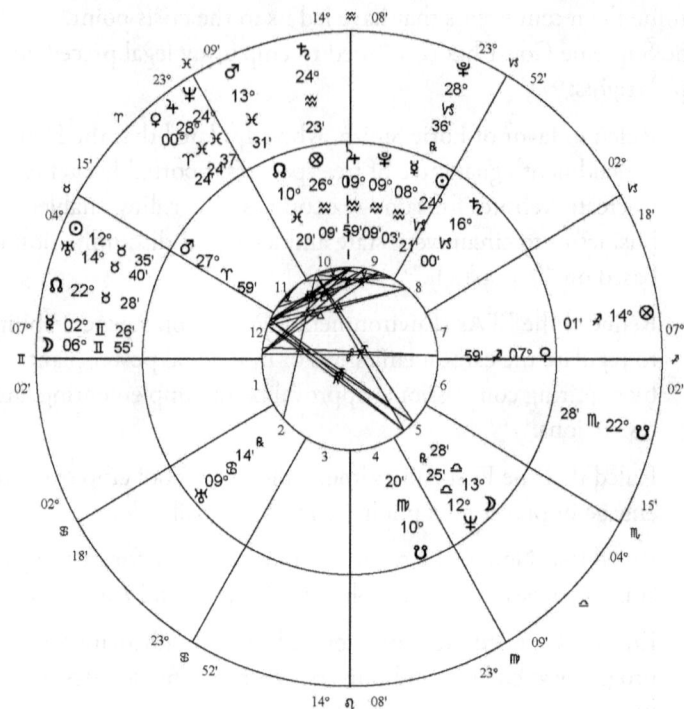

Figure 24-3
US chart/Roe v Wade leaked, May 2, 2022, 8:32 PM,
Washington, DC

(although it doesn't show in the comparison chart). It seemed to me to indicate further issues would be brought to our awareness, like religion versus government and, especially, federal versus states' rights.

Women reacted immediately to the shock. Angry protests by women's groups erupted all over the country, especially in the big cities. "'If it's a fight they want, it's a fight they'll get,' said Rachel Carmona, executive director of the Women's March, before the event."[11] Transiting Mars is conjunct the US North Node, bringing angry organized women together, which will continue for some time. Transiting Pluto continues its slow journey over the US Sun, bringing hidden issues to the forefront to increase the divisiveness. Exposure of startling cases, such as a 10-year-old girl who had been raped being forced to go out of state to terminate the pregnancy, brought national attention to the consequences.[12]

Since the overturn of Roe vs Wade, as of October 2023 fourteen states have banned abortion, most of them with no exceptions for rape or incest.[13] Some states have made it a felony for anyone attempting or completing an abortion, with varied sentence lengths in prison up to 99 years and related fines.[14]

Christian nationalism played a big part in some of these decisions and has greatly contributed to the division in the United States. It also evokes concerns about authoritarianism. The movement has increased its participation in the political arena since the 1980s (See Chapter 19). The ideas are not new in American history: a rise of evangelicals swept the country in the "Great Awakening" in the 1730s. However, when the movement became a powerful political bloc in the 1980s, it turned its efforts to electing conservative candidates who agreed with its agenda.

Demographic changes brought by immigration and increased rights for minorities and women have been seen as a threat to many in the movement. "As the country has become less white and Christian… these adherents want to hold on to their cultural and political power."[15] A Public Religion Research Institute and Brookings Institution survey found that "more than half of Republicans believe the country should be a strictly Christian nation."[16] According to the survey these adherents and their sympathizers "support the idea of an authoritarian leader in order to keep these Christian values in society."[17]

Correlations were also noted between Christian nationalists and "anti-Black, anti-immigrant, antisemitic views, anti-Muslim and patriarchal views." This small but powerful minority opposes pluralism and democracy.[18] They are against "wokeness," the quality of being alert to or concerned about social injustice and discrimination[19] and against critical race theory (CRT), a legal concept that posits that race is not an actual biological feature distinguishing human subgroups but is a culturally invented category used to oppress non-white groups. The goal of these theorists is to "eliminate all race-based and other unjust hierarchies."[20]

Such views have created a "culture war," dividing Americans further along ideological worldviews relating to beliefs about race, gender, religion, political affiliation,[21] and other issues we have discussed connected to the Yod. Culture wars have induced a moral panic that has promoted backlashes against LGBT groups and gender-affirming care for children and adolescents, resulting in legislation in at least 29 states to prevent schools from teaching about CRT and gender ideology.[22]

This movement also affected the public response to masking, safe distancing, and vaccines during the pandemic. Its anti-science view made directives from the CDC questionable, promoting defiance

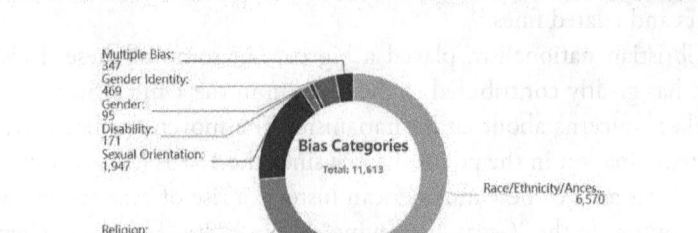

Figure 24-4: United States Hate Crimes by Bias (2022)

against health mandates and hostility toward health officials like Dr. Fauci. Government became the authoritarian tyrant trying to take away our freedoms while the rioters of January 6th became patriots.

Increasing division and hostility in the United States have resulted in a soaring of hate crimes as reported by the FBI in their 2022 report.[23]

The level of hate crimes in the US is the highest in over ten years. Anti-Black hate crime was up 40 percent. Crimes against Asians (tied to Covid-19) increased by 70 percent.[24] Some of these include mass shootings.

More than 647 mass shootings occurred in the US in 2022, including one in an LGBTQ bar in Colorado, and another in an elementary school in Uvalde, Texas in which 19 students and 2 teachers were killed.[25] The subsequent congressional bill did not address the problem of rapid-fire guns like the AR-15 and large magazines of bullets. Many Americans are ready to deal with this problem but cannot find support in their representatives, state or federal. Some groups have interpreted the 2nd Amendment to be almost a commandment. It may require a re-examination to assess its fitness in the present era.

Contributing to the anti-government movement are conspiracy groups that "spread disinformation and misinformation about government institutions and officials."[26] Conspiracy theorists have been with us since the Puritans in the Massachusetts Bay Colony started witch hunts, a term still used today. In the 1920s, the pseudoscientific theory of eugenics claimed that "bad blood of inferior racial groups was a threat to the country"[27] (See Chapter Eight), resulting in immigration legislation to dehumanize immigrants from everywhere but "Nordic" countries. These theories have continued down the decades to be incorporated into new groups. In the 2010s, for example, the Great Replacement theory became popular. This idea asserted that there were "left-leaning...elites... attempting to replace white citizens with non-white immigrants."[28] Fox News commentators Tucker Carlson and Laura Ingraham attested to the conspiracy, suggesting its underlying purpose was to create a large majority loyal to the Democratic Party. By 2022, one third of Americans and nearly half of Republicans accepted this view.[29]

Alex Jones, a right-wing extremist, has asserted the existence of a New World Order aiming to create a totalitarian world government.[30] Another conspiracy group appeared in 2017 when Q emerged on the internet, building a following of QAnon adherents who are antigovernment, claim that the election was stolen from Trump, and foster mistrust in the democratic process.[31] Conspiracies about the schools "attempting to sexualize and indoctrinate children"[32] have led to book burning, banning, and attempts to alter school curricula.[33] More recently, Florida Governor Ron DeSantis has supported a new Florida school curriculum that misrepresents Black history and suggests that slavery benefited Blacks by allowing them to acquire useful skills.[34]

"The paranoia and skepticism around the U.S.'s democratic processes eventually reached a boiling point under the Trump administration... old conspiracies were repackaged into such concepts as the 'Deep State,' 'Q Anon,' Migrant Caravans,'" etc.[35] This kind of propaganda relies on division, the "us vs them" rhetoric that arouses fear and anger in citizens, affecting their ability to think critically. One cannot disprove a conspiracy[36] because it uses self-confirming, circular reasoning "where questioning one premise or conclusion simply leads to stating another premise or conclusion."[37]

States' rights issues have furthered the authoritarian/democracy conflict. The overturning of Roe vs Wade was supposed to remand the abortion issue to the states. However, we have seen state legislatures try to override voters' decisions to maintain abortion access in their states, as well as congressional representatives attempting to pass a nationwide abortion ban. In other examples, Alabama state representatives have defied the federal government's directive regarding redistricting that violates the Voting Rights Act, and in Texas, Governor Greg Abbott has refused to "comply with a Justice Department request to remove floating barriers in the Rio Grande."[38] As noted by Daniel Ziblatt in *How Democracies Die*, conflict over democracy may be reflected in the confrontation between the federal government and the states. This conflict is at the highest level it has been in the last 70 years.[39]

The anti-government attitude has been perpetuated by many congressional members and state legislatures. They decry the government elites who are out of touch with ordinary people. The result is increasing deadlock, making it almost impossible to pass bipartisan legislation. Is it any wonder the American public has lost its faith in its own government? A government that does not "…establish Justice, insure domestic Tranquility…promote the general Welfare, and secure the Blessings of Liberty…" in fact, does not respond to stated public desires and needs.

The same questions plagued our colonial ancestors in the late 1770s under the rule of a distant, unresponsive British parliament and king. At that time, as is happening now, Uranus was transiting the American chart's twelfth house, arousing turmoil in the collective unconscious of America, bringing results of past actions to our awareness as we continue to search for our true identity. The division between Black and white, red states and blue states, North and South, liberal and conservative, wealthy and poor has reached a chasm that seems unbridgeable.

Two hundred and fifty years ago, America faced a crisis: should the citizens continue to live in an autocracy or make a different choice, a republic? Our Founding Fathers dreamed of a great republic where the citizens would elect men of wisdom, men of vision, who would put the welfare of all the nation's citizens before their personal interests. They believed in education for all people so they would know how to choose such men. They also feared that a tyrant could subvert that democratic republic, taking advantage of men's greed and manipulating them by fear and hate of "the other" to secure power.

We have seen the concept of the American Dream move from the hope of a better life into "I want what the rich have by any means I can get it," the seed of all corruption. The cries for freedom and liberty seem to apply only to those in the correct "tribe." The Founding Fathers promoted life under a system of laws, not under commandments of any religion. They believed in justice for all, not just those who could afford a better lawyer. They promised us the pursuit of happiness but did not guarantee it. They hoped that educated, thoughtful voters would choose leaders that would put the country first, promoting dignity, respect, and acceptance into one tribe, AMERICANS, which could lead to security for all.

The day that Uranus crossed the Ascendant of the American chart was the day the Declaration of Independence was signed: "…That to secure these rights, Governments are instituted among Men, deriving their just powers from the consent of the governed,— That whenever any Form of Government becomes destructive of these ends, it is the Right of the People to alter or to abolish it, and to institute new Government, laying its foundation on such principles and organizing its powers in such form, as to them shall seem most likely to effect their Safety and Happiness."

The Declaration of Independence gave us our right to Revolution; the Constitution gives us the voting power to make changes responsive to the people's needs. Now is the time, as Uranus repeats its transit over the Ascendant along with the return of Pluto to Aquarius, for every voter to think independently and remove the influence of political parties with their private agendas and deep pockets of donor wealth. We can do this without war or revolution. It is time to balance out the opposition of Saturn to Uranus so that we can prepare for and welcome the need for change.

As President George Washington noted in his first inaugural address: "…the preservation of the sacred fire of liberty, and the destiny of the Republican model of Government, are justly considered as deeply, perhaps as finally staked, on the experiment entrusted to the hands of the American people."[40]

CHAPTER TWENTY-FOUR NOTES

1. https://www.britannica.com/biography/Joe-Biden *Accessed 7/11/2023*
2. Joe Biden's 23 greatest achievements as president of the United States ... so far - The Smile News *Accessed 7/8/2023*
3. What the Supreme Court's LGBTQ rights decision means | CNN Politics *Accessed 7/11/2023*
4. https://usafacts.org/articles/what-does-government-data-say-about-the-2022-supreme-court-decisions/ *Accessed 7/11/2023*
5. Ibid.
6. Ibid.
7. Supreme Court reverses affirmative action, gutting race-conscious admissions : NPR *Accessed 7/11/2023*
8. https://usafacts.org/articles/what-does-government-data-say-about-the-2022-supreme-court-decisions/ *Accessed 7/11/2023*
9. https://thehill.com/regulation/court-battles/4222229-all-eyes-on-ethics-as-supreme-court-justices-return-to-washington/ *Accessed 9/26/2023*
10. Supreme Court approval ratings at record lows, poll says (fox5vegas.com) *Accessed 9/26/2023*
11. Thousands gather for pro-abortion rights protests across U.S. - CBS News *Accessed 6/23/2023*
12. www.nbcnews.com/nightly-news/video/10-year-old-girl-gets-abortion-in-neighboring-state-after-being-raped-144094789534 *Accessed 7/11/2023*
13. https://www.cnn.com/2022/08/31/us/abortion-access-restrictions-bans-us/index.html *Accessed 7/15/2023*
14. A state-by-state look at abortion laws in America | AP News *Accessed 9/26/2023*
15. Christian nationalism on the rise as it enjoys more Republican support : NPR *Accessed 7/11/2023*
16. Ibid.
17. Ibid.
18. Ibid.
19. https://blog.washcoll.edu/wordpress/theelm/2020/10/the-meaning-of-wokeness-explained/ *Accessed 9/26/2023*
20. https://www.britannica.com/topic/critical-race-theory *Accessed*

7/15/2023
21. https://en.wikipedia.org/wiki/Culture_war *Accessed 12/7/2023*
22. https://en.wikipedia.org/wiki/2020s_anti-LGBT_movement_in_the_United_States *Accessed 7/15/2023*
23. https://cde.ucr.cjis.gov/LATEST/webapp/#/pages/explorer/crime/hate-crime *Accessed 12/11/2023*
24. Chart: U.S. Hate Crimes At New Decade High | Statista *Accessed 7/19/2023*
25. https://www.insider.com/number-of-mass-shootingsin-america-this-year-2022-5 *Accessed 7/20/2023*
26. https://www.splcenter.org/fighting-hate/extremist-files/ideology/conspiracy-propagandists *Accessed 7/12/2023*
27. https://elpasomatters.org/2021/11/09/opinion-challenging-the-racist-underpinnings-of-laws-criminalizing-undocumented-immigration/ *Accessed 12/17/2022*
28. https://www.britannica.com/topic/replacement-theory *Accessed 8/22/2023*
29. Ibid.
30. https://en.wikipedia.org/wiki/Alex_Jones *Accessed 12/10/2023*
31. https://en.wikipedia.org/wiki/QAnon *Accessed 12/12/2023*
32. https://www.splcenter.org/fighting-hate/extremist-files/ideology/conspiracy-propagandists *Accessed 7/12/2023*
33. https://en.wikipedia.org/wiki/2021%E2%80%932023_book_banning_in_the_United_States *Accessed 12/10/2023*
34. https://www.washingtonpost.com/politics/2023/07/22/desantis-slavery-curriculum/ *Accessed 12/10/2023*
35. https://www.splcenter.org/fighting-hate/extremist-files/ideology/conspiracy-propagandists *Accessed 7/12/2023*
36. https://www.justsecurity.org/77078/the-propaganda-playbook-a-section-by-section-dissection-of-tucker-carlsons-communication-strategy/ *Accessed 7/30/2023*
37. https://helpfulprofessor.com/circular-reasoning-fallacy-examples/ *Accessed 7/30/2023*
38. https://www.theguardian.com/us-news/2023/jul/29/states-republicans-defy-washington-supreme-court *Accessed 7/29/2023*
39. Ibid.
40. https://www.archives.gov/exhibits/american_originals/inaugtxt.html *Accessed 12/3/2023*

EPILOGUE

"Where do we go from here, boys, where do we go from here?"
Howard Johnson and Percy Wenrich

We have explored America's journey from its beginnings to this point in time, 2024. A Pluto cycle is ending. A new beginning cycle is upon us. From 2024, Pluto will be transiting through the sign of Aquarius for 20 years, an anticipated transit with many astrologers offering suggestions about its significance for the United States and for the world.

In the past, Pluto's trip through Capricorn followed by Aquarius has toppled heads of state, bringing radical change throughout society. America's birth as a republic began at the last cycle's onset. Pluto represents the power of the collective will of the people, different from the will of the individual (Mars). Over time, it creates transformation- difficult because of continuous crisis with its accompanying anxiety, fear, and depression. Looking at prior cycles (see Prologue), we see the result is usually a whole paradigm shift in thinking and attitudes of society, especially toward authority. To understand the future, necessity requires a full examination of the past and how we arrived where we are now. That is what this book has attempted in a small way to do.

Historians also study cycles of the past to understand their meaning. These swings have been defined in various ways: conservatism vs liberalism; private interest vs public action; status quo vs innovation; capitalism vs democracy[1] (private property and freedom with social responsibility). You can see how the historical cycles found here reflect the Axis of Awareness of the Yod in the US chart, the opposition between Saturn and Uranus. However, it is important to recognize that cycles move in a spiral form, evolving ever upward.[2] Every solar return presents a new design in the chart to help us grow while on our journey. Similarly, the human body develops in stages of putting on weight and then getting taller. The brain also grows in two-year cycles of new learning and then accommodating that information with the old, being initiated by each

Mars return. Cycles are personal, worldly, and universal.

What initiates the change? Science and technology are one possibility. Consider the industrial revolution, a world war, the atom bomb, the computer age, or the growth of the internet. Events in an era may affect that era's generation. Consider the Depression years, World Wars I and II, the baby boomers, the hippie movement in the '60s, the moral majority of the '70s, the greed of the '80s. "Each new phase must flow out of the conditions – and contradictions – of the phase before and then itself prepare the way for the next recurrence."[3] After times of chaos and stress, humans need periods of recovery and stability.[4]

Another factor to consider is polarization. In every political system there are factions: groups joined together to pursue their individual goals and agendas. This is the source for political parties. At times these parties can work together and compromise their beliefs to serve the good of the electorate. At other times, they become gridlocked, especially if religious fervor or questions over morality are involved. The Civil War, for example, divided the country over the question of slavery, a highly passionate moral question. Another example was the era of Prohibition, in which the Women's Christian Temperance Union fought the "sinful" act of excessive drinking.

Unfortunately, when the masses align themselves with different sides, violence is often the result. In the first case, we experienced a bloody civil war and in the second scenario, the rise of crime, gangs, and the use of machine guns to maintain power.

Where are we today? "We are told that the nation's politics and government are becoming less engaging, less responsive, and less accountable to the citizenry. We are warned that the health of vital public institutions – the Congress, the courts, the executive bureaucracy, the news media – is endangered."[5] The people are subject to disinformation and misinformation on all sides, losing faith in what the Founding Fathers gave us so long ago. We've watched hate crimes rise, mass shootings rise, the rights of women, minorities, and voters eroded, along with the rise of corruption in every facet of our daily lives. Our elections are questioned, and a former president has been indicted on multiple felonies for the first time in our history.

In such times of chaos and stress, it is easy to become enamored of a charismatic strong man who promises to "fix it." If we abdicate our responsibility for our own right to self-govern, we admit that the "experiment" didn't work and turn the power over to an authoritarian to bring order to our chaos. I'm reminded of a statement about fascist leader Mussolini of World War II: that "at least he got the trains to run on time!" A rather large price to pay for transportation efficiency!

Each side of the division agrees that something is wrong with the government, but each side proffers contradictory solutions. What both forget is that the fault lies with ALL of us, the American electorate, who has allowed our government to fall into the state our Founding Fathers feared: one of luxury, power, and corruption. Little by little, we have watched the power of political parties grow, their different agendas funded by an increasingly wealthy group of citizens who promote their own personal goals. They select the people they want elected, leaving voters with a choice between two candidates they don't desire, forced to vote for the least bad candidate! Today both parties have grown far apart without hope for compromise, creating a deadlock and further polarization among voters. Right now, it looks like we may have another election between two unwanted candidates.

At the beginning of our republic, voter turnout was quite low. It reached about 40% in 1812, decreased to a low of 10% in 1820, then began to ascend, reaching 80% in 1840. It remained roughly between 70% and 80% until the end of the 19th century, then began dropping, reaching a low of 48.9% in 1924, even though the population of voters had risen with the franchise being extended to Black males, then later to women. Since then, it has remained in the 50% to 60% range, reaching 66.2% in 2020.[6]

If voters don't turn out for elections, they have abdicated their responsibility to maintain a virtuous republic, just as George Washington and Benjamin Franklin warned us. It is also the duty of the educational system to teach critical thinking, the difference between fact and opinion, and the importance of citizens studying the issues laid before them by various candidates. We need to ensure voters' ability to maintain that virtuous republic.

What are steps we can take to return to the vision of our Founding Fathers, a system which does what they promised us, "From Many, One"? We can remove private money influence from elections. Changes to our Constitution such as eliminating rules no longer relevant to democracy such as the electoral college should be discussed. We need to find enforceable ways to prevent corruption in the body politic. We must embrace diversity with acceptance and respect, keep our rule of laws without the influence of religious points of view. I believe the American people can find ways to set us on the correct course to maintain our democracy as well as "promote the general welfare."

Examine the chart of our next inauguration to see what a new president will bring to the country. I did not use an election chart because it is hard to determine the moment the winner is announced, and I don't find them useful.

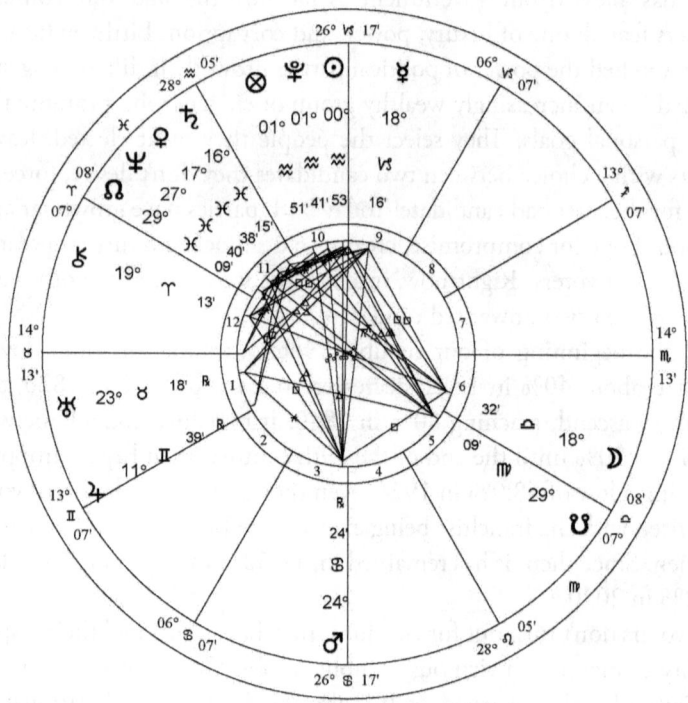

Inauguration in 2025
January 21, 2025, 12:00 PM
Washington, D.C.

The first thing to notice is the Sun conjunct Pluto in Aquarius in the tenth House of the administration, Pluto can represent the "healing principle which forces the collective, as an organic whole, to experience violent phases of self-healing, in order to become well again."[7] Of course, it can also be interpreted in a more sinister way that implies "secret police, organized crime and all self-destructive impulses."[8] Recall in Chapter 24, the chart of January 6, 2021 that transiting Pluto was exactly conjunct the US chart's Sun (President Trump) and the attack on the Capitol Building. This can be countered by Uranus trine the MC which suggests an opportunity to make important changes in the administration of government, along with Uranus trine the Sun, rulers of both legislative bodies of Senate and House. Since the first House represents the nation as a whole, Uranus posited there can represent the changes but it can also signify a disruption in the body politic as Jupiter (ruler of the eighth House) moves from the first House of good feeling in the people into the second House and squares Saturn implying reduction in funds for the budget. The opposition of Mars (ruler of the twelfth and seventh) to the MC shows that not everyone in the collective will be happy about change and will be hostile because it rules the collective unconscious of the twelfth House (the Jungian "shadow.") and will enter the fourth House of the people versus the government. It also rules the seventh House of foreign relations. With Chiron also in the twelfth House refers back to our wounds of "insecurity" discussed in the Introduction. One important point to note is that the ascendant is conjunct the US chart's Chiron (15 Taurus, 11 minutes) which reveals our collective unconscious issues to the public. They are forced to make a decision in this election on which side they will vote. If they choose the negative vibration of Pluto, it will create an awakening call which will eventually lead us to our real identity – that of "FROM MANY, ONE!" The positive side of Pluto begins with the transiting ascendant moving over our natal Chiron when we can see and heal ourselves of these issues. Hopefully we can make the right choices and evolve upward from where we have been. This can be countered by the Uranus in trine to the Midheaven, which suggests an opportunity to make important changes in the administration of government, along with Uranus trine the Sun, rulers of both parts of legislative bodies of Senate and House. Since the first house represents the nation as a whole, Uranus posited there suggests that the collective will accept the changes. Jupiter also in the first house suggests a sense of well-being in the nation reinforced by its trine to the Libra Moon in the sixth house of workers, health, civil service workers, and unions, as well as the military.

The opposition of Mars in the third house (and conjunct the fourth house cusp) opposing Mercury in the ninth house shows that not everyone in the collective will be happy about change and will be hostile with their arguments against it because it rules the collective unconscious of the twelfth house (the Jungian "shadow"). Venus, the ruler of the Ascendant, is in Pisces and makes sextiles to both Jupiter and Mercury, which eases some of the tension of its conjunction to Saturn which causes restraint.

One important point to note is that the Ascendant is conjunct the US chart's Chiron (15 Taurus 11), which brings us back to the collective unconscious issues that are becoming more transparent. Once the ascendant transits our Chiron, we can see and heal ourselves of these issues. Hopefully we can make the right choices and evolve upward from

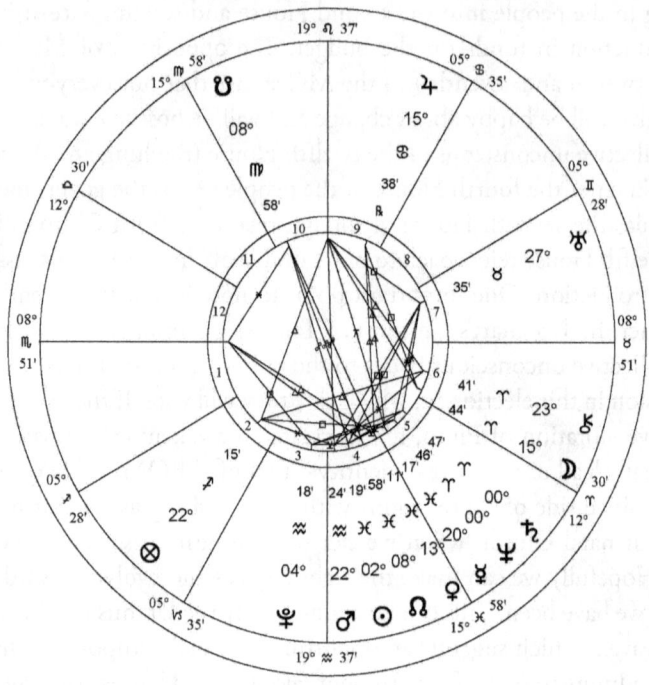

Aries Vortex
February 21 2026, 12:00 AM
Geneva, Switzerland

where we have been.

Looking at the North Node at zero Aries is crucial because in February 2026, Saturn and Neptune will conjunct at this degree while Uranus will make a trine to Pluto from Gemini to Aquarius whose midpoint will be close to zero Aries. This creates a double sextile aspect between Saturn/Neptune to Uranus and Pluto. Ray Merriman referred to this as the "Aries Vortex" and said, "It will look like an arrow with the zero Aries at the tip, hence acting like a cosmic vortex attracting powerful energy that brings together the principles of Saturn/Neptune and Uranus/Pluto."[9]

Nothing like this has happened before. All this energy suggests an enormous change in direction and the beginning of a new era for the United States and the rest of the world. Following this, Uranus will be transiting over the US chart ascendant from April 2028 to March 2029 while transiting Pluto will conjunct the US Mercury before its return to its own place at 9 degrees of Aquarius. Uranus will transit the US chart's first house for seven to eight years while continuing its trine to Pluto. This suggests a time of positive evolution and corrective changes.

The last two decades have been moving us to this culmination of geocosmic forces at which point we are forced to make a choice: evolve or die.

The next chart is of this Aries Vortex, which is the closest I could get to accuracy using a Geneva ephemeris with a midnight time. Please feel free to make your own personal interpretations of what this chart portends.

Begin with the fact that seven planets occupy the second quadrant (the "eternal child") which "describes the psycho-genetic blueprint of the tribe that we belong to, that we are incorporated into."[10] (Of course, some of us may feel we don't fit in with our tribe!) In this quadrant we have moved from childhood years to the period of pre-teens and puberty, then to adulthood and all that entails: moving from the family to learn about the outside world, our place in it, what we wish to accomplish, and to whom we wish to relate. We want to understand ourselves, so it is a very subjective period, especially when you realize all this concentrated energy is placed in the fourth quadrant in the US chart, which mirrors back to Americans what our "position in the world" should be.[11]

In comparison to the rest of the world, Americans are still in adolescence, a period of turmoil as we search for our national identity. We don't want to grow up and face all the heavy responsibilities that come with maturity. However, we are being forced by transcendental forces showing the end of a cycle and the beginning of a new one with all the energy pointing to zero Aries. The US chart will see a Nodal return which starts a new cycle, Pluto conjuncting the ruler of the US chart, Mercury, and the eventual return to its natal position. During this time, Uranus will cross the US Gemini Ascendant in June of 2027 and begin an eight-year tour through the first house while trining Pluto, bringing us scientific and technological advances as well as changes in the nation. One way to view the Aries Vortex is as a severe test, a crucible of concentrated forces that interact to cause a powerful change in society as we know it. The nature of that change is yet to be determined.

Let us recap our astrological journey of America. We began as a nation governed by a majority of white, male, Anglo-Saxon Protestants who cherished their independence and their right to freedom. The "We the People of the United States" phrase at the beginning of our Constitution basically meant white people. Our history has illustrated the next phrase, "in Order to form a more perfect Union" by the long struggle to realize that dream by becoming more and more inclusive.

Today, some people wish to reverse the flow of history, to return to what we were in the beginning, wiping out the lessons we've learned on our journey. They are threatened by the new diverse face of America, reacting by electing those prompted by fear, anger, and hate (America's unconscious shadow) of "the other," namely those who are different from our vision of what we were at the beginning. The rise of hate crimes, domestic terrorism, and conspiracy theories has brought this "dark side" of America to the surface.

The dark side is now visible. We can see it, understand it, and manage it. "To ultimately prevail in this defense of our democracy, we must clearly understand the underlying forces imperiling the nation, name the nature of the opposition, and summon the majority of Americans to unapologetically affirm that this is a multi-racial country."[12] We should expand that idea to include not only race, but religions, national origin, sexual orientation, gender, and economic class.

When Benjamin Franklin told questioning citizens about the kind of government the Constitutional Convention had given us, his answer was short but profound: "A republic, if you can keep it." We must remember that democratic republics not only require the people's consent, they "are also absolutely dependent upon the ACTIVE and INFORMED involvement of the people for their continued good health."[13] (capitalization is mine).

Our journey for now has ended. The road to the future lies ahead. I, for one, feel optimistic about the future. America has always faced challenges, but the evolution has always gone forward. We will always pursue a more perfect Union.

EPILOGUE NOTES

1. Schlesinger, Arthur M., Jr.: *Cycles of American History*; Houghton Mifflin Company, Boston, Massachusetts, 1986. pp. 24-26
2. Ibid. p. 24
3. Ibid. p. 27
4. Ibid. p. 28
5. Nivola, Pietro S. and Brady, David W., Editors: *Red and Blue Nation?* Vol. I, Brookings Institution Press, Baltimore, Maryland, 2006. p. 3
6. Voter turnout in U.S. presidential and midterm elections 1789-2020 | Statista Accessed 3/9/2024
7. Baigent, M., Campion, N. & Harvey, C.: *Mundane Astrology*; Thorsens, London, UK, 1985. p. 224.
8. Ibid. p. 224
9. https://www.mmacycles.com/free-weekly-forecast/mma-free-weekly-column-for-the-week-beginning-july-3-2023/ Accessed 9/4/2023
10. Schlieffen, Alexander Graf von: *When Chimpanzees Dream Astrology*; Centre for Psychological Astrology Press, London, 2004. p. 12
11. Ibid. p. 48.
12. https://www.theguardian.com/commentisfree/2022/oct/04/how-whiteness-poses-the-greatest-threat-to-us-democracy Accessed 9/29/2023
13. https://constitutioncenter.org/education/classroom-resource-library/classroom/perspectives-on-the-constitution-a-republic-if-you-can-keep-it Accessed 9/04/2023

APPENDIX ONE
URANUS TRANSITS

Uranus Transits	Dates	Major Events	Period
Transits US Chart 10th House	2/14/1748-3/13/1758	1) Ohio granted 200,000 acres between Ohio River and Allegheny Mountains 2) Georgia allows slavery 3) Iron Act forbids iron-finishing in the Colonies 4) Outbreak of French & Indian War 5) End of French & Indian War gives control of the Ohio Valley to the English and opens new lands.	French and Indian War opens up new lands for settlement
Enters US Chart 12th House	7/15/1770-1/10/1776	1) Boston Massacre 2) Embargo of British goods 3) Boston Tea Party 4) HMS Gaspee, British schooner enforcing Navigation Acts, is burned down 5) Samuel Adams organizes Committee of Correspondence 6) Intolerable Act passed by British Parliament 7) First Continental Congress meets in Philadelphia 8) Britain declares Massachusetts in rebellion 9) Patrick Henry gives "Liberty or Death" speech	Resistance among the colonists begins to grow and intensify

Uranus Transits	Dates	Major Events	Period
Enters US Chart 12th House	7/15/1770- 1/10/1776	10) Paul Revere makes famous ride 11) Battles of Lexington and Concord occur 12) Thomas Paine publishes "Common Sense" pamphlet	Resistance among the colonists begins to grow and intensify
Conjuncts US Ascendant and transits US Chart 1st House	6/1/1776- 1783	1) Declaration of Independence signed and ratified 2) Continental Congress replaces United Colonies with United States 3) Revolutionary War begins 4) Stars and Stripes becomes the national flag 5) Bald Eagle is declared national bird 6) Articles of Confederation adopted by Continental Congress 7) France recognizes colonies' independence and becomes an ally 8) Cornwallis surrenders, Revolution comes to an end 9) The Great Seal of United States adopted 10) Slavery abolished in Pennsylvania and Massachusetts	Period of Revolutionary War ending with Treaty of Paris

Prologue

Uranus Transits	Dates	Major Events	Period
Conjuncts US Ascendant and transits US Chart 1st House	6/1/1776-1783	11) Treaty of Paris between Britain and US is signed 12) Treaty of Paris is ratified by the US in January of 1784 and returned to Britain.	Period of Revolutionary War ending with Treaty of Paris
Transits US Chart 10th House	2/1/1832-5/5/1841	1) Nat Turner slave rebellion results in his hanging 2) First American Convention held in Baltimore by Anti-Masonic Party 3) Black Hawk Indian War begins on American Frontier 4) Andrew Jackson is elected for 2nd term 5) Slavery is abolished in the British Empire 6) First assassination attempt on Andrew Jackson 7) Siege of the Alamo 8) Sam Houston defeats Mexican Army and US gains more territory 9) Cherokee Nation moved westward on "Trail of Tears" 10) Slaves rebel on ship Amistad and John Quincy argues case before Supreme Court and wins their freedom	Jackson Era

Uranus Transits	Dates	Major Events	Period
Transits US Chart 10th House	2/1/1832- 5/5/1841	11) William Henry Harrison becomes president but dies in office so VP John Tyler becomes president	Jackson Era
Transits US Chart 1st House	8/03/1859- 5/15/1866	1) Financial panic due to overspeculation in railway securities 2) Lincoln-Douglas debates begin 3) First oil well drilled in Pennsylvania 4) John Brown's raid occurs at Harper's Ferry 5) Pony Express begins between Missouri and California 6) Lincoln elected President 7) South Carolina secedes from the Inion, fires on Fort Sumter 8) Civil War begins, ending with Lee's surrender in 1865 9) Lincoln is assassinated at Ford's Theater	Civil War Period and end of slavery
Transits US Chart 10th House	3/1/1916 - 4/12/1925	1) Woodrow Wilson becomes president 2) Black migration to Northern States begins 3) World War I begins 4) Armistice ends World War I 5) Spanish flu global epidemic	World War I followed by Spanish Flu Prohibition Years

Uranus Transits	Dates	Major Events	Period
Transits US Chart 10th House	3/1/1916 - 4/12/1925	6) US Senate rejects Wilson's plan to join League of Nations 8) 19th Amendment gives women the vote 9) Volstead Act ends Prohibition 10) Warren Harding becomes president 11) Tulsa race massacre 12) Harding dies and Coolidge becomes president 13) J. Edgar Hoover appointed Director of FBI 14) Scopes trial prohibits teaching of evolution	World War I followed by Spanish Flu Prohibition Years
Transits US Chart 1st House	7/9/1943- 1949	1) Casablanca Conference with Churchill, FDR, and Stalin 2) Allies invade Normandy 3) Germany surrenders 4) First atom bomb dropped on Hiroshima 5) Japan surrenders 6) United Nations established 7) Nuremburg trials of Nazis begin 8) Truman Doctrine and Marshall Plan starts 9) Truman ends segregation in the army	World War II and aftermath

Uranus Transits	Dates	Major Events	Period
Transits US Chart 1st House	7/9/1943-1949	10) Israel proclaimed nation by UN 11) NATO formed	World War II and aftermath
Transits US Chart 10th House	3/7/1999-3/22/2009	1) Dow Jones reaches 10,000 for first time 2) Columbine mass shooting 3) George Bush is certified president by the Supreme Court 4) 9/11 attacks in NYC 5) Invasion of Afghanistan 6) Dept. of Homeland Security established 7) Invasion of Iraq by US 8) Ronald Reagan dies 9) Bush elected second term 10) Hurricane Katrina kills 1836 people, causes 81 billion dollars in damage 11) Nancy Pelosi becomes first woman Speaker of the House 12) 2008 recession starts 13) Barak Obama is the first Black man to be elected president 13) Tea Party protests begin	Wars in Afghanistan and Iraq Bush and Recession Obama is elected

Uranus Transits	Dates	Major Events	Period
Transits US Chart 12th House	5/10/2022-6/18/2027	1) Roe v. Wade reversed 2) Midterm elections give GOP small majority in the House 3) Ukraine invaded by Russia 4) Inflation 5) Trump indictments 6) Culture War intensifies 7) Israel-Hamas war begins 8) Polarization at maximum 9) Unknown	Culture War 2024 Election will take place
Transits US Chart 1st House	4/5/2028	? ? ?	

APPENDIX TWO
TREATY OF PARIS RATIFICATION

January 14, 1784
Annapolis, Maryland

for settling the Marine Accounts, or of appointing a special Commissioner for that express purpose.

Since writing that letter the Commissioner on the marine accounts having been obliged in the course of his business to look at the commercial and secret committee accounts, has not only discovered some balances due to the United States; but has reported other matters which shew in a strong point of light the necessity of examining and settling those accounts. I think they could be more easily, speedily and effectually settled by that gentleman than by any other, and therefore the submitting of them to him, might be eligible in an economical point of view.

I come now, Sir, to observe (which I am sorry to do) that my report on M^r. Cowper's case must necessarily be suspended until after a reference to the Commissioner appointed to adjust the accounts of the Secret and Commercial Committees, I shall be possessed of such a state of facts as will enable me to report with propriety.

Before I close this letter, I must also observe that as the accounts in question originated with and were under the superintendance of Members of Congress, it is a kind of Duty, which Congress in their political capacity owe to themselves, to trace the applications of money thro' those channels with the same attention which has very properly been applied to other public expenditures.[1]

WEDNESDAY, JANUARY 14, 1784.

Congress assembled: Present, Massachusetts, Rhode Island, Connecticut, Pensylvania, Delaware, Maryland, Virginia, North Carolina and South Carolina; Mr. [Richard] Beresford having this day taken his seat; and from the State of New Hampshire, Mr. [Abiel] Foster, and from New Jersey Mr. [John] Beatty.

On the report of a committee, consisting of Mr. [Thomas] Jefferson, Mr. [Elbridge] Gerry, Mr. [William] Ellery, Mr. [Jacob] Read and Mr. [Benjamin] Hawkins, to whom were referred the definitive treaty of peace between the United

---

[1] This report is in the *Papers of the Continental Congress*, No. 137, III, folio 415. According to the indorsement it was read this day and referred to Mr. [David] Howell, Mr. [Jeremiah Townley] Chase and Mr. [Arthur] Lee.

January, 1784

States of America and his Britannic Majesty, and the joint letter of the 10 September, from Mr. Adams, Mr. Franklin and Mr. Jay,

Resolved, unanimously, nine states being present, that the said definitive treaty be, and the same is hereby ratified by the United States in Congress assembled, in the form following:[1]

THE UNITED STATES IN CONGRESS ASSEMBLED,

To all persons to whom these presents shall come greeting:

Whereas definitive articles of peace and friendship between the United States of America and his Britannic majesty, were concluded and signed at Paris on the 3d day of September, 1783, by the plenipotentiaries of the said United States, and of his said Britannic Majesty, duly and respectively authorized for that purpose; which definitive articles are in the words following:

In the name of the most holy and undivided Trinity.

It having pleased the Divine Providence to dispose the hearts of the most serene and most potent prince, George the third, by the grace of God, king of Great Britain, France and Ireland, defender of the faith, duke of Brunswick and Lunenburg, arch-treasurer and prince elector of the holy Roman empire, &c. and of the United States of America, to forget all past misunderstandings and differences that have unhappliy interrupted the good correspondence and friendship which they mutually wish to restore, and to establish such a beneficial and satisfactory intercourse between the two countries, upon the ground of reciprocal advantages and mutual convenience, as may promote and secure to both perpetual peace and harmony; and having for this desirable end, already laid the foundation of peace and reconciliation, by the provisional articles, signed at Paris on the 30th of November, 1782, by the commissioners empowered on each part, which articles were agreed to be inserted in and to constitute the treaty of peace proposed to be concluded between the crown of Great Britain and the said United States, but

---

[1] This resolution was also entered in Secret Journal, No. 4, and in Secret Journal, No. 6, Vol. III.

which treaty was not to be concluded until terms of peace should be agreed upon between Great Britain and France, and his Britannic majesty should be ready to conclude such treaty accordingly; and the treaty between Great Britain and France having since been concluded, his Britannic majesty and the United States of America, in order to carry into full effect the provisional articles above mentioned, according to the tenor thereof, have constituted and appointed, that is to say, his Britannic majesty on his part, David Hartley, Esquire, member of the parliament of Great Britain; and the said United States on their part, John Adams, Esquire, late a commissioner of the United States of America, at the court of Versailles, late delegate in Congress from the state of Massachusetts, and chief justice of the said state, and minister plenipotentiary of the said United States to their high mightinesses the states general of the United Netherlands; Benjamin Franklin, Esquire, late delegate in Congress from the state of Pensylvania, president of the convention of the said state, and minister plenipotentiary from the United States of America at the court of Versailles; John Jay, Esquire, late president of Congress, and chief justice of the state of New York, and minister plenipotentiary from the said United States, at the court of Madrid, to be the plenipotentiaries for the concluding and signing the present definitive treaty: who, after having reciprocally communicated their respective full powers, have agreed upon and confirmed the following articles:

ARTICAL 1st. His Britannic majesty acknowledges the said United States, viz. New-Hampshire, Massachusetts-Bay, Rhode-Island and Providence Plantations, Connecticut, New-York, New-Jersey, Pensylvania, Delaware, Maryland, Virginia, North-Carolina, South-Carolina and Georgia, to be free, sovereign and independent states: that he treats with them as such, and for himself, his heirs and successors, relinquishes all claims to the government, propriety and territorial rights of the same, and every part thereof.

ARTICAL 2d. And that all disputes which might arise in future on the subject of the boundaries of the said United States may be prevented, it is hereby agreed and declared, that the following are and shall be their boundaries, viz. from the north-west angle of Nova Scotia, viz. that angle which is formed by a line drawn due north from the source of Saint Croix river to the Highlands; along the said Highlands which divide those rivers that empty themselves into the river Saint Lawrence from those which fall into the Atlantic Ocean, to the northwesternmost head of Connecticut river, thence down along the middle of that river to the forty fifth degree of north latitude; from thence by a line due west on said latitude, until it strikes the river Iroquois or Cataraquy, thence along the middle of said river into lake Ontario, through the middle of said lake until it strikes the communication by water between that lake and lake Erie; thence along the middle of said communication into lake Erie, through the middle of said [lake,] until it arrives at the water communication between that lake and lake Huron; thence along the middle of said water communication into the lake Huron, thence through the middle of said lake to the water communication between that lake and lake Superior; thence through lake Superior northward of the isles Royal and Philipeaux, to the long lake; thence through the middle of said long lake and the water communication between it and the lake of the Woods, to the said lake of the Woods, thence through the said lake to the most north-western point thereof, and from thence on a due west course to the river Mississippi, thence by a line to be drawn along the middle of the said river Mississippi, until it shall intersect the northernmost part of the thirty first degree of north latitude. South by a line to be drawn due east from the determination of the line last mentioned, in the latitude of thirty one degrees north of the equator, to the middle of the river Apalachicola or Catahouche; thence along the middle thereof to its junction with the Flint river; thence straight to the head of Saint Mary's river, and thence down along the middle of Saint Mary's river to the Atlantic ocean. East by a line to be drawn along the middle of the river Saint Croix, from its mouth in the bay of Fundy to its source, and from its source directly north to the aforesaid Highlands which divide the rivers that fall into the Atlantic ocean from those which fall into the river Saint Lawrence: comprehending all islands within twenty leagues of any part of the shores of the United States, and lying between lines to be drawn due east from the points where the aforesaid boundaries between Nova-Scotia on the one part, and East Florida on the other, shall respectively touch the Bay of Fundy and the Atlantic ocean, excepting such islands as now are or heretofore have been within the limits of the said province of Nova-Scotia.

ARTICAL 3d. It is agreed, that the people of the United States shall continue to enjoy unmolested the right to take fish of every kind on the Grand Bank and on all the other banks of Newfoundland; also in the gulph of Saint Lawrence, and at all other places in the sea, where the inhabitants of both countries used at any time heretofore to fish; and also, that the inhabitants of the United States shall have liberty to take fish of every kind on such part of the coast of Newfoundland as British fishermen shall use, (but not to dry or cure the same on that island) and also on the coasts, bays and creeks of all other of his Britannic majesty's dominions in America; and that the American fishermen shall have liberty to dry and cure fish in any of the unsettled bays, harbours and creeks of Nova Scotia, Magdalen islands, and Labradore, so long as the same shall remain unsettled, but so soon as the same or either of them shall be settled, it shall not be lawful for the said fishermen to dry or cure fish at such settlement, without a previous agreement for that purpose with the inhabitants, proprietors or possessors of the ground.

ARTICAL 4th. It is agreed that creditors on either side shall meet with no lawful impediment to the recovery of the full value in sterling money, of all bona fide debts heretofore contracted.

ARTICAL 5th. It is agreed that the Congress shall earnestly recommend it to the legislatures of the respective states, to provide for the restitution of all estates, rights and properties, which have been confiscated, belonging to real British subjects, and also of the estates, rights and properties of persons resident in districts in the possession of his majesty's arms, and who have not borne arms against the said United States. And that persons of any other description shall have free liberty to go to any part or parts of any of the thirteen United States, and therein to remain twelve months unmolested in their endeavours to obtain the restitution of such of their estates, rights and properties, as may have been confiscated; and that Congress shall also earnestly recommend to the several states a reconsideration and revision of all acts or laws regarding the premises, so as to render the said laws or acts perfectly consistent, not only with justice and equity, but with that spirit of conciliation, which on the return of the blessings of peace should universally prevail. And that Congress shall also earnestly recommend to the several states, that the estates, rights and properties of such last mentioned persons shall be restored to them, they refunding to any persons who may be now in possession of the bona fide price (where any has been given) which such persons may have paid on purchasing any of the said lands, rights or properties since the confiscation. And it is agreed that all persons who have any interest in confiscated lands, either

January, 1784

by debts, marriage settlements, or otherwise, shall meet with no lawful impediment in the prosecution of their just rights.

ARTICAL 6th. That there shall be no future confiscations made, nor any prosecutions commenced against any person or persons for or by reason of the part which he or they may have taken in the present war; and that no person shall on that account, suffer any future loss or damage, either in his person, liberty or property, and that those who may be in confinement on such charges, at the time of the ratification of the treaty in America, shall be immediately set at liberty, and the prosecutions so commenced be discontinued.

ARTICAL 7th. There shall be a firm and perpetual peace between his Britannic majesty and the said states, and between the subjects of the one, and the citizens of the other, wherefore all hostilities both by sea and land, shall from henceforth cease; all prisoners on both sides shall be set at liberty, and his Britannic majesty shall with all convenient speed, and without causing any destruction, or carrying away any negroes or other property of the American inhabitants, withdraw all his armies, garrisons and fleets from the said United States, and from every post, place and harbour within the same; leaving in all fortifications the American artillery that may be therein, and shall also order and cause all archives, records, deeds and papers, belonging to any of the said states, or their citizens, which in the course of the war may have fallen into the hands of his officers, to be forthwith restored and delivered to the proper states and persons to whom they belong.

ARTICAL 8th. The navigation of the river Mississippi, from its source to the ocean, shall forever remain free and open to the subjects of Great Britain, and the citizens of the United States.

ARTICAL 9th. In case it should so happen, that any place or territory belonging to Great Britain or to the United States, should have been conquered by the arms of either from the other, before the arrival of the said provisional articles in America, it is agreed, that the same shall be restored without difficulty, and without requiring any compensation.

ARTICAL 10th. The solemn ratification of the present treaty, expedited in good and due form, shall be exchanged between the contracting parties in the space of six months, or sooner if possible, to be computed from the day of the signature of the present treaty. In witness whereof, we, the undersigned their ministers plenipotentiary, have in their name, and in virtue of full powers, signed with our hands the present definitive treaty, and caused the seals of our arms to be affixed thereto.

Done at Paris, this third day of September, in the year of our Lord, one thousand seven hundred and eighty-three.

"(L. S.)   D. HARTLEY,

(L. S.)   JOHN ADAMS,
(L. S.)   B. FRANKLIN,
(L. S.)   JOHN JAY."

Now know ye that we the United States in Congress assembled having seen and considered the definitive articles aforesaid have approved, ratified and confirmed and by these presents do approve, ratify and confirm the said articles and every part and clause thereof, engaging and promising, that we will sincerely and faithfully perform and observe the same, and never suffer them to be violated by any one or transgressed in any manner as far as lies in our power.

In testimony whereof, we have caused the seal of the United States to be hereunto affixed.

Witness his Excellency THOMAS MIFFLIN, president, this fourteenth day of January in the year of our Lord one thousand seven hundred and eighty four and in the eighth year of the sovereignty and independence of the United States of America[1].

On the question to agree to this, the yeas and nays being required by Mr. [David] Howell,

New Hampshire,			Connecticut,		
Mr. Foster,	ay	*	Mr. Sherman,	ay	ay
Massachusetts,			Wadsworth,	ay	
Mr. Gerry,	ay		*New Jersey*,		
Partridge,	ay	ay	Mr. Beatty,	ay	*
Osgood,	ay		*Pennsylvania*,		
Rhode Island,			Mr. Mifflin,	ay	
Mr. Ellery,	ay	ay	Hand,	ay	ay
Howell,	ay		Morris,	ay	

[1] The above text is from the copy in the writing of Benjamin Bankson, in Secret Journal, Foreign Affairs, No. 5.

Delaware,			*North Carolina,*		
Mr. Tilton,	ay	ay	Mr. Williamson,	ay	ay
McComb,	ay		Spaight,	ay	
Maryland,			*South Carolina,*		
Mr. Chase,	ay	ay	Mr. Read,	ay	ay
Lloyd,	ay		Beresford,	ay	
Virginia,					
Mr. Jefferson,	ay				
Lee,	ay	ay			
Monroe,	ay				

So it was resolved in the affirmative.

Resolved, That the said ratification be transmitted with all possible despatch, under the care of a faithful person, to our ministers in France, who have negotiated the treaty, to be exchanged.

Resolved, That Colonel Josiah Harmar be appointed to carry the said ratification.[1]

Ordered, That the Superintendent of Finance furnish Colonel Harmar with money to defray his necessary expences.

Resolved, That a proclamation be immediately issued, notifying the said definitive treaty and ratification to the several states of the union, and requiring their observance thereof in the form following:

By the United States in Congress assembled,

A PROCLAMATION.

Whereas definitive articles of peace and friendship between the United States of America and his Britannic Majesty, were concluded and signed at Paris, on the third day of September, 1783, by the plenipotentiaries of the said United States and of his said Britannic Majesty, duly and respectively authorized for that purpose: which definitive articles are in the words following: [Here insert the treaty as above.]

---

[1] A draft of these two resolutions, in the writing of Hugh Williamson, is in the *Papers of the Continental Congress,* No. 36, II, folio 287.

And we, the United States in Congress assembled, having seen and duly considered the definitive articles aforesaid, did, by a certain act under the seal of the United States, bearing date this 14 day of January, 1784, approve, ratify and confirm the same, and every part and clause thereof, engaging and promising, that we would sincerely and faithfully perform and observe the same, and never suffer them to be violated by any one, or transgressed in any manner, as far as should be in our power; and being sincerely disposed to carry the said articles into execution, truly, honestly and with good faith, according to the intent and meaning thereof, we have thought proper by these presents, to notify the premises to all the good citizens of these United States, hereby requiring and enjoining all bodies of magistracy, legislative, executive and judiciary, all persons bearing office, civil or military, of whatever rank, degree or power, and all others the good citizens of these states, of every vocation and condition, that reverencing those stipulations entered into on their behalf, under the authority of that federal bond, by which their existence as an independent people is bound up together, and is known and acknowledged by the nations of the world, and with that good faith which is every man's surest guide, within their several offices, jurisdictions and vocations, they carry into effect the said definitive articles, and every clause and sentence thereof, sincerely, strictly and completely.

Given under the seal of the United States. Witness his Excellency THOMAS MIFFLIN, our president, at Annapolis, this 14 day of January, in the year of our Lord, one thousand seven hundred and eighty-four, and of the sovereignty and independence of the United States of America the eighth.

Resolved, unanimously, nine states being present, That it be, and it is hereby earnestly recommended to the legislatures of the respective states, to provide for the restitution of all estates, rights and properties, which have been confiscated, belonging to real British subjects, and also of the estates, rights and properties of persons resident in districts, which were in the possession of his Britannic Majesty's arms, at any time between the 30 day of November, 1782, and the 14 day of January, 1784, and who have not borne arms against the said United States, and that persons of

January, 1784

any other description, shall have free liberty to go to any part or parts of any of the thirteen United States, and therein to remain twelve months unmolested in their endeavours to obtain the restitution of such of their estates, rights and properties, as may have been confiscated: And it is also hereby earnestly recommended to the several states, to reconsider and revise all their acts or laws regarding the premises, so as to render the said laws or acts perfectly consistent, not only with justice and equity, but with that spirit of conciliation, which, on the return of the blessings of peace, should universally prevail: and it is hereby also earnestly recommended to the several states, that the estates, rights and properties of such last mentioned persons should be restored to them, they refunding to any persons who may be now in possession, the bona fide price, (where any has been given) which such persons may have paid on purchasing any of the said lands, rights or properties since the confiscation.[1]

Ordered, That a copy of the proclamation of this date, together with the recommendation, be transmitted to the several states by the secretary.[2]

[Motion of Mr. Jacob Read]

That Congress do on Wednesday next celebrate the final ratification of the Definitive Treaty of peace. And that a public entertainment be given on that day[3] ~~to the Executive and other respectable Citizens.~~

---

[1] The committee's report, in the writing of Thomas Jefferson, is in the *Papers of the Continental Congress*, No. 29, folio 315.

[2] The proceedings for this day were also entered in the Secret Journal, Foreign Affairs.

[3] This motion, in the writing of Jacob Read, is in the *Papers of the Continental Congress*, No. 36, II, folio 301. The indorsement states that it was referred to Mr. [Jacob] Read, Mr. [David] Howell and Mr. [Hugh] Williamson.

APPENDIX THREE

- **Important Pluto Transits**

- **My own connection with the Treaty of Paris chart**

Some important Pluto transits to consider:

Pluto Transits	Dates	Major Events
Pluto at 8 degrees Aquarius in 9th House	September 3, 1783	The Treaty of Paris is signed between the US and Britain, recognizing the US as a sovereign nation. Within 6 months, Congress must ratify the treaty or it will need to be renegotiated.
Enters 10th House at 14 degrees Aquarius	January 17, 1787	Shay's Rebellion. Farmers are arrested and their farms foreclosed because they received little compensation for fighting in the Revolution and were struggling to pay mortgages. They rebel and fight the militia of Boston. This event makes Congress aware that the Articles of Confederation are inadequate for the colonies.
At 15 degrees Aquarius	May 1787	The Constitutional Convention meets in Philadelphia with the purpose of changing the Articles of Confederation but secretly creates the Constitution we have now.
At 16 degrees Aquarius	July 26, 1788	New York is the 11th state to ratify the new Constitution and the remaining colonies follow thereafter.
Pluto changes signs	Feb. 18, 1799	Pluto enters Pisces, still in the 10th House.
At 4 degrees Pisces	June 1800	Washington DC becomes the new Capitol of the United States.

Continued:

Pluto Transits	Dates	Major Events
At 4 degrees Pisces	November 11, 1801	The first Congress to sit in the new Capitol is convened. President John Adams is the first president to live in the Executive Mansion.
Pluto transits US North Node	March 2, 1807	Congress passes the act prohibiting African slave trade and importation of slaves into any place within the US after January 1, 1808

My own relationship to the Treaty of Paris chart:

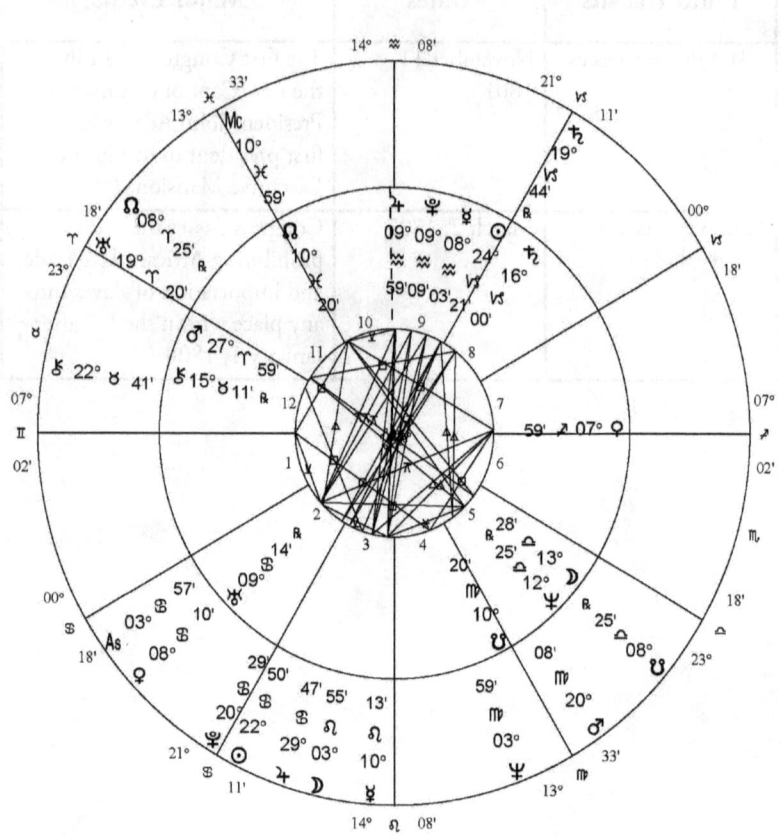

Inner wheel: Treaty of Pairs (ratified) 1/14/1784, 1:31 PM; Annapolis, MD
Outer wheel: Cornelia Hansen natal chart: 7/16/1931, 4:13 AM; New York, NY

Appendix Two

www.ingramcontent.com/pod-product-compliance
Lightning Source LLC
Chambersburg PA
CBHW050553170426
43201CB00011B/1678